The
Remembrance
of
Then

The Remembrance of Then

A Novel by

Michael Kaye

authorHOUSE

AuthorHouse™
1663 Liberty Drive
Bloomington, IN 47403
www.authorhouse.com
Phone: 833-262-8899

Published by AuthorHouse 03/19/2024

ISBN: 979-8-8230-2327-6 (sc)
ISBN: 979-8-8230-2328-3 (e)

Print information available on the last page.

This book is printed on acid-free paper.

This book is for Faye Salfinger,

my friend for over 50 years.

Acknowledgments

I am grateful to Richard Drake for his pen and ink artistry on the interior illustrations. He has my profound thanks.

My wife, Kristine, has my deep gratitude and love for her imaginative cover designs, as well as for her technical and editing contributions, which have improved this book beyond measure.

We cannot know how much we learn
From those who never will return,
Until a flash of unforeseen
Remembrance falls on what has been.

Edwin Arlington Robinson

Chapter One

$\blacklozenge \quad \blacklozenge \quad \blacklozenge$

The suggestion first came from my agent, Kay Collins, who strongly proposed I take myself off to Maine for a month. Work on the third book of my trilogy, *Intimate Strangers*, was way behind schedule, and Kay warned that the publisher was not happy that the completed manuscript wasn't in their hands yet.

"Vanessa," she forcefully pointed out, "you are under contract, a very generous contract, I might add, and the due date is less than three months away. Now, what is the problem, are you sick or something?"

Kay's insistent inquiry irritated me since I had always delivered on time – twelve full-length novels to date – but on the other hand I had to admit this one seemed to be a cause for worry. As an agent, Kay was nothing but the best. She cut me an extremely good deal for the three book series and I completely understood her reputation in the publishing world could not afford a slip up. My anger abated as I tried to explain.

"No, Kay, I'm not sick. It's the book itself. I'm three-quarters through but seem to be stuck at a crucial point. Don't worry though… it's nothing a few days of hard thinking won't cure."

"And that's what you told me a month ago, remember? No, Vanessa, this won't do," she continued, chastising me like a naughty child. "So, here's my plan, are you listening?"

It was then she informed me, much to my displeasure, that she had booked me into *The Ocean View Hotel* in Maine for a complete month.

"What?" I protested, angrily. "You've done what?"

"Oh, don't sound so alarmed," she countered. "This is just the place for you to settle down and finish the damn book. It's early in the season so there shouldn't be too many people around to bother you, and it's kind of remote with gorgeous views of the ocean. I've stayed there a couple of times myself. There's a decent restaurant and bar which will keep you well fed and watered. So there will be nothing much to do but buckle down and work."

"Kay, I just can't pack up and leave town for a month! I just can't!"

"Well, figure it out, Sweetie, because you're all booked in and there's no refund," she offered, with a laugh.

We finished the conversation curtly with me still protesting and her still insisting. After I'd hung up, I paced the room with a dozen different reasons why I couldn't go to Maine whirling inside my head. But the more I thought about her suggestion the more reasonable it sounded. A month away from all of life's distractions wouldn't actually be a bad thing. If I could get someone to take care of the dog and water my plants, then I really didn't have a valid excuse not to take Kay up on her offer.

By the morning I was due to drive the fours hours plus to Maine I had secured the promise from my good neighbor, Jean, to take the dog and also look after the house. I reluctantly called Kay to inform her that I was, indeed, on my way.

The drive, uneventful but scenic, went by quickly and a little before four I pulled into the almost deserted parking lot where a pleasant ocean breeze gently welcomed me to Maine. Unloading my things, I hustled into the lobby which, to my surprise, exuded a warm, oldy-worldy atmosphere not found in most hotels today.

Kay had booked me into a rather grand suite, complete with bedroom, bathroom and a small sitting room. At once, I felt at home, particularly as a small fruit basket and a half bottle of wine awaited me, compliments of the owners, Joyce and Keith Andrews. I relaxed for a while before dinner, calling Kay to thank her for her generosity, and taking a well-earned nap after my long drive.

Later, at reception, I thanked the owners for their kind gift and Keith, being a gentleman, escorted me into the dining room, picking out a quiet table with a view of the sea. The attendance in the room was sparse; only two other tables occupied but it did fill up a little while later since the restaurant was also open to the general public.

I have to say the food was delicious, with excellent choices and generous portions. The wine list, although small, contained some of my favorite reds and were served, conveniently, by the glass. So, all in all, I had to admit if I was going to be forced to spend a month away from home, this hotel seemed to be the perfect place. Kay, to my chagrin, appeared to have come up trumps once more.

After I finished dinner, Joyce came by and invited me to the bar for a nightcap. I graciously accepted and we had a pleasant conversation which eventually turned to my writing. Obviously, Kay had informed the owners that an author of some note was about to honor them with her presence, which turned out to be true and for which I apologized profusely for Kay's over expressive hype. We had a good laugh at that and the ice was now definitely broken.

To my dismay, Joyce then informed me that the next night the bar area was to be turned into a sort of dance club, complete with a dee-jay, which, she said, the locals liked and supported very well.

"We do it once or twice a week. Everyone has a good time and, of course, it gives us extra revenue during the slow season. We'd love it if you'd join us. The music is mostly Sixties and Seventies, which everyone seems to enjoy."

I smiled politely and said I would try but that the sole purpose of my stay in Maine was to complete my book.

"Of course, I understand," she offered. "I only hope the music won't disturb you too much."

I replied that I didn't think that would be the case since I usually worked around a barking dog, lawn mowers and a constant string of cars going by my house. We enjoyed another drink before I called it a night and retired to bed.

For a while I sat on my small balcony, enjoying the calm, warm night and the soothing sound of the gentle tide lapping the shoreline. For a long time I seemed to have forgotten some of the simpler pleasures in life, as I dashed from book to book, deadline to deadline and tour to tour. At once, this moment made me smile, made me realize that at seventy-two it might be time once in a while to stop and smell the roses. I went to bed relaxed and for the first time in a long time slept the sleep of the dead.

The next morning, before breakfast, I decided to take a brisk walk along the shore, often stopping to stare out at the ocean and marveling at the quiet solitude of it all. The tourist season was still a month away so I had the beach almost to myself. The walk also gave me a chance to arrange my work schedule in my mind so that I was productive but not overly stressed; creative but by no means forced to write just for the sake of it. By the time I returned to the hotel I was confident I had a plan that would enable me to finish the book and finally get Kay and my publisher off my back.

At breakfast, the dining room was again sparsely attended. The two couples from the night before were eating, as well as a family of four. We all exchanged pleasantries, commenting on the good weather and generally making small talk before settling down to the important issue of breakfast.

The two children, a boy and girl, eventually came over to my table and asked if I was on vacation like them.

"No, actually, I'm here to do some work," I answered, with a smile.

"What work is that?" the young girl enquired, as her mother told them not to pester me.

"Oh, it's quite all right," I replied. "They're not bothering me at all." I then invited them to sit at my table while I explained what I was doing in Maine.

"I'm a writer and I've come here to finish my latest book."

"What's it about?" the boy asked. "Is it adventure stuff or sci-fi?"

Laughing, I said, "No, not quite. This is the third book in a series and it's about a family that finally gets together again after many, many years apart."

The kids didn't seem very interested with that explanation so I changed the subject and asked if they liked to read.

"Yes, I do," the girl replied firmly. "We get to read books all the time in school."

"And do you also like to write your own stories?"

"Yes, do you?"

"Oh, very much. I seem to have been doing it since I was your age."

"I just like books about space travel," the boy interjected. "I'm going to be an astronaut one day."

"Then you'll be able to write all about that for everyone else to enjoy," I answered, now wishing they would leave me in peace to finish my breakfast.

Fortunately, my wish was granted as their mother called them back to their table. I watched for a while as the children relayed our conversation and, as the family left the room, the mother came over and stood by my chair.

"I don't mean to pry but are you Vanessa Parker?"

I nodded and agreed that I was.

"*Intimate Strangers,*" she offered. "I loved the first two."

"Well, thank you. It's always reassuring to receive a compliment like that."

We continued talking briefly about the third book before she apologized for interrupting me and diffidently took her leave. I was now fairly sure that my presence in the hotel would soon be known to all. As quickly as I could, I finished eating and made for the sanctuary of my room.

The schedule I settled on and promised myself I'd faithfully follow consisted of writing each day until lunch, then a mind-clearing walk either along the beach or on the many cliff walks surrounding the hotel, and a few more hours of bashing the laptop keys until dinner at around half six or seven. Depending on my energy levels, I would then either write into the evening, visit the bar for an hour or two or have an early night. Convincing myself that this was a plan I could keep to, I pulled out my laptop, plugged it in, reviewed the last few chapters I'd written and began composing.

Surprisingly, over the next couple of days, I managed to make a considerable dent in the on-going saga that was *Intimate Strangers*. That elated me and I could finally see the light at the end of the tunnel. I actually called Kay to inform her of my progress and to let her know I wasn't totally goofing off at her expense.

"Two long chapters finished, Kay, so I think your money is being well spent," I expressed, with a giggle.

"Good, that's good," she answered. "I knew Maine would do the trick for you. How's the hotel?"

"Just as you said; comfortable and nourishing."

"Not spending too much time in the bar, I hope," she asked, also giggling.

"My lips are sealed. However," I continued, "the night before last they had music and a dee-jay which kind of spoiled my enthusiasm for the sauce, at least, for that evening. So I took to my room and bashed away for a few more hours."

"Think I'll call them and ask if they'd do that every night," Kay offered, facetiously. "That way the damn book'll be done by next week."

"I'm sorry," I joked, "the line's suddenly gone dead. What did you say?"

"All right, all right," she responded, "you can have your evenings in the bar. But a little music now and again isn't a bad thing, is it?"

"All Sixties and Seventies stuff. The Beatles, Stones, Credence... you get the idea."

"Could be worse, you could have a piano man there in a tux playing real oldies. And, hey, Sixties and Seventies, you grew up with that, right?"

"Yes, you're correct. I have to admit hearing some of that stuff had me singing along in my room sometimes. Those guys wrote great songs back then."

"Well, there you go; sea, songs and sauce...what more do you want? By the way, many people staying there yet?"

"No, just a few. Nice family, two kids, and the mother recognized me and said some really touching things about the first two books."

"See, people love your writing, Nessa. Anyway, thanks for bringing me up to speed. Continue what you're doing and I'm glad you seem to be happy and productive. Keep it up."

"I actually am and I will. So, thank you for forcing this on me. Apparently, it was the kick up the butt I needed."

Kay laughed and informed me her fee had just risen by another ten per cent. And then she was gone and I made my way to the dining room for dinner.

As the week came to an end the other guests I had exchanged small talk with, as well as the family of four, all departed. We wished each other well and the mother of the two children again expressed her eagerness to read the final book in my trilogy. I asked for her name and address and promised her a signed copy, which seemed to thrill her beyond measure.

On Saturday afternoon I ventured into the nearby town to poke around the stores where, to my delight, I happened upon an ice cream parlor that had just opened for the season. Since my indulgence with ice cream was legendary among my friends, I made a promise to visit this heaven of sweet treats as many times as I could while in Maine. Although seventy-two, walking down the street, licking a cone for all I was worth, made me feel young again. It was a feeling I was to experience many times on this trip although, at the time, I was unaware of that fact.

Dinner that evening held a different atmosphere since the dining room was much fuller than normal. Keith had told me that bookings for the coming week were up significantly but, still, I was surprised by the number of occupied tables.

There were several families and a host of couples varying in ages from the twenties through, I imagined, to the eighties. Everyone seemed pleasant and I again exchanged passing small talk as I made my way to my regular table. As the meal progressed and I had a chance to take in some of the new guests, I was puzzled by an elderly couple, perhaps in their late seventies or early eighties, who were seated at a table quite close to mine.

The woman had a shock of white hair, beautifully coiffed, an expressive face that always seemed to be smiling or laughing at something, and sharp features that her large framed glasses failed to hide. The man she was with, her husband I supposed, had what I thought was too longish hair for his age. It looked untidy as it curled over his collar and, compared to her appearance, he seemed not to care that much about how he looked. He had a plump, fleshy face, pink skin but deeply lined and eyes that darted around the room as if he was afraid of his own shadow. But his conversation must have been stimulating and funny since the woman constantly giggled or laughed at something he'd said.

As I glanced at the couple I had a faint sense that I knew them or, at least, people who looked like them. Over the next few days I searched my memory to see if I could remember who they were or where I had possibly met them. But, despite my valiant efforts at recollection, I always came up blank. That is, though, until dee-jay night in the bar. I happened to have spent most of the day hunkered down with my laptop and decided after dinner I desperately needed a nightcap. As I entered the crowded bar I noticed, sitting in one corner enthusiastically enjoying the oldies' music, the couple whom I was having trouble recalling where and if we'd met. At that moment, the speakers started belting out the sometimes shrill, twangy rendition of *'Me and Bobby McGee'* by Janis Joplin. It was then it hit me; it was then I remembered that couple from long ago.

Chapter Two

---◆---

Memory is a strange bedfellow, recalling and forgetting at the same time. As soon as I heard the Joplin song in the bar I remembered quite clearly those faces from long ago but not the names. The whole incident jolted me and I quickly finished my drink and hurried up to my room.

As the music from down below continued and I sat in my comfortable easy chair, the flashes of remembrance began in earnest. Rainbow Falls…Aunt Sheila and Uncle Brian…the Barringtons' house on Market Street…*The Announcer*…the Barringtons' four children, Edward, Hugh, Simon and daughter Chloe…

At once, I was back in my youth, over fifty years before. I distinctly recalled the Janis Joplin song *'Me and Bobby McGee'* was playing the night Jack and Clare Kenwright arrived and made their first appearance at the Barringtons' house. Their names magically flashed into my head and I wondered how on earth I hadn't been able to bring them to mind sooner.

I decided the hour was far too late to begin what I knew would be a formidable walk down the halls of my past, so instead I bashed out two more important pages of the book before calling it a night. Tomorrow, I promised myself, I would seek out the Kenwrights to start the process of remembering.

I overslept the following morning so consequently when I arrived for breakfast I was dismayed not to find the Kenwrights there. Fortunately,

9

after I'd finished, I wandered past the lounge and saw them leisurely sipping their coffees. Venturing over, I sat in a nearby chair and introduced myself.

"For the past few days," I began quite boldly, "I have been trying to recall where and when we've met before."

They both looked at me with total surprise wondering, I'm sure, what this complete stranger was talking about.

"Really," the man replied, seemingly not giving a damn, "and have you figured it out yet?"

I nodded and told them I had.

"You're Jack and Clare Kenwright, aren't you?"

They both acknowledged the fact a little more enthusiastically this time.

"And we're supposed to know you?" Clare asked, frowning.

"Oh, it was a long time ago now, but yes, our paths crossed quite often. Does the name Barrington ring any bells?" I enquired.

"Barrington? Barrington?" Jack Kenwright repeated. "When was this again?"

"Oh, late Sixty-nine and early Seventy. My name's Vanessa Parker, and you and I, Mr. Kenwright, worked together for a while."

He seemed surprised at this revelation, cocking his head and paying more attention.

"We did, eh? Where would that have been?"

"Rainbow Falls," I offered, "just north of New York City."

I could see them both searching their memories for a clue, and no doubt still wondering if the person questioning them was for real or just a scam artist.

"Ah, yes," he finally acknowledged, "Rainbow Falls, you're correct, a long time ago now."

"At *The Announcer*," I explained. "You'd just arrived from head office."

"And you were some sort of young reporter, weren't you?" Clare correctly recalled. "I remember now that you loved to write. Do you still keep up with it?"

I told her I did, that in fact I write novels for a living.

She seemed mildly interested but didn't pursue that line any further.

"Which reminds me," I said, getting up to leave, "I need to get back to my room to finish up a few more pages of my latest. My agent and publisher are hounding me like rabid dogs. Perhaps we could meet later when we have more time?"

They agreed that would be very pleasant and I left them to hopefully stir their memories into action.

Up in my cozy room I did indeed finish the next chapter. I wasn't entirely happy with the result but the basis was there, and I knew I should be able to review it and rewrite those parts I was unhappy with at a later date. My mind now seemed to be taken up with the Kenwrights, the Barringtons and Rainbow Falls, which made me anxious to do some remembering of my own. I ordered room service lunch, ate it fairly quickly, made myself comfortable in the easy chair and began the business of recollection.

I wasn't originally from Rainbow Falls. As a family, we lived about ten miles away in the quiet town of Fairfield. I say as a family, but it was really only my mother and me since my father had passed away when I was about three from complications with polio. That would have been towards the end of Nineteen Fifty-four judging by the year I was born, but I had no memories of events from those early days.

My mother, Elizabeth, or Betty as she was popularly known, was a bookkeeper for an established company in town, and as far as I could recall I had a fairly normal childhood. I did remember she worked long, hard hours and I was often looked after until she could pick me up by my aunt and uncle, Sheila and Brian. I also recalled quite clearly how much I hated my mother working all those long hours because, being young, I often feared I would never see her again. Irrational as it seemed, the thoughts of the young sometimes are all that and more.

I know I really enjoyed my teenage school years, with plenty of friends and classes that both challenged and completed me. Particularly, I loved to write, even from an early age, and was especially encouraged by my high school English teacher, Ms. Fuller, who sent some of my essays and youthful takes on life to the local paper, *The Announcer*. Seeing my efforts actually in print for others to read thrilled me beyond measure. It was probably at that time I decided my future would be devoted to writing.

I stopped at that point in my remembrance, since the next part of my life was difficult and I needed some space and time to process what had happened after I graduated high school.

The weather had warmed considerably, so I decided to take a walk along one of the cliff paths to clear my mind. The walk overlooked the ocean and the rugged rocks, while all sorts of gulls, sandpipers and such screeched and dotted the pale blue sky. I stood, taking in the view, trying hard *not* to remember what I knew was coming next in my recollections.

Back in my room, I realized I needed to forget Rainbow Falls for a while and concentrate what talent I had on pushing forward with the book. Kay had called earlier and seemed genuinely pleased with the chapters I'd sent her.

"Vanessa, these are really, *really* good. Some of your best work yet. How you keep coming up with these different scenarios is beyond me," she gushed. "What's the prognosis for finally finishing it?"

"Kay, please," I pleaded, "don't keep pressuring me like this. It'll be done when it's done. This final part has to be perfect so I'm giving it a lot of thought and planning. It's coming together in my mind but I'm not quite there yet. Don't worry, you'll have your book on time."

She apologized but also said she felt I sounded strange somehow. "There's a stridence in your voice but with a touch of sadness. Is everything all right there?"

I assured her it was, but that I'd met a couple from my distant past and I was recalling some of those days. "It's nothing, really, except I'm trying to remember some things that happened back then. I'm sure they'll be gone in a few days and then I won't have to worry about them anymore." It was a hopeful statement, which I knew wouldn't be the case, but I hoped it would be enough to satisfy Kay's curiosity.

"By the way," she added, happily, "I'm coming to visit you in a week, so tell the boys in the bar to get the drinks ready!"

"Oh, Kay, I'd love that. It's been kind of lonely here, so that'll be great."

And I meant it, too, since Kay could always manage to squeeze a fun time out of almost nothing. We had a close working relationship and to simply see a familiar face would certainly help get me over the finishing line with the book.

The rest of the afternoon sped by with me bashing out six highly complicated pages. I suddenly felt confident that the ending to the book would more than satisfy the readers who had faithfully followed the previous two. To celebrate, before dinner I ventured into the bar and had Kay treat me to a well deserved glass of Chablis.

It was late when I ate dinner and to my dismay the Kenwrights weren't present. I had planned to stop by and see if they, too, had any recollections of those distant days. Perhaps they'd left, after all vacations don't last forever. But, to my great surprise and delight, I found them again as I went past the lounge on my way upstairs.

"Oh, good, there you are!" I exclaimed, maybe a tad too enthusiastically, as I hurried in and joined them.

To my surprise, they warmly welcomed me, even offering a drink to make the moment, I suppose, as friendly as possible.

"We were hoping to see you," Jack offered. "We've been trying hard to do some remembering of our own but some of our recollections have dimmed I'm afraid."

"You said you recall the evening we arrived at the Barringtons' house," Clare said, looking straight into my eyes. "How is that so clear to you?"

I smiled then chuckled, before saying, "Because it was Nineteen Sixty-nine and the Barrington boys were having a party. The other night when I went into the bar the dee-jay happened to be playing '*Me and Bobby McGee*' by Janis Joplin. And the evening you arrived at the house way back then, that was the song spinning on the record player."

Jack Kenwright nodded and smiled.

"Oh, we certainly liked rock and roll in those days, didn't we, Clare?"

As he spoke I took the chance to study her features and, despite her age, I could still see that cheerful face from over fifty years ago. The clear eyes and ready smile still emanated as easily as back then when she always seemed to play second fiddle to Jack.

Clare was agreeing with her husband's remark about the music but seemed eager to move on. That reluctance on her part pricked my memory, as though her not wishing to pursue that particular time mattered somehow. For now, I dismissed that thought and tried my best to answer her next question about my life after working for *The Announcer*.

"Well, while I was there I began my first novel, which eventually did well enough for me to leave the newspaper and concentrate full time on writing. That's what I've been doing ever since."

"Yes," she said, almost wistfully, "it's so important in life to do what you love."

Again, I felt a touch of sadness sprang from her voice, as though her life had been a disappointment in some way. I decided not to ask any more questions since my presence seemed to be making Clare somewhat uncomfortable. Also, I needed to search my memory now, to retrace my steps, fill in the gaps and discover what I knew I needed to remember. I bade them goodnight and said I hoped we might talk again at a later date. They were staying a few more days which gave me ample opportunity to bring some of my recollections to the fore.

Back in my room, I carried my unfinished wine from the bar onto my balcony, put my feet up on the railing and began thinking about the Kenwrights and Clare's apparent unease remembering those distant days of the late Sixties and early Seventies. I hadn't thought about those times in a long while, so I realized I would have to sort through my own memories to try and make some sort of sense of it all. Surprisingly, I actually looked forward to reliving what I could remember even though recalling some moments might stab me like a knife. So, I closed my eyes and, as the warm ocean breeze feathered across my face, I suddenly found myself back in Rainbow Falls just after graduating high school in the summer of Nineteen Sixty-nine.

Chapter Three

———◆————◆————◆———

After graduating in Sixty-nine, I spent most of the summer working at an ice-cream stand which, for me, was like having an alcoholic working in a bar. My shift usually began around noon and I stayed until the place closed at nine. The work was monotonous but I enjoyed my colleagues and, in general, our customers. The pay back then wasn't great but the shared tips helped grow my meager bank balance. That was important because by the end of August I was due to begin my college life at Amherst.

Since my mornings were mostly free I took the opportunity to write, something I'd done since grade school and which I decided would be my major at university. I didn't realize then that my dream of becoming a successful novelist would, in fact, become a reality years later.

During that summer my mother did her best, while working full-time, to ensure we spent quality time together since she knew the separation when I left for college would be difficult for us both. Weekends were especially full of fun as we hiked, watched movies and just enjoyed each other's company over some of her delicious dinners.

Unfortunately, her hours at her bookkeeping job often kept her late and I thought nothing of it one evening when she hadn't returned home before me. That was strange but I just assumed she had some complicated set of figures to sort out before she left for the night.

Shortly after nine-thirty I answered a knock on the door to find a grim-looking state trooper raising his hat respectfully to me. Gently, very gently, he informed me that there had been an accident involving my mother. Her car had veered off the road and hit a telegraph pole. I remember looking at him and frowning, expecting my mother to show up any minute in the driveway. I asked if she was all right and that was when he told me she had died in the accident.

A moment like that is totally unbelievable, more especially when we are young and have yet to come to terms with losing someone close and dear. I recall now that I kept asking where she was, could I see her, that I needed to go and be with her. My tears fogged my eyes but my clear recollection is of a policeman at a loss of what to do with someone like me. He kept looking behind him hoping, I imagine, for someone, anyone to come and comfort me.

That help came in the form of two kind hearts belonging to my Aunt Sheila, my mother's only sister and her husband, Uncle Brian. They lived only ten miles from us and apparently had been informed of the accident by the police and knew I would be in desperate need of help.

They took me in for the night, which turned into two nights and then weeks. Finally, we decided I should move from our rental home into their large house so that, at the tender age of eighteen, I was not alone with my grief.

My aunt and uncle were dear to me and I had spent a lot of time growing up in their company. They had quite different personalities; Aunt Sheila was always affectionate and warm but by no means anybody's fool. She ran her household exactly the way she wanted, which apparently suited Uncle Brian as well. When staying with her in my younger days she showed me how to bake and use a needle and thread, skills I resented at the time but later proved so useful. She had a lively sense of humor and enjoyed pulling Uncle Brian's leg at every opportunity.

He, on the other hand, while also loving and kind towards me, seemed always busy in his workshop, making or fixing something around the house. Indeed, it was my uncle who also taught me some practical lessons, including how to change a tire and the best way to wallpaper a room. The first actually came in handy several times in my life while the other one never did.

As the time came nearer for me to leave for college my mental state remained fragile. The sudden, totally unexpected loss of my mother constantly played on my mind, leaving me feeling lost and lonely despite the wonderful care my aunt and uncle gave me.

In the days after the accident I experienced puzzlement over how such a competent driver as my mother could lose control and crash into a telegraph pole. I thought she may have swerved to avoid a deer or a dog but that was not the case. The autopsy actually showed she had suffered a major brain aneurysm which rendered her unconscious and helpless. For a long time I blamed that on her stressful, figure-heavy job, which she needed to support us. I also blamed myself, irrationally, for her death in the sense that she only had to work as hard as she did to look after me.

So, even though my aunt and uncle assured me they would provide the necessary funds for me to attend Amherst, I felt I couldn't face a strange place and strange people at that moment.

Fortunately, my savior was my writing. Uncle Brian turned an upstairs bedroom into a kind of small apartment for me and it was there I spent most of my early days with them. Indeed, my first attempt at a novel took place in that room and it was that intense focus that helped drag me out of my despair and hopelessness. Immersing myself in a story took me to a completely different place, as I created characters that, for a while, seemed as real to me as my aunt and uncle. That feeling when I write even now has not changed; being able to submerge yourself, if only for a time, with characters and places enables one to lose oneself and feel refreshed.

But, as much as I lost myself with my writing, I also realized if I was not going to now attend Amherst then I had better start thinking seriously about getting a job. Of course, I only had a high school education to my name so my field of opportunity wasn't very wide. That is, until my uncle made a suggestion that I thought magical and perfect.

As I sat on my balcony at the Ocean View Hotel thinking and reminiscing about those long ago days in Rainbow Falls, I could still hear my aunt and uncle's voices bantering with each other, laughing at the silliest things and always encouraging me on. My mother never left my heart, even to this day, but my aunt and uncle also filled me with hope and promise which I like to think guided me down the years. Indeed, as I said, it was my Uncle Brian who inadvertently set me on the path as a real writer and subsequently a fairly successful novelist.

Uncle Brian worked as the senior maintenance technician for *The Announcer* newspaper. It was the same paper I had had some of my school essays and youth commentary pieces sent into by my English teacher, Ms. Fuller, and accepted. To this day I still recall the thrill of seeing my name in print. Uncle Brian had overall responsibility to see that the paper was properly produced every morning. The editor, Charles Barrington, relied heavily on my uncle's mechanical wizardry and over the years working together they became fast friends.

Charles Barrington was the quintessential small-town newspaper man, He kept the paper focused primarily on local issues and matters that were important and meaningful to people living and working in the area. For over twenty years he oversaw a dedicated group of reporters, staff and technical crew, and the daily paper was considered an essential part of life in Rainbow Falls.

As I floundered around town, enquiring at local businesses for the possibility of gainful employment, my uncle one Sunday afternoon after lunch made a suggestion which was to change my life.

"I was talking to Charles Barrington yesterday," he informed me, "and I told him about you."

Bemused, I can remember looking at him and frowning as to what he might be saying to the editor of the local paper about me.

"Yes," he continued, with a devilish twinkle in his eye, "and I mentioned you being a writer."

Again, I stared at him nonplussed, wondering what on earth he was talking about.

"And he would like to talk to you," he informed me, with a mischief smile.

"Uncle Brian, the editor of *The Announcer* wants to see *me*?" I asked, still mystified. "Are you pulling my leg here?"

"Not at all," he replied, this time more seriously. Pointing his finger in my direction, he went on to tell me about their conversation. "I know how much you like to write and since you're looking for a job I thought

I'd have a word in his ear. I mentioned the school articles you'd written and he seemed to remember them. Anyway, he told me he did have one vacancy for a rookie reporter and he was currently doing the interviews. *'Tell her to pop along and see me in a day or two. I'm not promising anything, Brian, but I'm always on the lookout for up and coming talent.'* So, I've arranged for you to come in with me early on Wednesday evening so you and he can speak."

This sudden news struck me like a thunderbolt from the blue. Simultaneously, I was both excited and scared out of my wits. To even *think* about being paid for my writing seemed totally incomprehensible. For a few seconds, I recalled quite clearly, my whole being seemed to be in limbo.

My Aunt Sheila gently shook my shoulder before saying, "Love, I think this is something you should do. Opportunities like this don't come around very often. And if nothing comes of it well, then, you won't have lost much."

Coming out of my temporary torpor, I nodded before saying, "Oh, wow, Uncle Brian, yes, I mean, of course I'll come with you. Thank you! Thank you, so much for thinking of me. This is like a dream come true."

"Well, don't get your hopes up yet. As he said, he has others to interview but at least you'll have your foot in the door. Although Charles is a good friend of ours I wouldn't expect that to play any part in his decision. It'll be on the merits and quality of your writing, nothing else if I know Charles."

I told my uncle that I completely understood and that was the way it should be. I certainly didn't want to be a charity case in any way, shape or form. So it was settled that on Wednesday evening I'd go and meet with Mr. Barrington to hopefully persuade him to give me a job.

To prepare for the interview I dug out some old pieces I'd written while in school as well as the first couple of chapters of the novel I'd recently started. I also jotted down a sort of primitive resume which listed, among other things, my participation in my high school's debate team and my interests, which included social studies, history and, of course, English literature.

My uncle mentioned that Mr. Barrington did not suffer fools gladly, but that he was a fair man who expected a fair day's work for a fair day's pay. As I recalled this momentous time in my life, sitting and gazing at the Atlantic Ocean, I clearly remember thinking that this might be the stepping stone to my loftier goal of becoming a full-time writer. Despite the warnings from my uncle I don't think I ever imagined *not* getting the job. Such is the exuberance and high expectations of youth that sometimes we think the world is just waiting for us to come and save it.

I smiled as my recollections took me back to that fateful Wednesday evening when, dressed as professionally as I could, I made my way with my Uncle Brian to the meeting with Mr. Barrington. My uncle made the introductions before leaving us alone to talk.

I made myself as comfortable as I could as I sat across from his large, imposing desk. Taking a few seconds to glance his way, I saw a distinguished man, probably in his fifties, with neat hair just turning grey at the temples and a kind, warm face that smiled often in my direction.

"So," he began, glancing at my pathetic attempt at a resume, "you want to be a writer. Why?" he asked me, bluntly.

I took a deep breath and told him I always seemed to have had a love of words, even from an early age. He smiled again and asked how old I was.

"Eighteen, but an old eighteen," I answered, with a smile of my own.

That remark seemed to break the ice between us and the rest of the conversation was warm, friendly, inquisitive and informative for me since Mr. Barrington detailed the requirements for a rookie reporter on his paper. As the interview drew to a close I felt I might definitely have a chance of being hired although he did emphasize there were also a lot of other qualified candidates he was considering. His decision, he said seriously, would be made in a day or two and he thanked me for coming in and presenting myself as well as I did.

I sought out my uncle afterwards and he kindly took a half hour break to drive me home. On the way, his words of encouragement helped ease my fear of failure and, by the time we arrived home, I began to feel I really had a chance. My Aunt Sheila echoed my feelings.

"We know Charles Barrington very well, Lovie, and he's nothing if not fair. As long as you did your best...well...that's all you can do. Now, go to bed and try not to think about it."

That sound advice unfortunately fell on my deaf ears. Being eighteen rendered me incapable of seeing very far into the future except to realize my dream of having a writing life would be over if I didn't get the job. The next two nights were mostly sleepless ones, and I moped about the house like someone whose dog had eaten their last five dollar bill. I largely remained in my room, still writing but wondering if my efforts were futile and pointless.

As I ventured down to breakfast three days after my interview, my Uncle Brian, who had just returned from his overnight shift at the newspaper, informed me Mr. Barrington wanted to see me that afternoon.

"He told me, Vanessa, that he wanted to break the news to you personally. I have no idea what that meant but you'd better get yourself down there to find out."

I took my uncle's comment that Mr. Barrington wanted to break the news to me in person as a sign that he would let me down gently because of my youth. Reluctantly, I said I would go, but the words came out of my mouth in a dejected fashion. My poor Aunt Sheila did her best to bolster my spirits, which only made me feel worse considering all the sacrifices she and my uncle had made for me.

By two o'clock, I was standing nervously in the lobby of the vast newspaper building, waiting to be called in to what I imagined to be the second worst day of my life.

"Ah, there you are," Mr. Barrington began brightly. "Sit yourself down for a minute."

I took a seat opposite and waited patiently as he sifted through some papers. Finally, he looked up and smiled.

"I wasn't sure at first," he said, waving the papers and tilting his head, "that these were as good as I thought. I actually had a couple of my top reporters look them over to give me their views, but they confirmed my own opinion. You, young lady, are one heck of a writer."

I clearly recall steadying myself in my chair at his remarks. Was I hearing things or did he say what I thought he said?

With a startled look, I'm sure, and eyes wide open, I replied, "You think my work is good?"

"Oh, not just good," he answered, "but mature, thoughtful and full of insight to a degree I seldom see."

"Mr. Barrington, I'm shocked that you would say that. I mean, I'm stunned, really, really stunned."

"Ms. Parker, let me tell you something. I've been in this business a long time and I've encountered all sorts of writers, essayists and op-ed folk. Very few have been worth reading week in and week out. Those that are now all work here at *The Announcer*," he continued, with a laugh. "So, yes, I think your work not only good but remarkable for one so young. This one in particular," he said, holding up an argument I'd put forward when on the debate team, "shows a level of understanding of human achievement and interaction that, quite frankly, is beyond your years. Are you sure you actually wrote this?" His broad grin told me he was, of course, joking.

"So, before I hire you as a junior reporter for the paper, I only have one further question."

I gulped at learning I'd actually been offered a job and stared at him like a startled deer.

"Okay," I offered, almost in a whisper.

"I want to know why you want to write for a career."

For once, I didn't hesitate and launched into all my reasons. By the time I'd finished I was breathless, flushed and elated. Mr. Barrington continually nodded as I spoke before finally holding up his hand.

"So many good reasons," he commented, still nodding and smiling, "that *I'm* now confused."

We both laughed at his joke before he officially welcomed me onto the staff at *The Announcer* as a junior reporter.

Chapter Four

As I finished my wine and watched the orange ball slowly slip down the horizon, the warmth of remembering that moment, when I officially became a reporter on *The Announcer*, washed over me like the distant, disappearing rays of the sun. I smiled... no I actually beamed at the memory, which made me feel elated all over again. Suddenly, I had the urge for a nightcap, to share that recollection with somebody, so I made my way down to the bar.

Hoping the Kenwrights might still be up and around, my spirits were raised even before I'd raised my spirits. Unfortunately, they were nowhere to be seen. In fact, to my surprise, the bar was comparatively empty. My savior this evening was Stu, the bartender, who I'd chit-chatted to a few times in the week I'd been at the hotel. I ordered my usual glass of house red and enquired about the lack of patrons.

"A combination of a beautiful evening and free movie night in town," he replied, with a shrug. "But those old folks, the Kenwrights, were in earlier. Actually," he continued, surprising me, "they were talking about you."

"Really, I'm intrigued."

"I didn't know you're a writer. That's way cool in my book."

"Yeah," I admitted, "except you probably wouldn't like any of the stuff I put out."

"As long as they're not that romance crap," he offered, with a fake sneer. "But I enjoy most things."

"Well, as long as you asked, I have written everything from suspense, murders, family drama and even one set in a nursing home. Right now, I'm trying desperately to finish the third book in my trilogy *Intimate Strangers*. That's what I'm doing staying here. My agent packed me off for a month," I said, with a laugh.

"Well, I'd certainly like to look them up if you give me the titles. It's Vanessa, isn't it?"

"Yup, Vanessa Parker. Amazon lists them all. Any purchases would be gratefully received," I answered, "since I have to keep the old Mercedes running somehow."

We both laughed before I enquired about the Kenwrights.

"You said they were discussing me...care to share?"

"Oh, they just mentioned you were a writer and that you all knew each other like fifty years ago. The guy did most of the talking... something about both of you working on a local newspaper. Mrs. Kenwright didn't seem very interested in joining in the conversation. It was almost as if she didn't want to remember stuff from back then. I've gotta tell you, Ms. Parker..."

"Vanessa, please," I interrupted.

"Oh, okay, thanks. Well, I've gotta tell you, Vanessa, she just seemed uncomfortable with his whole conversation. It got me thinking whether something bad happened back then, but she kinda shut him down and then they left."

I nodded at Stu's comments and for a few seconds remained silent.

Finally, I said, "When I first saw them in the dining room, I faintly recognized them but I couldn't put my finger on when and where. And then the other night...dee-jay night to be exact...they played Janis Joplin's version of *'Me and Bobby McGee'*. That stirred something in me and, so, over the last few days I've been searching my memory...such as it is...and I've narrowed it down to just after I'd graduated high school back in Nineteen Sixty-nine. And he's correct, we did work together on the local newspaper called *The Announcer*. In fact, it was my very first proper job...my first paid writing job, in fact."

"So, like, fifty years ago?" Stu asked.

"Yes, amazing, eh? It's been fun recalling those days but I realize

I've got a long way to go yet. Funny, though, that Mrs. Kenwright didn't seem to want to talk about those days."

"Maybe some deep, dark secret," Stu surmised, waving his hands in front of him like a scary horror character.

"Guess I'll find out," I answered, nodding. "When are they leaving?"

"Friday, I believe."

"So, I've only got three days to remember," I offered, raising my eyebrows. "Better get my skates on eh?"

"Oh, if it was important back then I'm sure you'll bring it to mind. Memories are funny like that…some things stick out more than others."

"Well, give me another red and I'll go back to my room and put my thinking cap on. Three days isn't long when you're trying to remember a lifetime."

Stu poured me a generous glass and I made my way upstairs and back to Rainbow Falls.

Although the hour was late, somewhere after ten, I again sat on my balcony listening to the tide recede this time and enjoying the twinkling lights splitting the darkness around the bay. I sipped my wine, closed my eyes and promised myself I would only spend a little time tonight thinking back into the past.

It began to amaze me that the more you consciously try to remember the more you actually recall, sometimes with extreme clarity and sometimes with sketchy details. For instance, my Aunt Sheila had a good friend called Joan, and I often found them in our kitchen baking for hours on end. Their laughter would echo throughout the house and I always knew when I heard it that good, tasty pastries or pies were soon to emerge from the oven. That made me hurry down as the aroma was too much to ignore. But, for the life of me, I could not remember Joan's last name, which I know I would have respectfully called her.

My next clearest memory, and one I grinned at recalling as a warm breeze ruffled my hair, was the Monday morning I reported for work on my first day at *The Announcer*. It was a week before Christmas and it seemed like a wonderful early present Mr. Barrington had given me.

Of course, my stomach was full of butterflies as I tried to keep my breakfast down that morning. My uncle had returned from his night shift and both he and Aunt Sheila were doing their best to calm my nerves.

"Lovie," she began, "everyone feels like this on their first day. Your uncle says all the folk at the paper are decent people and, knowing Charles Barrington like we do, I know he wouldn't put up with any nonsense from anyone, right, Brian?"

Uncle Brian nodded vigorously, adding, "We're a team there, the whole place is like one big family. You'll be all right, Vanessa, believe me."

While all those comments made me feel much better, the prospect of actually going into the building and meeting complete strangers filled me with dread. But as soon as breakfast finished my uncle whisked me out the door and into his car.

"This is another thing that won't do," he told me, as we drove to my new place of employment. "You need a car. You'll be expected to rush here, there and everywhere chasing down stories and you can't do that walking or waiting for buses."

I already had my license, but the thought of buying a car never occurred to me since the cost was way out of my reach. Two weeks later, courtesy of my aunt and uncle's generous Christmas present, I was the proud owner of my first automobile.

Until then, I relied on my uncle to drive me in each morning and pick me up when my shift ended. But for now, as we neared the newspaper building, my only thoughts were of not making a complete fool of myself in the company of seasoned reporters, and learning as much as I could from those same people.

My uncle, on purpose I suspect, dropped me at the front door, wished me well and was gone. For a few seconds I stood on the steps like a shipwreck survivor marooned, alone, on a desert island. After what seemed like an age, I pushed my way through the doors and introduced myself to the receptionist.

"Oh, yes," the young woman replied, brightly, "Mr. Barrington's waiting for you. You can go in that door over there."

Inside the small conference room Charles Barrington and three other people were waiting for my arrival. That terrified me realizing people had been waiting just for me, but Mr. Barrington soon came over, warmly welcomed me into *The Announcer* family, and introduced the other folks.

During the next half hour he ran through the types of stories and articles the paper usually concentrated on, making sure I understood the importance of always serving the community. The other staff members then highlighted some of the current work they were doing as a way, I supposed, of emphasizing the consistent message and image they wished to display to their readers. Their words were eye-opening and I really wondered if I would ever be able to come close to matching their high ideals and obvious professionalism.

Mr. Barrington, a shrewd, seasoned newspaper man, must have noticed my apprehension. He told me he quite understood if everything I'd heard was somewhat overwhelming, but that he expected nothing more of me in my first few weeks except to listen and learn. To that end, he asked one of the reporters in the room, Betsy Clarke, to take me under her wing and show me the ropes.

I finished my wine as some of the lights along the bay began disappearing with the lateness of the hour. I decided my recollections for now could stop, that I needed a good night's sleep in order to concentrate my efforts tomorrow on bringing another chapter of the book to its, hopefully, rightful conclusion.

As I lay in bed trying to drift off, I couldn't help thinking again about my start at *The Announcer*. Although totally petrified, I also clearly remember how proud I was of myself, that my dream since grade school and beyond may actually come true. It was with that pleasant thought I slept undisturbed until morning.

In lieu of the fact that Kay was to descend upon me in a few days, I made a concerted effort to concentrate most of my energy the next day to completing at least another chapter of the book. This was by no means an easy task since wrapping up a three-book series required not only satisfying myself but also my readers, of which for *Intimate Strangers*, there were now thousands according to the latest sales report from Kay. Certainly, the pressure I felt to deliver an authentic, meaningful ending to the whole endeavor also caused mixed emotions for me. When I eventually penned the last word of the last chapter it would mean I had to say goodbye to characters I now considered to be near and dear to me. On the other hand, presenting my readers with a true, compelling finish would please me in a way that was hard to explain. In other words, I needed to be completely satisfied that what I had written did justice to the story, the characters, myself and, of course, my readers. That is why I needed to be careful, thoughtful and totally honest, and certainly not rush the conclusion in any way.

Breakfast came and went and, although I saw the Kenwrights and exchanged the usual pleasantries, I decided not to engage them at that moment in any type of remembrance. I hurried up to the sanctuary of my room, opened my laptop and carefully began to craft the next chapter.

At the end of my morning's work I felt extremely pleased with the way things had gone. I managed to bring together a lot of the crucial elements that would enable me to fashion the last few chapters into a believable and satisfying conclusion, not only to this book but to the series as a whole. The trilogy proved to be a monumental undertaking, the scope of which I never envisioned when the idea for the story first took root in my mind.

Lunch was a welcome break and, surprisingly, I shared it with Jack Kenwright. His wife had taken off for an hour or two into town, so when I entered the dining room he beckoned me over and asked that I join him. I did, reluctantly, but I hoped the conversation would be about anything except the past. I still had a lot of remembering to do on my own terms without Jack putting any sort of slant into the equation.

Unfortunately, after our burgers and salads arrived, he launched into a series of questions and statements about his time in Rainbow Falls, which I strongly felt were designed to taint my own recollections.

"So, you actually became a novelist," he began, pleasantly. "I do recall your passion for writing even then. What kinds of stories do you make up?"

Again, I sensed he was trying to head me off, as if to infer that whatever I managed to remember might just be folly and fantasy on my part. But I knew what I knew and my thoughts so far had been mostly clear and distinct.

Smiling sweetly, I answered, "Oh, any number of subjects, as the fancy takes me. None, I'm happy to say, involve my past which would be too close to the truth."

"Yes, yes," he offered, weakly, "not much point I always feel in dragging up the past. Some things, I believe, are better left undisturbed. My wife's of the same opinion, sort of what's done is done type of attitude. Very commendable, I think. The lives we've lived, I mean, so much happens, really."

At this point, despite his convoluted argument, which was becoming hard to follow, I felt sure he was trying to warn me off remembering too much and, more importantly, not involving his wife in any meaningful way. I decided I wasn't having any such nonsense.

"Oh, Mr. Kenwright, you are so correct there," I responded, brightly. "I mean, take me for example; first job as a rookie reporter and now earning my living as a novelist. I never in my wildest dreams imagined that. Which reminds me, I know you came to Rainbow Falls to participate in some way at *The Announcer*, but were you a writer, too?"

He studied me for a few seconds before shaking his head.

"No, nothing as grand as that," he offered, dismissively, "just sent from head office to make a few necessary changes. We were only there, I believe, for six months."

"Remind me what your wife did in those days," I asked, pointedly.

"Oh, Clare was an artist…loved to paint…that kept her pretty busy."

His comment sparked a faint memory in me.

"Oh, yes, I do seem to remember that about her now. Landscapes, wasn't it?"

"Indeed. She'd take herself off for hours on end into the countryside. Produced some fine work, a few of which, I might add, we still have."

As he spoke, my previous faint recollections of the pair sharpened somewhat. I did remember that his wife was an artist and that the couple didn't seem to spend a great deal of time together. She was always off painting and he, I recalled, seemed to be consumed with *The Announcer*. My memory still couldn't quite grasp what exactly he did at the newspaper, except that after he arrived the place was never quite the same.

"You worked closely with Charles Barrington, didn't you?" I ventured, still finding it hard to recall what this man's role actually was.

"Barrington? Barrington?" he answered, vaguely. "Now, who was he again?"

At once, I sensed he was purposely choosing not to admit knowing Mr. Barrington very well, so I reminded him in a rather curt fashion.

Almost scowling, I replied, "Well, actually, he was the *editor* of *The Announcer*. I'm surprised his name's not more familiar to you."

He thought for a moment or two, frowning then opening his eyes wide.

"Oh, yes, Charles Barrington. Sorry, but it's been a long time. Had some sons, didn't he?"

"Yes," I agreed, "three and a daughter."

It was here that he changed the subject, rather abruptly, I thought, and asked about my writing. Briefly, I told him about the novels which, since we'd finished our lunch, gave me the perfect excuse to escape upstairs ostensibly to write, but in reality I desperately needed to return my thoughts to Rainbow Falls.

Chapter Five

◆——————◆

My first two weeks at *The Announcer* were a whirlwind of activities. Betsy Clarke duly took me under her wing, treating me with kindness but also with her no-nonsense attitude. As I traipsed around after her covering a variety of local stories, she began teaching me a number of important journalistic lessons.

"Personal contacts and building relationships," she stated firmly, "are the bedrocks of being an effective reporter. Whether it's with a local councilman or woman, the police, store owners or just the general public, you will need to gain their trust and prove your reporting will be honest and true. Do that early on, Vanessa, and you won't go far wrong."

To prove her point, we dropped in at the village police department where Betsy was greeted warmly and with even a few hugs. She introduced me to some of her main contacts who offered their cooperation whenever it was appropriate.

Outside afterwards, she strongly reminded me never to take advantage of the privileged position we enjoyed, and to always write only the facts as they were known. "Once you've lost their trust," she emphasized, "it's gone forever. You only get one chance."

That piece of advice I have followed consistently with my prose writing; never take advantage of a source and always try to be faithful to whatever you've been told, usually in confidence.

Back in the office, which I clearly recall as always being smoky, noisy and full of people typing furiously or talking animatedly on the phone, Betsy walked me through how to report a story from start to finish. Of course, back in the late Sixties and early Seventies producing a newspaper was vastly different from the technology existing today. Betsy tried to explain the process to me, as did my uncle, who was heavily involved with that side of the paper. I could never quite grasp how the whole thing worked, but I do remember the typesetting was done by using a hot metal process called linotype. My uncle worked on the presses, which were either the rotary type or a flatbed machine. The actual newsprint paper came in a reel or on a huge roll called, if I recall correctly, a web.

Once a reporter had filed the story and it was approved, the typesetters worked their magic on machines that seemed, to simple me, as complex beyond words. They could automatically justify lines, assemble and type the story, and lock the finished piece into usable frames ready for my uncle and the press. The whole system boggled my mind and I tried my best to stay away from that side of the business.

The newsroom was full of characters, but all of the reporters were serious about their work. There were perhaps twelve of them, along with two photographers and a crusty old guy who specialized in sports. Before I came onto the scene Betsy was the only woman in the newsroom. I do recollect being treated well and accepted almost immediately into this close-knit society.

After a week trailing Betsy around town, she suggested it was high time I wrote my first piece. It concerned a suspicious fire in a house on the outskirts of town, and the assistant editor wanted me to find out as much as I could, if arson was involved and, if so, who might be responsible. Discovering all that information involved talking to the police, the fire department and, of course, the homeowners.

I still didn't yet have a car so Betsy kindly loaned me hers for a few hours each day. The police told me as much as they were allowed, not officially calling the fire arson, while the fire chief, after I pressed him, admitted an accelerant had been used. The fire, which pretty much destroyed the house, left the three occupants homeless. I managed to catch up with them at a nearby motel, where they were staying temporarily, courtesy of the Red Cross.

At first they were reluctant to talk to me, but I presented myself as the person who could get their story out into the world in a true, straightforward fashion. That seemed to work, I recalled, and the moment, I clearly remembered, filled me with pride that I'd managed to pry some very important details from them.

Later, at Betsy's desk, I wrote the story with her considerable assistance and, to my great surprise, it passed the assistant editor's approval for actually going to press for next day's edition. My Uncle Brian, having printed the actual issue during the night, presented me with my own copy at breakfast the next morning. He and Aunt Sheila reminded me, as if I needed telling, that this was a moment in my life I would never forget. It turned out they were right and, indeed, I still have that paper, with my very first article, sealed in plastic in my house.

Charles Barrington also took the time to congratulate me.

"Well, Vanessa," he began brightly, the next morning, "how does it feel?"

"A little surreal to be honest, but amazing at the same time," I replied, as confidently as I could.

"Well, get used to it," he continued, with a broad grin, "because if you keep producing stories like that, well written and full of crucial insight, then you'll be keeping our typesetters in business."

My next memory of that time concerned an office Christmas party, which for someone like me, basically straight out of a sheltered high school life, brought me face to face with raucous behavior, laughter and booze. Fortunately, the three females in the organization – Betsy, Sharon, the receptionist and me – stayed together. I worried, I recalled, being concerned that some of the guys might get out of hand, but, actually, the opposite was true. Although they were loud, sometimes bordering on inebriation, they all behaved with respect towards us. Charles Barrington was present, I remember, making the rounds and, I assume, keeping the young fellows in check. And I have to say, during my time at the newspaper, no one ever made even the slightest off-color remark to me.

As I sat on my balcony, feeling the sun and gentle breeze on my face, the remembrance of that party clearly brought to mind the first time I was invited to the Barringtons' house. It must have been a day or two before Christmas because my aunt and uncle were also invited, being close friends with Mr. and Mrs. Barrington. It was also the first time I met Mrs. Barrington, the three sons and the daughter.

As I recalled the evening there were probably twenty to thirty guests present, with a few of the senior reporters like Betsy Clarke, but mostly they were close personal friends of the Barringtons. Uncle Brian looked after me that evening knowing I was really shy around new people. To make me more comfortable, he first introduced me to Mrs. Barrington and then the four children.

"These are the troublemakers," he joked, as he got to the three boys and the girl who stood politely before me. "This one's Edward, this is Hugh, Simon and finally Chloe. And this," he continued, "is my niece, Vanessa, who's just started at the paper."

The three boys didn't seem particularly interested in meeting a gawky and awkward looking nineteen year old, pimply-faced girl, but the daughter, who I guessed to be around seventeen, asked how I was enjoying working at the paper.

"So far," I began cautiously, not wishing to give even a whisper of negativity, "so good. Everyone's been very nice and helpful to me, especially your father."

"Well, from what he said to us after your interview, I know he thinks highly of your writing, and Daddy doesn't make mistakes when it comes to the newspaper."

By this time the boys had wandered off, so Chloe took me to a quiet corner where we chatted for quite a while. I asked about school, what she enjoyed and what were her hobbies.

At this time, at the end of the Sixties, the whole country was in upheaval with the war raging in Vietnam. Chloe told me she didn't really know or understand too much about it, except that Edward had completed his tour, while Hugh could be called up at any time. Simon, she mentioned, was at Columbia and wouldn't be called on account of some medical condition.

"Daddy's so against the war that he's cost the paper some readers, but he's adamant it's wrong and that following Nixon is wrong, too. I'm sheltered from a lot of what he goes through and am just mainly concentrating on school."

She went on to tell me she loved fashion and her dream was to be a designer one day. I told her mine was to be a novelist and that being hired as a reporter on *The Announcer* was the first stepping stone. As we chatted, I noticed a tall, slim, very pretty young woman talking to Edward and Hugh. They were laughing and seemed completely comfortable with each other. Chloe must have noticed me looking and informed me that she was Edward's girlfriend, Samantha, known to the family and her friends as Sam.

Later that evening, just before we left, Aunt Sheila introduced me to Samantha. She didn't have to, but she spent about ten minutes with me enquiring about my writing and mentioning, in passing, that she was a singer, also just starting out, but hopeful to make it into the big time some day. I clearly recall we both laughed at our ambitions and how she said nothing in the world was impossible if you just wanted it badly enough. Of course, the music of the day was all rock and roll or protest songs, and Samantha said she covered a lot of Stones, Janis, Carly Simon and Joan Baez. All these years later, I could still see her as I attended a few of her local shows, and my memory was of a tremendously talented performer who seemed to love life and lived totally in the moment.

Suddenly, I recollected how, despite their apparent closeness and laughter, she and her boyfriend, Edward, didn't really seem to go together. At the time it was just an impression on my part, that here was this free-spirited soul, an obvious extrovert who loved performing, tied somehow to a more staid individual from a prominent family in town.

That party at the Barringtons was the first of many visits to their house. Over the next few months I became a regular visitor and the whole family gradually came to accept me into their tight, inner circle.

Christmas morning brought a tremendous surprise for me as my aunt and uncle presented me with the keys to my first car. It was a Ford, black, with leather seats and less than fifty thousand on the clock.

"Take care of it," my uncle advised, "and it'll take care of you."

Those words of wisdom proved to be correct. I had that little car for ten years and never in that time did it break down or get a flat. Several years later, when my novels started producing some significant income for me, I repaid my aunt and uncle's kindness by buying them a brand new Mercedes.

That car, in my early days with *The Announcer*, proved to be a boon, allowing me to cover my assigned stories quickly and, also, giving me a new found freedom in my off time. I loved nature, and hiking became one of my great pleasures, as it still remains to this day, although I'm a lot slower now than I used to be.

The car provided me, as well, with a way to enjoy some of the movies and plays in town and all over the county, which fed my artistic love as they still do today. My Aunt Sheila sometimes came with me, which made the whole experience that much more enjoyable.

Work at *The Announcer* after the Christmas break proceeded at an alarming rate. I took to going in an hour early to catch up with my copy and sometimes stayed well into the evening if a story merited it. My introduction to the world of journalism bordered on the manic most of the time. It was frenetic and pressure driven, but oh, so, rewarding when a story you'd researched and written hit the pages the next day.

The plum assignments were obviously given to the senior writers, but once in a while they corralled me into helping them with some leg work. Those times became magical for me since it let me inside the minds of people I respected and from whom I could learn.

One of those people, Vincent Spencer, specialized in investigative stories, which usually ended up being three or four part series, stretching over a two-week period. His particular interest centered on rooting out wrong doing within local government and exposing any corruption by elected officials. Down the years, apparently, Vincent had garnered quite a reputation for honest, in-depth reporting of these stories, and I was excited to join him on one when he approached me.

"First and foremost, Vanessa," he emphasized, as he began schooling me in the way he worked his stories, "always keep what you learn to yourself until you're ready to write it up. No blabbing to anyone just to show off what you know. Number two," he continued earnestly, his deeply lined face focused on my eyes, "only report those facts you know for certain are true. That means verifying everything of note from as many different sources as you can. Don't ever, ever, make stuff up. That's hard sometimes because you might know so and so is guilty but you can't prove it. That's not good enough for this paper. And I can tell you, you won't last long around here if you don't play your reporting straight down the line. Now, tell me you understand completely what I've just said?"

I assured him that I would follow his directions to the letter, after which he started telling me the hot story on which he was currently working. As it unfolded, I thought how much it seemed like a novel, not, in fact, the real life corruption it was. In the years that followed, my early connection to Vincent stood me in good stead when my novel writing really began cranking up. His attention to details, facts and writing a compelling narrative never left me over the years and I always felt I owed Vincent so much for being a major influence in my subsequent success.

My days working on that story of Vincent's filled me with a new respect for newspaper reporters. But at the same time the whole process awed me into wondering if I would ever reach those heights of quality writing. Much to his credit, Vincent allowed me a great deal of latitude as a contributing writer on his story. In fact, when the series was published both our names were listed under the headline. I still don't know if Vincent talked to Charles Barrington but, soon after the collaboration, my solo assignments became much more interesting.

Chapter Six

———————◆———————

The afternoon of remembering taxed my mind and, since the weather presented itself with sunshine and a warm breeze, I decided to take a leisurely stroll along one of the cliff walks. This part of the Maine coast intoxicated me with its stunning views way out into the ocean, its rugged rocks spilling from where I walked and disappearing into the foaming, sun dappled sea, its paths that sometimes meandered through canopies of fresh-leafed trees and, of course, the constant companionship of the squawking gulls, the soaring black and white winged kites, the always scurrying, long-legged sandpipers, and the sleek, plane-like, black-headed terns. It was a kaleidoscope of images that I felt privileged to witness.

When I first ventured back in time all those day ago, I wasn't sure if it was wise revisiting the past to discover…what?…jumbled memories, perhaps a pleasant recollection or two of some good times…I didn't really know then. But, ever since I began recalling in earnest, I now found I enjoyed the experience. Those times at *The Announcer* were foundational for me and they still hold such a special place in my heart. Also, bringing back to life my Aunt Sheila and Uncle Brian meant everything they did for me, both in practical and personal terms, had stayed with me as a sort of guidepost for my life.

But, as much as I relished all those things, I found myself becoming most intrigued with the Kenwrights and the Barringtons. Having only just started to scratch the surface of those folk, I somehow suspected they held much more in the way of meaningful and, perhaps, discoverable explanations to what I strongly felt needed to be explored when I first set eyes on Jack and Clare in the dining room. My memory was jarred by the sight of them and then, as now, I surmised something important must be lying dormant in my mind and which, for some reason, I had to revisit.

Halfway along my walk I found a convenient bench and plopped down to take a few minutes' rest. I closed my eyes and let the rays warm my face, as the sound of the incoming tide gently soothed me. Soon, I heard the presence of someone sitting down next to me and upon opening my eyes was greeted by the sight of Clare Kenwright.

"Oh, I hope you don't mind me disturbing your siesta," she offered, brightly, "but the cab driver told me of this gentle walk back to the hotel, which…well…for me," she continued, shaking her head and frowning, "wasn't so gentle after all. So, I'm glad of the rest."

Pulling my senses back into the present, I assured her she wasn't bothering me in the least.

"Your husband said you'd gone into town for a bit," I told her, "We had lunch, you see. Hope you don't mind," I said, with a broad smile.

She laughed, telling me it was good he could spend some time with someone who didn't tend to nag him all the time.

"Actually," I countered, "I asked him about your time in Rainbow Falls. He seemed to have some vague recollections, so I filled in a few of the blanks for him."

"Ah, yes, Rainbow Falls," Clare replied, nodding, "such a long time ago now. I don't think we were there for very long."

"No, that's right, only about six months, as I recall."

She cocked her head and her white hair seemed to shimmer in the late afternoon sun. As I briefly studied her face I could still see her as she was over fifty years ago, her sharp features softened somewhat but prominent enough to give her the regal look I clearly recalled. Her smile also hadn't changed in all that time, lighting her face as though she was permanently happy and nothing nor anybody could change that.

"Your husband reminded me that you painted in those days," I continued, wondering if she'd try to shut me down as she did with Stu, the bartender.

"It was in the blood," she responded, nodding. "My father was artistic and I suppose some of his magic rubbed off on me. And back in those days an artist's life greatly appealed to me. It was a sort of freedom, very few rules, do what you want when you wanted to. Probably the same for you, too, wasn't it, being a writer, I mean?"

Shaking my head and ruefully smiling, I told her my aunt and uncle kept me on a tight leash.

"I'd led quite a sheltered life up until I got the newspaper job. And after that my sights were always firmly focused on becoming a full-time writer."

"Not like me," she replied, rather sadly, I thought. "Jack was the breadwinner, always has been. Oh, I'm not complaining, he's given me a comfortable life, but sometimes you look back down the years and wonder... what if... what if I'd made other choices? You just wonder sometimes, that's all."

"Where did you two go after you'd left Rainbow Falls?"

Looking out at the ocean she answered, "Oh, probably another city in another state. Jack was a sort of troubleshooter for his father's company that owned a group of nationwide local papers. He wasn't home a lot, that much I do remember. So I painted, went to rock concerts, did some pot, you know...the usual Seventies' things."

As she reminisced, a few memories of my own about Jack popped into my head. Whenever he came into the office I recalled being a little intimidated by him, that his demeanor was brash and very self-assured. I also remembered how on a number of occasions he would take some of us aside, particularly the younger reporters, and offer advice on how our stories should be framed and written, which I clearly recollected annoyed the assistant editors and, of course, Charles Barrington himself.

Being a writer, which made me naturally nosy about and interested in other people's lives, I asked Clare how they ended up together.

She smiled as she said, "Oh, I gather he was quite a handful in his teens. Liked the ladies and the booze, so his father packed him off into the Army when he turned nineteen. He did his four years...the last in Vietnam...and then went into the family business. I met him through a mutual friend and, after dating for a year, we married in '68."

As she spoke, another recollection of Jack Kenwright pricked my brain, one that was fuzzy but which I somehow knew seemed important to my whole remembrance of my time at *The Announcer.*

After a few more of my probing questions, I got the impression Clare was becoming increasingly uncomfortable with the way the conversation was progressing. She slowly arose and said it was time to head back to the hotel, while I decided to continue my walk a little while farther.

Before she'd gone more than a couple of steps she stopped and called out to me.

"I hope your remembering doesn't upset you too much," she offered. "We were all different people back then."

Shaking my head, I replied, "Oh, no, not at all and, yes, it's true, we were all different back then. See you later."

Her remark, the more I thought about it on the rest of my walk, seemed strange to me, as though she knew something I hadn't yet recalled. That notion intrigued me and I couldn't wait until I picked again at my recollections.

Before that could happen I had to attend to the pressing matter of finishing my trilogy of *Intimate Strangers.* By the time I returned to my room it was past four o'clock and I decided to spend the hours before dinner working out the final, crucial, last two chapters. Kay, my agent, was due to show up sometime on Friday and I wanted to at least have a definite outline and road map to assure her I had, indeed, been writing diligently as per her instructions.

The three-book series represented my proudest writing achievement. Not only did I feel I'd created a continuous compelling storyline, but I also felt the thousands of loyal readers who had taken the ride with me believed in the work as a credible piece of fiction. The first two books were obviously the foundation for the final one, which meant there could be no room for disappointment as the story finally concluded. I felt the pressure to produce an appropriate and convincing end, but I wasn't daunted by the prospect. But it needed to be thought about carefully and that effort consumed me for the rest of the day.

Surprisingly, the two hours or so before dinner produced clear, creative ideas, which, after my evening meal, I quickly transformed into what I thought to be an impressive start to the penultimate chapter. The words flowed almost effortlessly and by eleven I had the basic concept tucked away. I went to bed that night feeling more than satisfied that the end of *Intimate Strangers* would please me and my readers alike.

When I awoke the next morning I decided to have breakfast in town, at a smart little café quite near the ice cream store. For some reason I couldn't face seeing the Kenwrights again for a while, especially since I knew I needed to sort out some more important memories which Clare had stirred up in me yesterday.

I ordered coffee and a blueberry muffin, and really began to enjoy the cozy atmosphere and aromas surrounding me like warm hugs. I chose a corner table from where I could observe the other patrons, something I'd always done and which I found useful when having to describe people for my books. Writers never know when a certain trait, walk, mode of speech or affectation in someone will be needed, and I certainly had pulled a lot of stored characteristics in my time and used them to, hopefully, great effect.

As I lavishly buttered my muffin I noticed coming through the door a striking young woman, perhaps in her mid-twenties, dressed casually but, I guessed, expensively, in fashionably holey jeans and a bright yellow tee-shirt. Accompanying her was a very good-looking man, again maybe in his mid-twenties, who guided her to a table and then went to the counter to place their order. After a while, he carried their coffees and Danish back to the woman and they began to enthusiastically enjoy their treats. There was nothing particularly remarkable about that whole scene except for the way the young man seemed, from his behavior, to be completely enamored of his companion. He smiled and laughed a lot, letting her do most of the talking while he constantly nodded and held her hand or touched her face whenever possible. From my brief observations I surmised this young man was besotted with the woman, while she, although attentive, utterly understood it was she who drove this bus not him.

Of course, I may have been wrong on all fronts but the incident immediately jabbed my memory and, at once, I remembered something of importance to my Rainbow Falls recollections. A sudden light bulb switched on in my mind and I left the café silently thanking the couple for the revelation.

On my walk along the beach on the way back to the hotel, I excitedly looked forward to settling down on my balcony and taking myself back to those early weeks of January 1970. But as soon as I entered the lobby Joyce Andrews, one of the owners, politely stopped me for a chat.

"So sorry to bother you," she began, as she served me a cup of tea in her private lounge, "but I've been asked to see if you'd do a favor for the local library."

Puzzled, I frowned as I wondered how on earth I could help the local library.

"Oh, well, yes...what do they have in mind?"

"Well, you see, word has gotten around that there's a famous author staying here," she continued, with a wide grin.

I cocked my head and returned the grin.

"And I wonder how that happened?" I countered.

"Sorry, so sorry," Joyce apologized. "It was a friend of a friend who spilled the beans. Anyway, our librarian got wind of your presence, is obviously very familiar with your work and wants to know if you'd be prepared to come in and give a talk at the weekend?"

I was taken aback by the offer but immediately accepted.

"Of course, I'd be delighted."

Giving talks and promoting my books was something I'd done quite often and was used to. I would use my standard presentation, take a few questions and then sign some books if anyone wanted to make a purchase.

"Okay, thank you so much," Joyce replied, appreciatively. "The library patrons are going to love this. We seldom get anyone of note like you around this neck of the woods. I'll let them know and get back to you with the day and time."

Knowing Kay was coming for the weekend I called her immediately to let her know of this new arrangement. She was always thrilled when her authors gave talks and that was certainly the case this time.

"Oh, just wonderful, Nessa," she gushed, "especially as the new book will be out soon. All good for sales, and," she continued, "I'll bring in a generous supply of your other titles for you to sign and people to buy. Oh, this is so exciting!"

Kay was nothing if not a great promoter of her authors, whereas this time I just wanted to give the locals a genuine insight into the writing process rather than peddling my books. But I supposed making a few sales wasn't a bad thing after all. I told her I was really looking forward to her visit, asked her to drive safely and left it at that.

Back in my room I took a few minutes before settling down once more to revisit my time in Rainbow Falls. As I sat on my balcony closing my eyes, I took myself back to my early days at *The Announcer*. I particularly wanted to recall the moment the Kenwrights appeared on the scene and the eventual impact Jack Kenwright had on the newspaper. I thought hard for a while but finally brought that memory to mind.

It was halfway through January and the Barrington family was throwing a party to celebrate Edward's twenty-sixth birthday. Surprisingly, I had been invited, mostly, I suspected, because my aunt and uncle, being close friends of Charles and his wife, were included among the guests. Samantha, Edward's girlfriend, and her close friend, April Sinclair were there, along with maybe four or five of the Barrington boys' pals.

I clearly recall how loud the party was, mostly because the record player was belting out rock and roll for all it was worth. I was taken under April's care, since both she and I weren't used to such noise and merriment. But Samantha seemed to be in her element, standing in the middle of the room lip-syncing to most of the songs.

Both the music and booze flowed freely that night, which allowed the event to be a happy, joyous occasion. Halfway through the evening Samantha insisted Chloe, the boys' younger sister, who seemed to be in charge of playing the music, put on and turn up 'Me and Bobby McGee' by Janis Joplin, apparently one of Samantha's favorites and one she performed regularly with her band.

True to form, Samantha joined Janis in the song, while the rest of us stood around clapping, hooting and urging her on. The moment was spellbinding for me and I truly felt a part of the family.

Just before Janis and Samantha's final, explosive lyrics ended we were surprised to see a couple of strangers standing in the doorway. As the song ended and the room fell quiet, all eyes swiveled towards the pair.

"Oh, sorry," the man began, "but we did ring the bell but obviously no one heard us. We just came round to let you know we've arrived... Jack and Clare Kenwright."

Mr. Barrington, ever the gentleman, immediately went over and introduced not only himself but everyone in the room. That was the first time we set eyes on the Kenwrights...in the middle of *'Me and Bobby McGee'*.

Chapter Seven

◆———————◆

A fter my initial bright beginning at *The Announcer* I was brought down to earth by one of the senior editors who assigned me for the time being to some mundane areas. These included covering local council meetings, school board sessions and sometimes even local flower and dog shows. Apparently, it was all part of my training on the path to becoming a 'real' reporter. I minded not at all since I was writing and that always made me happy.

We didn't see much of Jack Kenwright at first as most of the time he seemed to be sequestered with Charles Barrington in his office. The official story, for his sudden appearance at the paper, was that his father wanted him to gain valuable experience by visiting all the papers in the group, with a view to eventually taking over the running of the company. Once or twice during their meetings most of us in the news room heard loud exchanges and, more than once, Mr. Barrington stormed out with a face like thunder. We assumed his reaction must be serious since, for the most part, he was a man of calm, deliberate temperament.

Of course, being the newest addition to the staff, I wasn't privy to a lot of the inside gossip, but I heard enough to know things were not well. After a week matters calmed somewhat when Jack Kenwright began attaching himself to different reporters ostensibly to learn the business from the ground up. He certainly wasn't well liked in the office mainly because his demeanor came off as brash and condescending. But he never seemed to complain when trailing around with his current partner, even if the story was dull, or in his words, 'trite'.

About this time April Sinclair, Samantha's good friend, sought me out and wanted to know if I'd like to go hiking with her at the weekend. April seemed at loose ends particularly as Samantha was heavily involved with rehearsing with her band as well as still seeing Edward. One of my passions was walking and hiking the hills around Rainbow Falls, so I immediately agreed to accompany her. Since leaving high school I'd lost contact with a lot of my friends, so I welcomed the chance to make a new one. April and I seemed to have quite a lot in common when we spoke at Edward's birthday party. She worked as a veterinary assistant and was going to school part-time for her license. I loved animals, too, so I knew the conversation wouldn't lag.

Unfortunately, my Aunt Sheila got wind of our expedition and asked, as a favor, if I would take her neighbor's nine year old son with us. My aunt looked after him sometimes when the neighbor worked and this particular Saturday was one of those times.

I knew him as Jimmy and the few times he was at our house he tended to follow me around like a puppy. I surmised the boy must be lonely, so I did my best to talk to him before I usually made an excuse and headed to my room to write. I remember he liked to ask questions all the time, which was all right up to a point. As I got to know him better I realized Jimmy was very intelligent, not just nosy. He loved to ask about my writing, so I would tell him the basic storyline and suggested he give me some ideas about what should happen next. Of course, the results were always way off from where I was headed but through these exchanges I encouraged him to do some story writing of his own.

Jimmy's attempts, although obviously childish in nature, definitely held promise, and I did my best in all the time I knew him to support his ever growing interest. He didn't seem to have many friends his own age and, whenever he was around my aunt and uncle, Jimmy, I clearly recall, never seemed confident or very communicative. My Aunt Sheila, bless her heart, tried her best whenever she looked after him to encourage him to talk about school and his interests, but Jimmy never seemed comfortable around adults. On the very few occasions my Uncle

Brian happened to be home when Jimmy visited, my aunt would ask my uncle to show Jimmy whatever he might be working on in his workshop. After a while that stopped because Jimmy showed little interest in woodworking or mechanical projects.

On this particular Saturday I loaded him and our hiking gear into my car and headed out to pick up April at her apartment.

"I wish it was just you and me going," Jimmy said, rather sadly, as we drove along.

Frowning, I replied, "Oh, c'mon, Jimmy, April's a lot of fun. She loves to hike, too, and she knows a lot about animals. She's learning to be a vet, you know."

He thought about that for a few seconds before saying, "That's what I want to be when I grow up, but I want to work at a zoo." He then wanted to know about my latest story, which just happened to be about a dog.

"Maybe you could help me with it," I offered, as I related the main points. "I seem to be stuck on the ending."

He made a couple of suggestions, both of which didn't fit with my own vision for a good finish, but I thanked him for giving me some possible new options. By this time we'd reached April's apartment and soon all three of us were on our way on the ten mile journey to Beecher's Woods.

After parking the car we set out on the main trail which, because of the mild winter was mostly devoid of snow, for the five mile hike to our destination – Hollow River, where we planned to rest and eat our lunch. For most of the walk Jimmy went ahead, returning now and then to inform us of some birds he'd seen or, once or twice, a few deer.

That actually suited April and me since it meant we could go at our own pace while chit-chatting about our lives. It turned out she'd known the Barringtons for about five years and considered herself to be a close friend of the family.

"I went to school with Hugh, so we hung out quite a bit. I got to know Edward, Simon and Chloe through him, although Edward was away most of the time in the military. Have you heard about Simon's illness?"

"No, I hardly know them at all. What's the matter with him?"

"He has epilepsy and has seizures some times. It's very sad and quite disturbing when you see it happen. He's also highly strung. He's in college but I understand it's a struggle for him. His parents are very protective but his brothers and sister seem to take it in stride."

As we walked on I asked about Hugh, the middle brother.

"Oh, he's a real sweetie. Very funny, teases people a lot and is very protective of Chloe. Unfortunately, he could be called up at any time, so that's a worry for everyone. By the way," April continued, "we're all going to Sam's concert tomorrow night. Why don't you come, too?"

"I'd love to but I don't want to intrude on a family occasion."

"Oh, they won't mind and, besides, you work with Mr. Barrington and your aunt and uncle are their really good friends. As long as you'll feel comfortable they won't care."

"All right, then, I'd like to go, thanks."

"Come to the house around six. We'll probably have a few snacks before we go and then after the concert there's usually a late dinner."

It was all agreed before I knew it but, along with a little trepidation, I actually found myself looking forward to the occasion. The Barrington family, it seemed to me, exuded the kind of closeness I felt with my mother and my aunt and uncle. I guess it was a sense of belonging, of being a part of a group of people who I could look up to and learn from. At this point in my young life I suppose I needed that feeling and the Barringtons in my eyes supplied it in abundance.

We finally made it to Hollow River where, bundled up, we ate lunch, skipped stones into the water, and persuaded Jimmy not to venture too far from shore since April warned us that the river was deep with a wicked undertow. Fortunately, he heeded our warnings and instead wandered off a little way down stream where he found a small animal skull.

"Vanessa! Vanessa!" he yelled, running back. "Look what I found."

He placed the skull at our feet and quickly removed a frog from his pocket, which he then thrust almost under my nose.

"Treat it gently," April advised, as she proceeded to give Jimmy some interesting facts about frogs. He listened while stroking the creature and, surprisingly, asked April to tell him more about them. For the first time I witnessed Jimmy really paying attention and being totally interested in what April had to say.

"I'm going to write a story about this," he informed us, proudly. "It'll be an adventure story."

"Oh, I like that idea, Jimmy," I told him, encouragingly. "And if you need help, we're always here for you. Now, why don't you put the frog back where it belongs?"

He obliged, carefully placing it on a rock near the river's edge.

"Did you know the Barringtons have a place just over that ridge?" April asked me.

I shook my head and she suggested we hike the small distance and take a peek. The building was more like an oversized cabin but large enough to host the family and a few guests.

"We come up every other weekend in the summer," she informed me. "Next time you must come, too."

I told her that sounded like heaven and we began our trek back to the car. Jimmy skipped ahead again and made us laugh by hiding behind trees and jumping out at us as we passed. It was great seeing him laugh, too, and having a really good time. As we crossed a field on the last part of our journey back to the car we came across Clare Kenwright sitting at an easel she'd set up with a gorgeous view of one of the distant hills.

Jimmy ran ahead and the two began talking. By the time April and I got there Clare was showing Jimmy her palette, various brushes and bits and pieces of different colored charcoal.

"And this is how you get the trees to look real," we heard her telling him, as we arrived on the scene. She looked at us and smiled before handing Jimmy a brush with a dab of blue on it and told him to carefully paint a small section of sky. "He's a natural," she offered, still smiling. "My work just increased in price by fifty dollars!"

Laughing, I thanked her for taking the time with him.

"It's Vanessa, isn't it?" she asked, looking at me. "You work at *The Announcer* don't you?"

"Yes, very junior reporter, but I'm learning," I offered, with a smile.

"I'm sorry," she said, turning to April, "I don't think we've met. I'm Clare Kenwright."

"Actually, Mr. Barrington introduced us when you stopped by the house when you first arrived," April replied, "but it was quite noisy. I'm April Sinclair."

"Oh, yes, sorry, well it's nice to see you again. Your friend, I remember, was quite the singer. Even my husband was impressed."

"That's Samantha, yes. She has her own band."

Clare didn't seem to be too interested after that, and by this time Jimmy had finished the spot of sky. Clare turned her attention to him and offered a tiny patch of grass to fill in.

"I didn't know you were an artist," I said, surprised. "This looks very good to me," I continued, admiring the landscape.

"Thank you, I try. But, yes, it's a passion. And, I have to do something with myself since my husband's so busy most days. I imagine you see more of him than I do," she added, with a faint smile.

"Oh, I think he's tied up a lot in meetings, and I'm out and about chasing down stories, so we don't tend to bump into each other much." I noticed Jimmy had finished his patch of green, so I told him it was time to go so that Mrs. Kenwright could continue with her landscape.

He frowned but complied, and I asked him to thank her for letting him paint a little, which he did very politely.

"If you'd like," Clare said, patting his arm, "I could help you paint your own picture some time."

"Would you?" he answered, almost yelling with delight. "Vanessa, can I? Can I?"

"Don't see why not, but let's talk about it with you mom and dad. Okay?"

"Okay."

"That's so kind of you," I told her, as we gathered up our stuff and headed back to my car.

On the drive home, April reminded me to be at the Barringtons' house at six the next evening for Samantha's rock concert, and I assured her I'd be there. We dropped her at her apartment where she thanked me and Jimmy for the hike. I felt, as she left us, that I'd now made a firm friend in April, as though she might well be the big sister I never had.

The next evening I duly presented myself at the Barringtons' house at a little after six. April met me at the door and I was soon ushered inside and greeted warmly by Mr. and Mrs. Barrington.

"So glad you could make it, Vanessa," Mrs. Barrington said, smiling, as she called Simon over to take my coat. "And, Simon," she continued, "please make sure Vanessa has a drink and something to snack on."

"What's your fancy?" Simon asked, as he guided me over to the drinks' table.

"Oh, just a soda, thank you."

As he poured me a glass I studied him for a few seconds, finding a clean-cut, dark-haired young man, who grinned pleasantly as he handed me my drink.

"Chips? Dip? Maybe some crackers and cheese?" he asked, as he passed me a small plate.

We helped ourselves to a few snacks, found a quiet corner and started chatting.

"How's the old man treating you?" he continued, almost laughing.

"So far, so good. No complaints."

"And this new guy...Kenwright, isn't it? What's he like? I think my dad's wary of him right now."

I shrugged and replied that I hadn't seen much of him around the office. Simon was making me uncomfortable talking about matters that really were none of my business, so I changed the subject and asked about college.

"What's your major? Have you decided yet?"

"Mom and Pop want me to go into business like Edward, but that kind of stuff bores me. So, right now, I'm thinking I'd like to go into the movies."

"What, like being an actor?"

"No," he laughed, "don't think I've got the looks. More behind the camera, I'm thinking. I fancy directing."

As I stood there I could actually see him in a few years doing exactly that, although I didn't tell him. Instead, I asked what kind of films he liked.

"Something with a good story where you really connect with the characters. Have you seen *'Five Easy Pieces'*?"

"Not yet. Is it good?"

"So good," he exclaimed. "Jack Nicholson and Karen Black blew my mind. Great family story, very intense and you don't see a lot of it coming."

I was beginning to warm to Simon and was glad he seemed to be orienting towards the arts, which is what I, too, eventually wanted to pursue with my writing. Just when I was about to ask him some more questions we were ushered out of the house and into two cars for the short journey to Samantha's concert.

Chapter Eight

---◆---◆---

My morning of remembering astounded me in that I actually recalled so much. The whole process excited me, too, for it enabled me to relive in my mind some really happy occurrences from my youth. Although so long ago now, my recollections pleased me in a way I never expected. The past is the past and I never found myself dwelling much in it before. But this whole experience brought me joy and also a certain amount of pride in some of my early accomplishments, which, at the time, meant very little to me.

I was anxious to return to Rainbow Falls so I asked Joyce Andrews if she could arrange for me to have my lunch in my room. My feeling was that I did not want to see the Kenwrights or engage them in any conversation at that point which might infringe upon my remembrances. Joyce duly obliged and brought my meal up personally.

"Here we are, Vanessa, fresh fish and chips."

I thanked her profusely and asked if she'd stay for a few minutes.

"I just want to run a couple of thoughts by you, if you wouldn't mind?"

"Oh, no, absolutely not. I could do with something other than reservations and bills to think about," she offered, with a laugh.

She called down to the bar and had Stu, the bartender, send up a couple of glasses of my favorite red.

Settling down, I began telling her a little about my journey through the past. I didn't cover everything, of course, but just enough to give her the gist of my endeavors.

After ten minutes I said, "So, my question is, to someone like you who really knows nothing much about me, am I chasing some pleasant memories in the hope of making them seem more important than they really were, or am I searching for answers to some long ago buried situation that I now feel I have to confront to finally have peace of mind?"

Joyce surprised me by immediately understanding the dilemma.

"Vanessa," she began, after taking a long sip of her wine, "we all need to know certain things about our past. I, for instance, confronted my mother a few years ago about stories that began surfacing about my grandfather, long since gone now, I might add, which suggested he was not at all how I remembered him.

"He was a business man, a successful one, too, but the rumors were that he had attained his wealth through, shall we say, shady dealings with disreputable people. This was important to me since I was just starting out on my own career in town and I was fearful my efforts might be harmed by my grandfather's alleged misdeeds.

"As well as enlisting my mother's help, I also talked to some of his still-living old friends who knew him much better than me. And it turned out my recollections of him were spot on, that it was other jealous people who had tried to ruin him with lies concerning his business practices, because he was successful while they struggled.

"But having to recall the past for me not only validated my grandfather as I remembered him, but also strengthened the fact that how I recalled him was true, not only in my mind, but in actual fact. That was so important for me. So, Vanessa, what you've told me about your own recollections will, I hope, provide you with some sort of resolution to whatever it is that's still concerning you. And it seems, from what you've told me, that something certainly is. Now, it may not always be good news, but at least when you're done you'll hopefully have that finality you're seeking."

Joyce's words of wisdom washed over me like the refreshing breeze I sometimes felt sitting on my balcony. In such a short time she had put my worries and doubts into clear perspective. I wasn't wrong in trying to remember; I really had a duty.

"Joyce, thank you. Thank you. I feel like I owe you two hundred bucks for a therapy session," I replied, giggling. "What you've said helps so much."

"You're very welcome, and I'll add my fee to your bill," she responded, with a laugh.

We finished our wine and my lunch and left each other with a meaningful hug.

Before returning to Samantha's concert I decided to try and tie down at least a couple more pages of the book. Although I'd done a great deal of remembering, I'd also managed to frame in my mind exactly how the trilogy should end. Most of the ideas came to me when I was in bed, restless and unable to sleep. I always kept a pad handy to jot down whatever came across so that in the morning I still had the gist. Of course, much of what I thought of at that time of night was nonsense and, upon reviewing it in the morning, I scrapped most of it. But, once or twice the germ of a real possibility presented itself for me to work on and improve.

Over the last few days from those jottings, I clearly formed a credible but unexpected ending to, not only this book, but the whole trilogy. Wrapping the series up in this way exhilarated me, and as soon as Joyce left I settled down and began writing the beginning of the end. Before I knew it four hours had flashed by but the work I'd accomplished pleased me beyond measure. Now only the final chapter remained to be written.

Since I'd been cooped up in my room most of the day I decided to have dinner in town, at a smart little Italian restaurant only recently opened for the season. Again, I didn't wish to meet or mingle with the Kenwrights, so this was the perfect solution. I managed to slip out of the hotel unnoticed and, after eating, was able to get back in without attracting their attention. Stu, the bartender, supplied my usual glass of red and I carried it carefully up to my room where I changed, got comfy and prepared to take myself back to Samantha's concert some fifty years before.

The Chelsea Morning Coffee Bar was the perfect setting for the concert. By day it served the neighborhood as a decent breakfast and lunch location, while at night it transformed itself into an intimate venue for local bands and singers. Tables were set up in the main dining area where customers and fans could order and enjoy drinks and fast food from a limited menu. The Barringtons, being regular patrons, apparently always reserved three tables to accommodate their large throng.

We arrived a half-hour before the start, ordered our goodies, made small talk and looked forward to Samantha putting on a great show. Just before she came on Jack Kenwright buzzed through the door and, finding it hard to find an empty table, was invited to join us. He was alone, telling us that Clare had caught a chill from spending too much time painting in the nippy January weather.

Soon, he ingratiated himself into our group by ordering a round of drinks for everyone. And, I must admit, for the first time I saw a different side to him than the one he portrayed around the news room. His amiable disposition belied the almost arrogant demeanor he usually showed and, even to Mr. and Mrs. Barrington, he was respectful, quiet and funny. He seemed interested in learning about the family, engaged the boys and Chloe in some easy banter and even asked April and me a few questions. This pre-concert episode on his part seemed genuine and, as the evening wore on, I sensed our whole crowd became more comfortable with him.

Just before eight the owner of the Chelsea Morning Coffee Bar took to the stage, thanked us all for attending and supporting the up and coming musicians and introduced Samantha and her band. Our reception was loud, particularly from the boys, but it was soon drowned out by the first number, a cover of Creedence Clearwater Revival's Proud Mary. Samantha, the lead singer, began the song quietly but soon the bass and rhythm guitarists and the drummer upped the tempo to match her rising, intense voice. For me, a recent high school graduate, seeing a fierce young woman on stage, in charge and apparently fearlessly taking over the room, filled me with awe and amazement that someone had the courage to do that.

But that was only the start of what was to become a night to remember. Samantha and the band followed the opening with covers of The Stones, The Eagles, Bad Finger and so many more rock legends. Interspersed were a few she'd written herself. The one I recall best even now was called *'My Time'*, a gentle folk-rock song, which seemed to be a road map for Samantha's musical ambitions.

As I remembered that evening from all those years ago, I still saw Samantha strutting her stuff like a seasoned performer and giving her audience the time of its life. We cheered her, clapped her and yelled for more, only letting her go after she sang an extended version of Joni Mitchell's *'Both Sides Now'*. It was a fitting close to an extraordinary performance for me; a performance that told me anyone can be anything they want to be.

After the concert ended and the praise and congratulations for Samantha and the band finally died down, we headed out for our late dinner. The other band members preferred hanging out at the Chelsea Morning's bar, so Samantha rode with me, Edward and April.

"Oh, Sam," April gushed at her friend, "that was so good. At this rate you'll be bigger than Janis," she joked. "Am I right, guys?" she asked me and Edward.

I agreed immediately. "I could hardly believe what I was seeing and hearing, Samantha. Only wish I had half your talent."

"Well, the star of the show thanks you," Samantha replied, outrageously milking the moment, grinning and high-fiving us. "We aim to please."

Funnily enough, Edward, who was driving us to dinner, seemed lukewarm with his compliments. He told Samantha, "Good job, as usual, Sweetheart. Great set but I missed the softer side of you."

"Eddie," April butted in, "this is rock and roll, man, not tango night for the over seventies! Don't listen to him, Sam," she continued, giving her a hug, "it was just what the crowd wanted."

Sam shrugged, as though she was used to Edward's comments. That moment between the two of them hit me like a hard slap. I instantly felt, as I had before, a certain amount of tension with them, as though Samantha didn't quite match up to Edward's ideals, that her singing career was some sort of threat to him.

"Am I right, Vanessa?" April asked, as we pulled into the restaurant parking lot.

"Yes, amazing, just amazing!" I responded, shaking my head. "Best music and singing I've heard in a long time. Just amazing," I repeated.

Beaming, Samantha turned from the front seat and high-fived me. After we left the car and headed inside, I noticed Edward and Samantha hanging back, in deep conversation which, at times, seemed intense and angry on her part. But, once inside and seated with the family, they acted civilly towards each other.

My next recollection of that evening suddenly filled me with a chill, as I recalled the frightening moment it happened. The dinner was nearly over and, as we were finishing our coffees and desserts, Simon let out an almighty wail and, shaking and jerking uncontrollably, fell off his chair onto the floor. I found out afterwards he was experiencing a grand mal seizure which he'd had a few times before, but which was completely foreign to me.

Paralyzed, I could only watch in horror as the sad, frightening event unfolded before my eyes. Quickly, as though on cue, Mrs. Barrington and Hugh jumped up, gently turned Simon on his side to assist with his breathing, placed a coat under his head and stayed close until the seizure abated. This one lasted what to me seemed like an age and, indeed, since it went on for over six minutes, an ambulance was summoned.

When Simon came around he was disoriented and unaware of his surroundings or what had just happened to him. Mrs. Barrington went in the ambulance with him, while the other family members told her they'd meet her at the hospital. April and I said we'd go there, too, while Samantha, distraught and crying, said she just wanted to go home. Edward told her to get a cab, but instead, she took up Jack Kenwright's kind offer of a ride since he lived quite close to her.

As far as I recalled we stayed at the hospital until we knew Simon was resting comfortably. He'd suffered a slight concussion from hitting his head on the wooden floor but other than that the doctor told us he was none the worse for wear. Mr. Barrington gave April and me a lift home, while Edward took care of the others.

The next morning Mr. Barrington sought me out to tell me Simon was now home and how much the family appreciated my support. He reassured me that, although the situation with Simon looked scary, the seizures were few and far between, and both he and the family were used to them. His kind words put my mind at ease and, indeed, for the whole time I knew and mixed with the Barringtons, I did witness quite a few more of Simon's seizures. The incidents, of course, never failed to upset me but at least I understood they were somewhat of a normal occurrence for him.

To protect myself, and I suppose, my sad feelings, I remember purposely staying away from the Barringtons for a few weeks. I kept in touch with April, went on another hike or two, but generally stayed home after work to concentrate on my own writing projects.

By the time these vivid memories began to fade I noticed the time had slipped past one o'clock. I finished the last drops of wine, brushed my teeth and settled down in bed for what I hoped would be a restful sleep. For the most part that's what happened, but once or twice I awoke to be bothered by a constant thought that somehow Simon's seizure that evening was actually the beginning of something worse for the family.

Chapter Nine

———◆———◆———

"Vanessa, this outline is phenomenal!" My agent's voice and face appeared in front of me before I'd hardly had a chance to wake up.

"Kay, really, did you have to call this early?" The time was six-thirty.

"Yes, yes, I did. The ending you've imagined is just magnificent. Oh, god, this book's going to be a smash!"

The ideas I'd firmly worked out in my mind as a fitting end to, not only this book, but the trilogy, I'd emailed to Kay the day before. I was pleased and reassured that she sounded so excited because if anyone recognized a winner it was Kay.

"Oh, that's a relief, Kay," I answered. "You're a tough nut to crack and satisfy," I added, with a laugh, "so if you think it's okay, I'll start the last chapter as soon as I can."

"Don't forget I'm coming in at the weekend. Really looking forward to it. Sun, sea and wine…couldn't ask for more. By the way, how's your remembrance of times past going?"

I felt Kay seemed a tad flippant with her question but I resisted the temptation to bark back at her.

"Actually, Kay, the process has been revealing, rewarding and sometimes, I'll admit, somewhat disturbing. But I have to say I am enjoying the recollections and meeting again all those people who meant so much to me, if only in my mind's eye."

"And what about those people in the hotel you mentioned were familiar to you in some way? Have you figured them out yet?"

"Oh, yes, and they seem to be an integral part of the whole story."

"Story?" she asked. "What story? This is beginning to sound very interesting."

"I'm not sure yet, Kay, but the more I remember and keep digging the more I feel I'll uncover something that's obviously been laying dormant in my mind."

"Or something you've chosen to deliberately forget?"

"That, too, perhaps, I just don't know."

"Has it upset you all this going back and dredging up the past?"

"No, not really. I mean there have been moments that have been painful to recall, like my mother's death, but on the other hand, I now realize how lucky I was having so many people supporting me and seeing me through that bad time. And, also, reliving my time at *The Announcer*, which actually set me on my professional writing path. So, it's been good and bad so far. But honestly, Kay, I really feel I've only scratched the surface. As I've remembered stuff it pricks my memory into areas I'd quite forgotten. That in turn gives me the feeling that somewhere buried in all this is something really, really important that I know I'll eventually discover."

"This has all the makings of your next novel, Vanessa," Kay only half joked. "If I'm intrigued I'm sure your faithful readers would be, too."

"Hold that thought, Kay, and let me at least finish the trilogy first. But, yes, you never know where all this remembering will end up."

"Is your talk at the local library still on for Saturday?"

"It is, yes."

"Good, because not only have I a ton of your books for sale, but I've also alerted the local media."

"You've done what?" I asked, incredulously. "Oh, for goodness sake, Kay!"

"No, no, listen to me, Vanessa. The anticipation for your new book is palpable, and the more we can feed your faithful readers the more that anticipation and interest grows. I mean, you want it to be a success, don't you, a validation that the trilogy as a whole worked?"

"Of course, but this is just a teeny-tiny library, in an out-of-the-way-place in Maine, not New York City," I argued, forcefully.

"Well, that's the whole point," Kay responded, firmly. "The publicity this event will manufacture will soon be picked up by the nationals. And from there the anticipation for the book knows no bounds. Stephen King does this type of thing all the time. He builds anticipation which eventually pays off in massive sales. Trust me here, Vanessa, I'm right."

"But I just want to give the locals who don't usually have a chance to perhaps meet an established author that opportunity. I don't want them to think they don't matter, because they do. This town is full of good, decent, hard-working people who go about their daily lives without asking for much in return. All I want to do, Kay, is make them feel appreciated, that I cared enough to give them my time and a personal look inside a writer's life."

"Yes, yes, I understand all that and very commendable, too. But, Vanessa, this is also a business…a very tough business. You must trust me here as your agent and friend. It will be fine, I assure you of that. I will make sure the locals have their moment in the sun, so to speak."

"As long as they're not treated as after thoughts…not there just to make the numbers up…then, okay. But I warn you, Kay, I will take matters into my own hands if I feel they are."

"You sound like a tough character from one of your books," she answered, with a chuckle. "It'll be fine, Vanessa, it'll be just fine."

I knew from her last comment that my message had gotten through.

"Oh, you don't know the half, Kay," I offered, with a sinister laugh. "I've killed lots of people in my books, so throttling you if this all goes wrong will just be another day at the office for me."

We both laughed before I told her I had to go, and that, despite her interference, I was still looking forward to seeing her on Friday.

As I entered the dining room for breakfast, Jack Kenwright waved at me and insisted I join him and Clare. This was the last thing I wanted to do but, not wishing to seem standoffish, I reluctantly did so. For a few minutes we made polite conversation, until Jack said Clare had been doing some remembering of her own and wanted to ask me a few questions, if I had no objections. I told them that I didn't and it was then she mentioned my young friend from all those years ago.

"I wanted to ask about that inquisitive little boy who hung around with you a lot back in the day."

"Jimmy. His name was Jimmy."

"Ah, yes, Jimmy. Now I recall. Bright thing, I remember. Very curious."

"He loved to watch you paint," I offered. "You were so patient and kind to him."

"Thank you. Yes, he joined me on several occasions. He was amazed that a picture could appear like magic on a blank canvas."

"I recollect you offered to teach him how to paint. He was tickled pink at that."

"Did he ever show you his masterpiece?" she asked, with a chuckle.

"He did. He was so proud of it."

Turning to her husband, she said, "Jimmy loved animals and wanted his picture to be of a dog. So, that's what I helped him draw and paint. And, as I recall, it wasn't half bad."

"Not at all," I agreed. "He proudly showed it to everyone. Had pride of place in his house, too."

"Any idea what happened to him?" Clare wondered.

"No, I'm afraid not. After I left *The Announcer* we lost touch. A shame, really. He was a good kid, just a little lost at times."

I noticed Jack Kenwright giving us, what I thought to be, a false smile, before saying, "Well, you know, a long time ago now all those people. Imagine they've all scattered to the wind."

I sensed he was eager to wrap up Clare's recollections and, to be honest, I was, too. I needed to remember those times on my own terms, so, as quickly as I could, I finished my breakfast, made my excuses and left.

The morning, again, greeted me with sunshine and a warm breeze, so I took advantage of the good weather, put on my stout shoes, packed a beach towel, grabbed some goodies and headed for a cliff walk. As I set out I admitted to myself that my time in Maine had been quite therapeutic. The gorgeous weather helped, of course, but the sea air and brisk, pleasant walks along the cliffs brought my mood to a level I hadn't felt in a long time.

As I glanced at the rocky coastline I noticed a secluded stretch of sand which seemed to beckon to me. I gingerly made my way over the rocks, found the perfect spot, laid out my towel and settled down to enjoy the sun and the fantastic view.

The gulls and sandpipers quickly gathered nearby hoping for any scrap of food I might throw their way and, indeed, from my bag I took a cookie from my snacks, crumbled it up and tossed it as far as I could in their direction. In a short time their numbers increased rapidly, but the sight of them made me smile.

The smell of the ocean soon became intoxicating and before I knew it I was back in the Barringtons' house a few days after Simon's seizure. He didn't seem any the worse for the experience and, indeed, headed back to college two days later. Until then, he, Hugh, Chloe, April and me took in a couple of just released movies – '*The Owl and the Pussycat*' and '*A Man Called Horse*'. I didn't care much for the Richard Harris film, which was too violent and sometimes cruel for me. A lot of the dialogue was spoken in Sioux, which I found difficult to follow, and I recalled the others felt much the same, although April liked the fact that a lot of the movie focused on the Sioux culture, which had largely been forgotten.

The '*Owl and the Pussycat*' was a wonderful comedy that we all loved. Of course, I enjoyed it because George Segal played an aspiring novelist, while the boys liked it because Barbra Streisand played a prostitute.

Going to the movies, mixing and spending a great deal of time with the family, only increased my love of being part of what I considered them to be - the most important group in town. They were well known, respected and, above all, looked up to. For me, in my youthful mind, to be in some way connected with that identity, however tenuous, made me happy and wanted.

As we became more used to each other I remember finding myself organizing my life mostly around theirs. If they were going to a concert or a movie I was invariably asked to go, and whatever I had planned I put aside just to be a part of the group. At work, Mr. Barrington often stopped by my desk, telling me how pleased he was with my efforts. So, all in all, I now considered myself to be on a par with the family in the same vein as April. But it was she who one day on a hike tried to put me straight with regard to my apparent increasing reliance on the Barringtons for my emotional and practical needs.

We had been discussing them in general and I commented how much I appreciated being taken under their wings, so to speak. I went on to say how I felt so much a part of the family, and how I owed them a lot for including me like they did. April frowned and shook her head.

"Vanessa, listen to me for a second. You shouldn't blow the Barringtons up into more than they are. Of course they're fun to be around, but at the end of the day they are just flesh and blood like all of us."

Her strong words took me by surprise and I immediately screwed up my face.

"Oh, April, have I been making an ass of myself?"

"No, not at all, but you shouldn't care too much about them. Enjoy them, yes, but please don't think of them as exceptional or superior to you. They're not."

"I know that, April, but all I meant was they are people I look up to. I'm just starting out, trying to make some friends and figure out where I'm headed in life. I suppose I just need some sort of attachment outside of my aunt and uncle."

"All right, I understand that, but try not to see or follow them as your ideal image of what you should be. Don't think everything in your world has to revolve around them."

Her words continued to sting me, but the more I listened and thought about what she said, the more she made sense. If I was honest I'd have to admit that since I'd known the Barringtons I had pretty much lost myself within their circle. And it was true what April said about living my life vicariously through them. Slowly, I now realized, I had done just that.

Defiantly, and not wishing to admit my situation, I responded, "Honestly, April, I think you're overreacting, but I do appreciate what you've told me."

She shrugged and added as a final piece of advice, "All I'm saying, Vanessa, is don't become mesmerized with them. You are the only one in charge of your life...not them."

We said no more on the subject and continued our hike. Throughout my years of meeting and dealing with all sorts of people, I often remembered April's words of advice and I have to say, even now, they served me well. It took a while before I became confident enough in my own skin to know the decisions, thoughts and actions I was taking were the correct ones for me and, indeed, made me who I am today. Often, I smile and silently thank April, wherever she is, for caring enough in trying to help a young, struggling girl to find her own way.

Chapter Ten

———◆———

C harles Barrington never disguised his abhorrence of the Vietnam War. Indeed, under his leadership *The Announcer* often carried opinion pieces by prominent members of the community who shared his views. However, not once did he attack the members of the military who were doing the actual fighting; his objections were always aimed at the government which he strongly felt was leading the country down a disastrous path.

As 1970 moved from winter into spring, the number of demonstrations against the war increased around the country. These protests were largely led by young people and Rainbow Falls every so often held their own shows of discontent. They were well advertised and supported, as well as being reported on but not in any great depth. It was a surprise then one day when Mr. Barrington called me into his office to discuss my next assignment.

"Vanessa," he began, seriously, "you're probably well aware of the big anti-war demonstration planned for next weekend in City Park?"

"Of course, Mr. Barrington, one of the biggest yet around here."

"Exactly," he emphasized, almost giddily, "which is why I want you to do a piece on it."

"Oh, okay," I responded, taken aback, "I'd love to."

"Not just an article," he continued, "but a three-part series."

Again, I was astonished by his offer since three-part stories always went to the most senior reporters.

"Oh, Mr. Barrington," I countered, not sure whether my journalistic abilities ran that high, "are you...?"

"Yes, absolutely, I'm certain you are the right person for the job otherwise I wouldn't have suggested it."

His comment made me feel both elated for his trust in me and somewhat ashamed having almost questioned his judgment. He then went on to elaborate his ideas for the series.

"Since most of the participants in the rally will be around your own age I want you to interview some of them and delve deeply into their rationale and reasons for their participation. This is a real chance for our community to understand and be exposed to the passion these young people have for opposing the war."

He continued to expand on his vision and it was at that moment I realized the enormity and responsibility of what he was placing in my lap. For him, this was not the standard, run-of-the-mill piece, but a real chance to cement his views in the minds of his loyal readers. For me, the whole scenario scared me to death. On the one hand, I could hardly believe the importance of what he proposed handing me, but I also understood my career as a writer now stood on the line.

Personally, I knew little about the war, so I welcomed this opportunity to discover as many facts as I could. I understood the country as a whole was divided about its support and that young people especially were mostly adamant about its lack of validity and worth.

The more I talked with Mr. Barrington the more excited I became. He convinced me that I was the right person for the job, that my youth would be an advantage when conducting the interviews, since the young folk, he felt, would be more comfortable and forthcoming talking with someone around their own age.

But to be fair to both sides, Mr. Barrington also asked me to interview a few people who held opposing views to his, so that the reader could contrast the differing opinions. This directive further enhanced my respect for him, making me aware that I should always try and see that my reporting was balanced.

When I related my latest assignment to my aunt and uncle, they took it as a sign that my writing ambitions were not misplaced, and that this direction I was headed seemed to be the right one.

"I've told you before, Vanessa," my Uncle Brian stated firmly, "he doesn't make mistakes when it comes to journalism or his paper. He trusts you now, lass, otherwise he wouldn't have given you this story to write. And I know from speaking with him a few times how much he thinks of your talent…that's what he told me you have. High praise, I'd say, coming for the likes of him."

It was indeed high praise but the accolade only made me feel more nervous, more apprehensive about the upcoming piece.

"Listen, Vanessa," my aunt joined in, seeing my obvious discomfort, "look at this as an opportunity, nothing more. Your career as a writer will not depend on the outcome of these articles no matter what you think. This is just one small step. All you can do is the very best you can. This is just another learning experience for you, one you should grasp with both hands, but remember there will always be other chances that come your way. So, put your nerves aside," she continued, reminding me of my mother's wisdom, "and do what you know you can do."

As I prepared in the next few days to begin the series my aunt's wise words often came back to me, bolstering and focusing my spirits in the right direction.

My days leading up to the actual rally in City Park on Sunday were spent preparing for the best way to structure the three-part series. Obviously, I had no experience in this area so I asked Betsy Clarke, the reporter who originally showed me the ropes at *The Announcer*, to give me some advice and counsel. This she did willingly, and before the day was out I had a firm plan as to how to proceed.

The protest was well advertised so I had no trouble reaching out to the two main organizers. They were only too happy to sit down with me, explain their position with regard to the war and their aims for the positive outcome for the rally. This first part of the series appeared on the day before the event, with the intention being that our readers could glean some idea of its purpose and seriousness.

The rally was held at noon on Sunday and I made sure I had a great vantage point to hear not only the speeches but also gauge the atmosphere in the park. The mood of the crowd ranged from joyful at being able to express their opposition to the war, to morbid and angry as one of the organizers read out the number of casualties on our side. The protest lasted three hours and I estimated some four thousand people were in attendance. That, to me, said a lot about the passion and deeply felt view of the war, since Rainbow Falls was only a town of perhaps ten thousand folk.

As soon as the event ended, I hot-footed it into the office and wrote the copy for the next morning's paper. A senior editor came in especially to help organize the finished piece. By eight o'clock we had it finalized with both of us more than satisfied with the end result. He sent it through the usual printing channels and I went home feeling elated that I'd managed to accomplish such a polished, informative article. The next day I planned on interviewing a few dissenters and supporters of the war to get the views on how they thought the rally had served their respective sides. I slept very well that night and couldn't wait for tomorrow to arrive.

The next morning I left home early with my Uncle Brian's praise for a job well done echoing in my ears. He'd read article two late the previous night as he prepared the final edition of the paper.

"You, young lady," he began, after giving me a hug, "have hit the jackpot. I've read a lot of stuff over the years and this series ranks right up there with the best of them. Congratulations!"

It was high praise indeed and immediately made my day. On the way to the office I stopped to pick up a coffee and bagel from the local bakery. The store, popular for quick breakfast items, also had a few tables towards the back for those who preferred a more leisurely morning meal. As I waited for my order I casually glanced around and noticed, to my surprise, Jack Kenwright and a woman sitting, with their backs towards me, at the farthest table. They seemed to be animated in conversation and laughing quite a lot. I naturally assumed the woman was his wife, Clare.

After my order came up and I paid the bill, I turned to leave at the same time as the woman sitting with Mr. Kenwright slightly moved her head. From where she sat she couldn't have seen me, but from the quick sideways look at her I was astonished to see it was none other than Edward Barrington's girlfriend, Samantha. I hurried to my car wondering all the time what that incident may have been about.

I spent part of my morning contacting some of the rally goers. To be fair, I lined up interviews with both the war protesters and those who supported the conflict. Mr. Barrington stopped by my desk to let me know how well I'd done with the first two articles.

"Vanessa," he began, sitting down opposite, "very good work. Of course, I'm pleased you gave more weight to the antis than the pros, not only from my personal point of view but from the opinion of most of our readers judging from the letters we've received on the subject. We have to stop this thing, we really do."

Although still relatively new to the intricacies of the war I had learned so much in the past few days talking with both sides and in particular hearing the speakers at the rally. I was now convinced in my youthful mind that the war was wrong and we should withdraw as soon as possible. I tried my best not to let my views taint the articles but I was also sure I probably was unconsciously biased in favor of the protesters. But hearing Mr. Barrington's strong condemnation of the war eased my worries, and if he felt I had accomplished good work with the articles then I considered it a job well done. He left me feeling proud of what I'd achieved so far and I couldn't wait to finish up the series, which would conclude in Friday's edition.

About an hour after Mr. Barrington's visit I was joined at my desk by Jack Kenwright. I was still confused about seeing him earlier that morning in the bakery with Samantha, so his appearance now for some reason made me feel uncomfortable.

Since his arrival at *The Announcer* in January I'd had very little professional contact with him. He was either holed up in Mr. Barrington's office or following one or other of the senior journalists around as they sought and reported on their various stories. But that all changed now as he perched nonchalantly on the corner of my desk, folded his arms and looked at me with a frown.

"Yes, Mr. Kenwright?" I enquired, anxious to learn what he wanted with me.

"Read your first two articles, Vanessa," he began, seriously. "Have a few comments, d'you mind?"

By the look on his face this conversation, I suspected, wasn't destined to bode well for me.

"Oh, yes, okay, fire away, Mr. Kenwright."

"Absolutely good writing," he started, with a smile, "but too much pushing one point of view, I feel."

Cocking my head, I frowned this time, not quite understanding what he was saying.

"I'm sorry, not sure I'm following you, Mr. Kenwright."

"Aren't you? Well then, let me explain." His tone, condescending and forceful, immediately put me on edge. "I imagine you're aware that my father owns not only this newspaper but some twenty more like it scattered around the country."

He waited for my acknowledgment and I told him I'd certainly heard that.

"What you may not be aware of is that my father and, indeed, the whole Kenwright family, are fierce supporters of President Nixon. To that end," he continued, his eyes laser focused on my face, "we also totally endorse his Vietnam War policy."

His last remark at once brought a stab to my heart for I now well knew what may be coming next.

"Oh, okay," I meekly replied. "It is a free country."

"Yes, except my father and the whole family feels Nixon isn't receiving the recognition he deserves for safeguarding our country. So, through his network of newspapers he's trying to change that, which brings me to your articles on the past weekend's rally."

I cocked my head again and frowned.

"You didn't like them?" I asked, honestly.

"Vanessa, I don't know for sure your opinion of the war but I suspect you are against it. Clearly, those first two articles show that."

I raised my eyebrows at that comment. I personally thought I'd bent over backwards to be fair to both sides, and Mr. Barrington's comments had made me feel that way, too.

"Mr. Kenwright," I responded, with a voice slightly thin and shrill, "I spent a great deal of time interviewing people with differing opinions.

My articles reflected those opinions as truthfully and as accurately as I could. I'm sorry if they disappointed you but, honestly, I told it like it was. In fact, Mr. Barrington seemed very pleased with the outcome."

"Well, yes, he would, wouldn't he? The man's practically a walking billboard in opposition. Anyway, the point is you have one article left in the series, I understand?" I nodded and pursed my lips. "Therefore," he continued, "I think it might be in your best interests to, shall we say, modify somewhat your extreme views and give some more air to our supporters.

"You have a very promising future as a journalist, Vanessa, and I know my father looks forward to having you within his organization for a long time to come. Editors come and go, so we're always on the lookout for talent such as yours. My advice to you is not to let this viewpoint prevent you from moving up the ladder, so to speak. Do the right thing, young lady; do the right thing."

He left me, and I slumped back in my chair feeling confused but absolutely sure I had just been threatened with basically the end of my career before it had really begun.

Chapter Eleven

◆————◆

"What is this?"

An irate Charles Barrington almost shouted at me after I was summoned to his office on Thursday morning. He held part three of my series in his hand, waving it in front of my face like a flag. I had spent the previous two days on the article which I was finally glad to be rid of. He didn't let me reply before he continued his unfamiliar rant.

"Vanessa, what the hell happened here? This is about as one-sided as it gets. I told you to be fair, but this is ridiculous! And we're certainly not printing it."

As my face reddened and my throat dried up, I tried hard to respond as best I could.

"Oh, Mr. Barrington, I'm sorry, I'm sorry," I whimpered. "I did what I thought was right after Mr. Kenwright directed me to soften the criticism of the war."

"He did what?" Mr. Barrington exploded, his voice booming around the office. "He directed you to do what?"

"He came to see me just after you'd told me how much you liked the series so far. Apparently, his father and the whole family are big supporters of President Nixon. He said they didn't feel he was getting enough credit for protecting the country. He indicated that my future in journalism might be affected if I didn't play up the support for the war."

"Wait. Wait. He threatened you? Is that what you're telling me?"

"Not in so many words but the inference was clearly there. I felt I had no choice but to do as he asked. I mean, his father does own the newspaper, after all."

"Yes, and I'm still the editor. He threatened you...unbelievable. All right, Vanessa, I want you to accept my apology for the way I behaved just now. This clearly is not your fault. That he would coerce *any* of my reporters, let alone someone just starting out, is totally unacceptable. All right, take this," he continued, thrusting the article into my hand, "and rewrite it as *you* wish it to appear. And let this be a lesson to you that you should never, ever, compromise your ethics to please someone else. Now, go and get busy. I have complete faith in you."

I tried to thank him for his kind words and advice but hurried from the room as fast as I could. His last remark stayed with me, not only for the rest of my time at *The Announcer*, but for the rest of my writing career.

I immediately went to my desk and began revising the whole article until I was satisfied it met my true intentions as a suitable finale to the series. I did give some acknowledgment to the supporters of the war, but by and large it reflected the growing feeling in Rainbow Falls that the war was wrong and we, as a country, should not be involved. The next morning Mr. Barrington again called me into his office, but this time it was to praise me for a job well done.

As a way of relieving some of the obvious tension I was feeling, April very kindly took me to the movies to see a latest release, *'Airport'*. The mish-mash of a convoluted plot certainly did the trick, as we immersed ourselves in a horrendous snowstorm and a mad bomber.

Afterwards, we went out for pizza, which gave us a chance to catch up since we hadn't really spent much time together due to our busy schedules. I enjoyed talking with her because, being a few years my senior, she always seemed to give me good advice.

"I read those articles," she began, nodding enthusiastically, "great job, my friend."

I thanked her and told her the Mr. Barrington and Jack Kenwright story.

"Yes, I heard all about that from Hugh. He said his father was furious with Kenwright and the two of them had a real set-to. I guess

Kenwright finally backed down but Hugh's pretty sure he and his father aren't the kind of people you want to upset or go against in any way. For some reason just because they own a bunch of papers they think they can and should control everything in them. Mr. Barrington apparently told him in no uncertain terms that while he was editor of *The Announcer* it would remain the independent voice of the community it's always been."

"What d'you hear from Samantha?" I asked.

"Oh, she seems to spend a lot of time rehearsing with her band. Haven't seen a lot of her lately."

"Are she and Edward still tight?"

"Sure, as far as I know. She hasn't said anything, why?"

"I dunno, I was just wondering."

"Vanessa," April replied slowly, while cocking her head expectantly, "why do you ask?"

I shrugged, before answering, "Well, a few days ago I was on my way to work and stopped at that little bakery/café place for coffee and a bagel. As I waited I noticed a couple at a table in the back. The guy I recognized as Jack Kenwright and I assumed the woman was his wife because I didn't have a clear view of her. But before I left she half-turned and I saw who it was. It was Samantha."

April frowned before shrugging her shoulders, too.

"Maybe they just bumped into each other. I think they live fairly close." Her reply seemed bland and not at all convincing, but she said she'd mention it the next time she saw Sam.

"Well, I don't want her to think I was telling tales out of school," I answered, "so please keep my name out of it."

April assured me she would and we let the matter drop. After some more small talk April told me the Barringtons were having a get-together the following weekend at their place in the woods we stopped at some weeks ago while hiking.

"You must come, Vanessa. These things are always a lot of fun. Good food and drink and Sam'll probably get up and give us a couple of songs."

I told her I'd love to, then we hugged and said our goodbyes.

I roused myself from my remembrance, looked at my watch and

discovered I had been on the beach for over three hours. I hurried back to the hotel, ate lunch without seeing the Kenwrights and retreated to my room to do some more work on the final chapter of the book. With Kay coming on Friday I was anxious to at least have a rough draft with which to assuage her anxiety about me finishing it on time. And, indeed, I did manage to accomplish that much before I put it aside to consider my morning's musings.

It amazed me that I remembered so much, most of which had obviously been buried deep inside for so many years. But my remembrances also stirred many different emotions in me as the various moments and incidents danced before my eyes. And yet, despite the vast array of recollections, I still felt there was something more that lay hidden among the ashes of my past. And this nagging obsession in my mind made me fairly certain it centered most definitely on the Kenwrights.

As I pondered, a call came through from the front desk. It was Joyce Andrews informing me of a visitor and could I come down? Wondering who it was I hurriedly put on a fresh top, tidied my hair, put on my game face and wandered, as casually as I could, down to the lobby.

"Ah, there you are, Vanessa," Joyce said, greeting me with a huge smile, "someone here to see you."

She promptly introduced a stunning black woman who looked like a cross between Michelle Obama and Jennifer Hudson. Her name was Olivia Pearson and Joyce further introduced her as the local librarian.

"Take her into the dining room, Vanessa," Joyce instructed, "and dinner's on me tonight."

I did as I was told and before long Olivia and I were deep in conversation about my upcoming appearance at the library.

"This is so generous of you to spare the time," Olivia began. "An author of your note is a rare find around here."

Her compliment caught me off guard since a writer is never truly sure how wide an audience he or she has.

"Not at all," I replied. "The honor is mine. How are the arrangements going?" I asked, trying to gauge what I might expect crowd-wise.

"Full house, no doubt, with standing room, too. Everyone's so excited to have you here. We've even alerted the local media…well, we didn't, your agent did," she replied, with a laugh.

"Oh, that's Kay all right," I murmured, shaking my head. "She never misses an opportunity to promote her authors."

"Quite okay," Olivia responded. "We're actually enjoying the limelight."

Over dinner we discussed the program which seemed sensible and well-structured to me. Olivia would moderate the evening, introducing me before I discussed the trilogy and some of my other works. I would then read an excerpt from the third, as yet, unpublished book and then take any questions from the audience. Finally, I would spend however long it took to sign copies of my previous books, which Olivia assured me Kay was definitely bringing with her.

"Sounds like a full and fun evening," I offered.

"And one more thing," she proposed, quite guardedly, "we have had a request from a professor at the University of Maine to record the whole event for later showing to his English major students. Would you give your permission?"

Raising my eyebrows, I shrugged and replied, "I don't see why not if it helps him with his classes."

"Oh, he assured me it would, particularly as a lot of them are following your trilogy. To hear you speak about your craft would be worth its weight in gold. I guess he's a big fan, too."

"Well, all right then…let the cameras roll!" I told her, as we both laughed.

During our dinner I really warmed to Olivia, and I told her that anything else I could do for her library to just call. I gave her my number before we parted for the evening, telling her how much I was looking forward to speaking on Saturday.

The evening was again warm so I took a glass of wine up to my room, sat on the balcony and took myself back to Rainbow Falls. A picture of the Barringtons' house in the woods immediately sprang to mind, and I began recalling my first visit in late spring with April, who had invited me in the first place. My aunt got wind of our plans and asked if I would take Jimmy with me. I'd seen him several times since our last excursion, when we chanced upon Clare Kenwright, and we seemed more and more comfortably with each other. He continued to be full of a nine-year-old's fascination with animals, fish and nature in general. April and I enjoyed his silliness, and we think he appreciated our paying attention to him since he hardly ever seemed to mix with friends his own age.

I picked them up and we drove again to the parking area before hiking the short way to the house. It was short - a mile or less – but the path meandered through the woods and by the river Jimmy had found the frog the last time. Finally, we climbed the hill, descending the other side to the house.

Most of the family was there already, laughing and engaged in some animated conversations. We were greeted warmly by Mr. and Mrs. Barrington, who told me, genuinely I felt, how pleased they were that I could come. Mrs. Barrington took Jimmy under her wing, whisking him off to find something to eat and drink.

Simon and Edward weren't there; Simon was away at college and Edward was working. Hugh, as soon as he saw us, came over and told us he was going to pick sides later for a friendly game of softball. After a while we all settled down on the large porch for a pick-up lunch and I was fortunate to be seated next to Samantha. Although not in her league I had, since working at *The Announcer*, gained more and more self-confidence.

Dressed casually like all of us but looking stunning as usual, she kindly asked how I was enjoying life at the paper. In turn, I was eager to know about her next concert and she told me the band planned a mini-tour of some of the local states in the next month. Rehearsals, she said, were going almost non-stop.

As we spoke I watched, to my surprise, the sudden arrival of Jack Kenwright. Samantha noticed, too, quickly apologized and headed off to greet him. The move startled me, especially since Jack was alone. I watched as the two of them hugged and began what seemed to be an intense conversation. In a while they parted, and Jack made his way into the fray and seemed to be warmly greeted by Charles Barrington. This did not surprise me since Mr. Barrington always made sure not to mix business with pleasure. Whatever differences the two had over my Vietnam series would have been buried for that day and not mentioned.

In fact, during lunch, Jack Kenwright sought me out and

half-heartedly, I thought, apologized for his previous criticism of the articles.

"Don't want you to get the wrong idea, Vanessa," he began, in a patronizing manner, "about what I said to you the other day. It's just that my father feels strongly about the war and I wanted to make sure you were being fair to both sides of the coin, so to speak. I now understand the deep feelings of the people around here and your writing was on the whole quite balanced."

He made no mention of his veiled threat to my future career which I knew was real and on-going. I tried hard to pass off his comments with a pleasant reply before we parted company to take part in the softball game.

Hugh picked the sides, with me, April, Jimmy and himself on one team, while Mr. and Mrs. Barrington, Chloe and Jack made up the other. Samantha didn't want to play until Jack went over to her, said a few words and handed her a mitt. They bantered for a while before Samantha took her place in the field close to him. Again, I noticed their closeness and wondered if anyone else had, too.

The game was lighthearted, of course, with lots of good-natured ribbing from both sides. But, again, all through the game I watched as Jack and Samantha never seemed far apart, as well as talking in closeness sometimes. To me, the whole scene with those two appeared quite strange considering Samantha was supposed to be Edward's steady girlfriend.

After the game, as the party wound down, Samantha announced Jack was kindly going to drop her off at her band's rehearsal since it was on his way home. They said their goodbyes and it seemed to me were very anxious to be on their way.

As the afternoon drew to a close, I rounded up Jimmy and April, thanked the Barringtons for their hospitality and headed back to the car. On the way, as Jimmy hunted again for frogs and turtles, I mentioned my thoughts about Jack and Samantha to April.

"They seem very close all of a sudden," I began. "Did you notice?"

April frowned, shook her head and stopped.

"Vanessa, what d'you think's going on here, that they're having an affair?" she asked, bitingly

I shrugged before I replied, "Not saying that, just that they seem awfully close all of a sudden. And where's his wife? She never seems to be around much."

"Away, apparently, visiting family...somewhere. But what does that matter? I asked Sam about being seen with him in the coffee shop... oh, don't worry, I kept your name out of it...and she told me everything was very innocent, that they just bumped into each other as they were going in and decided to sit together, So there, miss conspiracy theorist," she said, with a wry smile before punching me playfully on the arm, "nothing more than plain coincidence."

Her explanation sounded plausible but too easy, as if she wasn't particularly interested in the whole scenario. Of course, April hadn't seen Jack Kenwright in the same way I had, so I imagined her perspective was different from mine and I gave her the benefit of the doubt. It was quite clear, however, she really didn't wish to discuss the matter further, so I changed the subject.

And that's where I left my recollections for the night, with nefarious thoughts of Jack Kenwright and Samantha.

Chapter Twelve

$\bullet\quad\blacklozenge\quad\bullet$

I had a little over thirty-six hours before Kay was due to honor me with her presence, and another day after that before my scheduled appearance at the local library. So, my two main objectives were to almost complete the final chapter of the third book in the trilogy, as well as preparing somewhat for my talk before the locals.

As much as I wanted to continue my recollections of times past I knew those thoughts had to be put on hold until my other responsibilities were met. All these obligations presented me with delicious conflicts – finally finishing the book; being a star for a while at the library and delving, and hopefully discovering, more revelations of my time in Rainbow Falls, but the first two simply had to be my priorities for the next few days.

I thought, as I settled down to write, that completing the last chapter would be a breeze considering I had already written an in-depth outline which Kay gushed over. But when I reviewed those words I knew it wasn't nearly good enough to bring the trilogy to its just conclusion. Parts of the draft were okay but the ending didn't seem to capture my original vision of how I wanted to tie everything up. So, once again, it was back to the drawing board or, in my case, back to my laptop.

I was nothing if not dedicated to my craft and, rather than being frustrated by my previous efforts, I now knew clearly the direction I should and would go. And my hunch proved to be correct since, in a little over five productive hours, I wrote everything except the last page.

I went to bed that night feeling one journey was nearly over; one was just beginning and the other halfway through.

The Kenwrights, I learned from Stu, the bartender, were not leaving at the weekend but staying on another week to take advantage of the glorious promised weather. Upon hearing that news I wasn't sure if I was pleased or disappointed. On the one hand, their reticence about engaging me too much as I remembered certain facts dismayed me somewhat because I felt they could help fill in some of the gaps in my memory. Conversely, perhaps, not having them around when I recalled whatever it was I managed to remember wouldn't hamper or divert my intention of pursuing those memories wherever they might lead. But, apparently, the decision had been made and I was stuck with them for another week.

On Thursday, I took off after breakfast for my favorite spot on the beach to think hard about my appearance at the library on Saturday. Having done quite a few of these talks over the course of my career I wasn't nervous, but I did want to give the locals a rare look into a writer's life. Accordingly, I mapped out what I thought was an ambitious, interesting program, which included my general approach to writing a new book; where ideas came from; how to pace and develop a story; the invention of the main characters and supporting ones; the art, as I liked to call it, of meaningful and appropriate dialogue and, of course, the creation of a compelling narrative.

I also planned to give examples of each facet with short readings from my various books, as well as finishing up with a reading from the last book of my trilogy, *Intimate Strangers*. Questions, I hoped, would then be asked and the last act would be for me to sign copies of my books for interested patrons. Of course, I'd run the proposed program by Kay when she arrived on Friday, but on the whole I felt my ideas perfect for this occasion.

I caught lunch in town knowing I would have to spend the rest of the afternoon deciding which excerpts to read and, more importantly, which segment of the *Intimate Strangers* last book to share with the audience. This was tricky since I wanted to give the audience a meaningful snippet without giving too much away.

Back on my hotel balcony I briefly ran the plots of my twelve novels through my mind, discarding the three that had been made into movies or television mini-series. These would be well known and I assumed of very little interest to the library patrons to hear me read. I narrowed my choice down to four, selected some of my favorite passages and left it at that. I felt each segment would aptly demonstrate different parts of the writing process. All that remained now was for me to pick a fairly lengthy passage from the final book and, within an hour of hard review, I found the perfect example. For those who were familiar with the previous two books in the trilogy, it contained teasing references without revealing a lot of relevant context; just enough to whet the appetite but not enough to compromise the overall plot. With my mind finally at ease with regard to the upcoming library appearance, I headed down to the bar for a well-earned drink.

The bar, crowded with newly-arrived vacationers, wasn't my idea of a place to enjoy a quiet drink, so I grabbed my usual from Stu, the bartender, and headed for one of the lounges. To my dismay, the only other occupants were the Kenwrights, who motioned for me to join them.

"Haven't seen you in a while," Clare began, pleasantly. "Imagine you've been busy with your book."

"Yes, indeed," I replied, setting down my wine and pulling up a chair. "My agent is dropping in tomorrow for a few days so I needed to earn my keep." We all laughed at that remark but I felt they were not too interested in my writing. However, they did surprise me by saying they were looking forward to my appearance at the library and that they hoped to attend.

"You've been in the writing business a long time," Jack Kenwright added. "A lot of wisdom to impart, I'm guessing."

"Not sure about that," I countered, with an easy smile, "but I have had quite a few great teachers along the way, starting with Charles Barrington, the editor at *The Announcer*, who gave me my first chance. So many of my memories have been about him and his family…good ones, I might add. Well, you knew him, too, for a while," I continued, eager to confront him with some of my recollections of *his* time at the paper and around the Barringtons, "so you probably understand what I mean?"

Jack Kenwright shifted in his chair as his wife turned her head expectedly towards him, as though keen to hear *anything* he had to say about those times. I waited patiently for his response with a bright smile beaming back at him.

"Good man, as I recall, Barrington. Yes, lovely family, all top-notch. Ran a good newspaper, too, but very liberal minded. That caused some problems, I remember, but it was all long ago now so what does it matter, eh?"

"The war…it was mostly about the Vietnam War," I reminded him, perhaps a little too forcefully, although I was sure he still knew exactly what the problem was. "He was against it and your father and your family were for it." I smiled pleasantly again waiting for his reaction.

"Well, there were many opinions both for and against. We had the right to express ours," he countered.

"But, as I remember it, you tried to use your newspapers as sort of propaganda platforms. Once, you even instructed me to rewrite an article because you felt it was too biased for the other side."

"Oh, did I indeed? Can't say I recall doing that, but I'm sure Barrington had something to say about it if I did."

"Oh, you most certainly did, Mr. Kenwright and, yes, Mr. Barrington told me to ignore you instructions as long as I was fair and balanced in my reporting." I looked him squarely in the eye and continued, "He also said to me, remember, Vanessa, when you author an article of any kind you are essentially writing a first draft of history. And he was correct and I've never forgotten those words of wisdom."

He shrugged, which made me more than a little angry, so I decided on the spot to bring up a name from the past to gauge his and, possibly, his wife's reaction.

"In my recollections I came across the name of someone called Samantha. She was the girlfriend of one of the Barrington sons and a singer with her own band, as I remember her. Weren't you and she close, Mr. Kenwright?"

Upon hearing Samantha's name, Clare yawned, told us she was tired and would we excuse her? To my mind, her response to my question spoke volumes…it was a name she'd rather forget for one reason or another. After she'd left us Jack Kenwright feigned puzzlement over Samantha's name.

"A singer, you say? And how am I supposed to know her?"

Deflecting my question back to me was an old trick I'd used many times in my books when a character didn't want to answer directly a difficult query.

"As I've been recalling things," I offered, still pleasantly but insistently, "I seem to remember you and her meeting up quite a lot. You'd give her rides home on a number of occasions, as well as having early morning breakfasts."

Again, he dismissed my line of thought, brushing it off as if he had no idea what I was talking about.

"Sorry, the old memory's not what it was," he countered. "I'm sure I was just being helpful or neighborly or something along those lines. Why, is it important?"

That question I couldn't honestly answer just then, so I thanked him for his time, and took in an early night since Kay was due to show up in the morning bright and early.

As I drifted off to sleep, I knew Clare's reaction and Jack's convenient memory lapse were important indications that my recollections in the days to come would hopefully produce a lot more answers to the nagging suspicions lurking in my head about my remembrances of all those years ago.

As promised, Kay showed up mid-morning so, after introducing her to Joyce and Keith Andrews, I ushered her into one of the lounges where we could talk and catch up over coffee.

"First," she asked, excitedly and expectantly, "the book? Is it finally done?"

"Last page to go, literally. I need to think long and hard about it, but other than that, yes, it's all done."

"Pleased, are we?"

"Very. The road's been a long slog but I really feel, Kay, that I've tied everything up in an appropriate, true way. I'm very happy with the way the trilogy turned out."

"You realize this book…these three…will be your legacy, don't you?"

"My, my, a legacy and a legend." I joked. "Dickens had better watch out!"

Kay laughed, too, before adding, seriously, "No, Vanessa, I don't think you completely understand your standing within the literary world. You *are* a legend and *Intimate Strangers* will only cement that for all time."

It was high praise and I didn't believe a word of it.

"Kay, I think you're mistaking me for someone else," I joshed. "There are hundreds of great writers out there and if I could squeeze myself into perhaps the bottom three or four then I'd be happy. I never started writing to become famous or a household name. I just loved creating meaningful stories which I hoped a few people might appreciate."

Kay shook her head and wagged her finger.

"Oh, no, missy, you're not getting off that lightly. What you've done, and I believe deep down you know it, too, is bring characters who normally wouldn't have had a voice to everyone's attention. You have extolled their virtues and exposed their frailties. You have told extraordinary tales about them in a unique way, whether they were villains or heroes. You have opened the eyes of so many people to so many different aspects of the human mind and condition. No, Vanessa, you are, indeed, a legend and I won't hear anything different."

I bowed my head before looking her in the face and smiling.

"Kay, thank you. Thank you. You are the one who's always believed in me, guided me, bucked me up and steered my career in such an unselfish way. If anyone here is a legend in the publishing world, it's you!" I got up and hugged her for the longest time.

"My, my," she responded, with a giggle, "two legends in the same room. However will we be able to get our heads through the door?"

I punched her playfully on the arm before she brought up the matter of my appearance at the local library the next day.

"I think the program you've come up with is just right. You don't want the readings to drag on too long and these won't. It'll give you ample time to answer questions, of which I'm sure there'll be many, as well as at least an hour for signing your books. My trunk is full, probably thirty of each of your books, so we might be able to make a little money, too! And after your bar tab I think I'm going to need every cent I can rustle up!"

"Well, in my defense, all I can say is the wine helps my creative juices flow…so don't complain, Miss Twenty Per Cent!"

By this time the lunch hour had rolled around, so we headed to the dining room for a well-earned bite to eat.

The only other topic Kay wanted to discuss was about the two people I'd faintly recognized in the hotel shortly after my arrival. I'd mentioned it to her some time ago but hadn't gone into any details.

"So, spill the beans," she began, like an eager child wishing to know a deep-dark secret, "figured out yet who they are?"

"Oh, yes, indeed, Jack and Clare Kenwright."

"And from how long ago?" she asked.

"Nineteen-Seventy."

"So, you would've been what…twenty?"

"Actually, nineteen…just."

"So, what's the scoop?" she pestered, eagerly. "Is there a book in here?"

I told her as much as I wanted her to know but left out the parts I still struggled with or hadn't yet resolved.

"No, Kay, no book, but some of the recollections have shaken me up quite a bit. I still feel there's a lot more I need to recall and the Kenwrights seem to be at the root of it."

"Oh, I can't wait to meet them," she answered, with a wicked grin. "Are they here?" she wondered, darting her eyes around the room.

"No, but they're not leaving for another week so I'm sure we'll bump into them soon. But, Kay, you have to promise me you won't badger them for details," I more or less ordered. "It has been very difficult trying to get them to talk about those days and I haven't finished with them yet."

"I will be on my best behavior," she offered, "honest. But you said some of your thoughts had shaken you up. Why, may I ask?"

"Because I feel they may have been responsible for something… something…" and here I hesitated not really knowing how to describe a few dark thoughts I had, "…something that possibly changed lives back then, and not in a good way. But right now, Kay, I just don't know until I give those months back then some more of my time. Anyway, this is only about an old lady remembering and nothing else. It was so long ago now, as Jack Kenwright keeps telling me, so what does it matter?"

"Well, obviously, it matters a great deal to you or you wouldn't have invested so much time on it," Kay advised. "And memories are important, so I say stick with it until you find some sort of peace within yourself."

After lunch she told me she'd made an appointment with the local librarian to discuss my appearance, and that's where we spent the rest of the afternoon.

Chapter Thirteen

———◆———

My appearance at the library was set for two o'clock so I took Kay into town for a leisurely breakfast. Since she was due to leave the next day she eagerly talked about an upcoming book tour she was in the midst of arranging for me to coincide with the publication of the last book of *Intimate Strangers*.

"Very long, I'm afraid," she told me rather sheepishly, since she knew I was not a fan of such things. "Right now twenty stops, but spread out over three months. Can I persuade you?"

"Do I have a choice?" I answered, with a frown, as I opened up my hands.

"It's something I feel you have to do, Vanessa. I know how much you dislike these things, but you have an army of faithful fans just waiting to meet you and buy the book. And, of course, it's in your publishing contract so, no, you really don't have a choice unless you're dead."

Playfully poking my tongue out, I replied, "Well, okay then, but Kay I have something to tell you, something I've been thinking about for quite some time now."

"Sounds intriguing, I'm all ears."

"I'm fairly certain that *Intimate Strangers* will be my last novel. I'm…"

"What," she exclaimed, horrified, "your last novel, why?"

"A number of reasons," I continued, "but mostly because I'm seventy-two now and I want to do other things. Sitting, pounding out stories on my laptop for the next ten years isn't my idea of fun anymore."

"But, Vanessa," pleaded Kay, "this is your life and you're so good at it. I know you have quite a few more novels inside your head and heart, as well as having a lot more to say. Please don't do this."

I took a moment to answer, to form my response in the best possible way, to try and make Kay understand the whys and wherefores.

"Kay," I began, with a pleasant smile, "you have been nothing but the best as my agent and close friend for so many years. I owe you everything but I think there comes a time for all of us to recognize when the time is right to move on. That time is now for me.

"I have a Pulitzer and Honorary Doctorates from Columbia and USC. And, as you've said, I have a legacy within the literary world, for what it's worth, as well as thousands of loyal readers. For me to stain that recognition and, hopefully, esteem in which I'm apparently held, would be a huge mistake; one that I don't want to make. I want to go out on top, Kay, and I think *Intimate Strangers* will do that. I'm sorry if this disappoints you but for me I know it's the correct choice."

"I'm not disappointed, Vanessa, just shocked that you would even consider giving up what has essentially been your life for so long now. I wonder how you'll cope and what you intend to do?"

"After the book tour ends I'd just like to go back to my house and veg out for a while. No more late nights turning a plot over in my mind; no more deadlines; no more book tours and no more wondering where the next idea will come from."

"You're going to get bored very quickly, Vanessa. I know you, and you have to have a purpose."

"That's so true and what I've been thinking I'd like to do is pass on some of my writing knowledge to college students."

"You mean become a writer-in-residence somewhere?"

"Yes, exactly. Over the years I've had a few of those offers but could never take them because I was always working hard on a book and couldn't spare the time. But now I can and so, I will."

Kay slumped back in her chair, closing her eyes as she processed the information. I knew this revelation would hit her hard, mostly because she would know it was the end of our close working relationship which we'd enjoyed for over forty years. Her next question told me my prediction was correct.

"Will you promise me you won't close the door forever? Please, Vanessa, promise me that much."

I didn't have the heart to tell her my mind was made up and nothing she could do or say would alter that. So, I made her the promise knowing full well I would never need to honor it.

"Thank you. Thank you," she replied, like a drowning person clinging on for dear life. "I know you will change your mind, I just know it, and when you do I will still be there waiting for you as usual."

Again, I couldn't stab her in the heart so I told her I knew she would always be there for me whether as an agent or a dear friend. To soften the blow, I offered to do some personal appearances when and if she needed me to promote any of my books, as well as making sure we would meet on a regular basis to catch up on each other's lives.

She came over and hugged me before saying, "Vanessa, as long as I'm in this business I will never have the privilege of representing anyone who could come close to meaning what you do to me. Quite simply, you are the best!"

We left the matter at that point and headed back to the hotel to get ready for the session at the library. I changed into a smart pair of white, cotton pants and a bright yellow top, a combination Kay thought just right for the occasion; chic but casual. Then we ventured into the bar for a quick drink and a 'good luck' from Stu, the bartender.

By one-thirty we were in librarian Olivia Pearson's small office quickly running through the afternoon's program. She seemed more than pleased with our proposal, which Kay assured her was typical for these types of events.

"Your patrons," Kay offered, "will be more than happy with Vanessa's talk, particularly the time allotted for questions."

"Oh, I can't tell you how excited we are," gushed Olivia, as she took my hand. "This is a thrill, I can tell you."

"I've done a lot of similar events like this and after a while they get to be somewhat routine, but I have to say, Olivia, I'm actually looking forward to this one, mostly because of you and your warm welcome."

"The mayor is here," she told us, "as well as a number of our high school teachers eager to hear from a writer of such esteem. And there's also that professor from the University of Maine, who teaches a writing class, as well as being a huge fan. He'll also be taping the whole event to show to his students. So, if you weren't nervous before, well now you can be!"

We all laughed at her comments before she ushered us out into the standing-room only audience. After acknowledging the applause I sat down facing the excited crowd as Olivia made the introductions. As I quickly glanced around the room I noticed Jack and Clare Kenwright sitting in the second row. We smiled pleasantly at each other as we listened to Olivia.

"Oh, my, wow, what a crowd we have here this afternoon!" she began, full of genuine enthusiasm. "This is only appropriate, of course, since we are privileged to have as our guest speaker today the renowned novelist, Vanessa Parker." Olivia's introduction was interrupted by long, loud applause. I smiled back, deeply touched by the reception.

"To her many fans, avid readers and followers, she is internationally known, a Pulitzer Prize winner and holds Honorary Doctorates from Columbia and USC. And as many of you know some of her more famous titles have been made into movies or mini television series. Quite simply, we are lucky to be in the rare presence of one of the most treasured writers of the past forty years." More applause followed these remarks which, again, made me feel more than humble.

"Vanessa Parker's legacy will certainly be cemented with the publication of the last book in her trilogy *Intimate Strangers*, which I'm assured is almost complete." I nodded at Olivia as more clapping rang out. "Along with Vanessa, we are also joined this afternoon by Kay Collins who, as Vanessa's agent for all of her writing career, has been such a supportive figure and close friend down the years. Kay," Olivia said, nodding in her direction, "welcome to our modest library and thank you." Kay dutifully smiled as she glanced around the room, completely taken aback, I felt, by Olivia's remarks.

"Well, I've prattled on for too long, so without further ado please give a warm Maine welcome to our guest speaker, Vanessa Parker."

I stood for a few seconds before the applause abated, then sat down clasping my notes. Turning to Olivia, I thanked her for her kind introduction, jokingly adding that she must be a connoisseur of the hyperbole; either that, or she was mixing me up with someone else. The audience chuckled at my attempted humor but I felt it broke the ice.

"When I was a very young reporter just starting my career at the now defunct local newspaper *The Announcer* in Rainbow Falls, New York," here I looked directly at Jack Kenwright, "I envisioned excitement, glamour and scoops by the truckload. Little did I realize that writing of any kind was just hard work, but I was fortunate in having an editor who believed in me from the start and, through him and the other wonderful writers at the paper, I managed to learn an awful lot very quickly.

"Due to some unforeseen and unfortunate changes at the paper," here, again, I looked straight at Jack Kenwright, "...most fortuitous for me, although I didn't think so at the time...I was offered a job at a literary agency run by a man who ran a weekly writers' group in town, which I had attended on a regular basis. He knew my work at the newspaper and thought my first attempt at a novel very promising. Of course, I accepted the job and over the next few years met his daughter, who eventually joined the agency after graduating college. When I'd finished my first novel, *Cards*, she represented me and the rest, as they say, is history. That person was Kay Collins, who has remained my agent and friend ever since. Thank you, Kay.

"The novel was taken up by a large publishing house, which offered a three-book contract. I signed on the dotted line faster than I could sneeze. I'm very fond of that book even now, all these years later, and would like to read a short passage to illustrate my writing style as it was then."

For the next ten minutes I read an excerpt, stopping now and then to briefly discuss why I used a certain phrase or piece of dialogue. I even picked out a paragraph which was written in a particular way back then but which if I was writing it now, in a more modern novel, would be penned in a completely different manner.

Throughout the rest of my time 'on stage' I discussed how my writing had changed over the years, and how it had remained the same. I covered pacing, plot development, creating realistic dialogue as well as a lot of other areas I felt the audience might appreciate learning about. Finally, I told them that as a treat for such an amazing audience, I would read a passage from the last book in the trilogy *Intimate Strangers* without, I hoped, giving too much of the story away. This proposal was received with rapturous applause.

I began, "For so long the gulf between them seemed unbridgeable, a chasm too deep to be approached. But Lizzie knew she had to try; knew she needed to have a resolution one way or the other. She took a moment, a breath, before saying to him, 'What is it you want? Tell me? If we have any hope of resurrecting our life together you must be honest. There is no other way.' This was the moment, then, the time for a conclusion. She waited and stared almost blindly at this person she once called her 'other heart'. Would he respond at all? Would he care? Finally, Patrick faced her and answered, 'There are no words, honestly, no words at all. Nothing I can say will make a difference. You know that now. But if you believe in me again, trust me, take me under your wing for however much time we have left, then I promise, promise to love you as once I did, as once we did. There is nothing more for me to tell you.' Lizzie looked at him for what seemed an age, drinking in his features she knew so well. Bowing her head before piercing his eyes with hers she replied, 'I don't know, Patrick. I just don't know.' And that was how it was left for another day."

I closed my notes and waited as a stunned audience just looked at me for a few seconds before thunderous applause broke the eerie silence. There were even hoots and hollers as the crowd rose as one. The moment completely awed me, almost overwhelmed me to the point of tears. I couldn't have asked for a better response if I had scripted it myself.

"Thank you! Thank you!" I shouted over the throng. "Thank you!"

Olivia came over and hugged me before settling the audience down and requesting questions. Over the next half-hour I fielded a variety of questions, ranging from where my ideas for my books originated, to how some of them might get their own novels published.

Finally, Jack Kenwright got up slowly and raised his hand. I cocked my head, surprised by this turn of events, and wondered what on earth he would ask me.

"Yes?" Olivia offered, pointing at him. "What is your question, sir?"

"I would like to know from Ms. Parker how she differentiates between fact and fiction, both with her writing and in her personal life, considering she appears to spend most of her time making things up?" he asked, accompanied, I thought, with a false smile.

I grinned broadly at Jack Kenwright to let him know his question didn't bother me at all. I understood immediately how he was trying to undermine my recollections of Rainbow Falls and particularly of the short time he spent there. I wrote fiction therefore I must make a lot of things up and my memory could not be trusted to tell the truth. Of course, the audience had no idea of the context of the question or how it related to our brief intertwined lives all those years ago.

Looking him firmly in the eye, I replied, "That is such a great and interesting question, and one I'm only too pleased to answer if it helps to dismiss the notion that all fiction writers must be good liars or that they have difficulty distinguishing fact from fiction in their day-to-day lives.

"When one is writing and constructing a novel one is indeed immersed in that world at that particular time. And I have to tell our questioner that that is a good thing sometimes for it allows the writer to put him or her in a completely different world to the one they know. Of course, fiction writers must have a great imagination to conjure up the make-believe stories they are building chapter by chapter for their readers. Depending on the complexities of the plot, that necessitates the writer having a very good memory, a very acute ability to recall accurately details he or she has written about earlier, sometimes much earlier in the book. For instance, one may have described a character as having blue eyes and blonde hair in chapter one and, then perhaps, a hundred pages further on the writer must correctly remember those characteristics if wishing to describe them again.

"Now, the questioner wonders if this writer, me, has difficulty differentiating between fact and fiction in my personal life? And my answer is absolutely not. Fiction is fiction and reality is reality and, as they say, never the twain shall meet." Still staring solely at Kenwright, I ended my monologue by saying, "I hope this dispels forever your obvious worry that a writer's memories, recollections and remembrances are somehow tainted by the fictional world in which they sometimes dwell."

I sat down to resounding applause, at which point Olivia stood and thanked the audience for attending the proceedings, and me for giving them all an incisive insight into a writer's life. She then invited anyone who was interested in having a signed copy of any of my books to form a line at the pre-arranged desk. I was still signing away an hour later but Jack and Clare Kenwright were not among the purchasers.

Chapter Fourteen

———◆———

T he book signing while being most enjoyable was also exhausting. My hand ached from scratching my signature or writing personal notes on some of the gathered masses' books, as well as keeping up a polite but interesting conversation with those who wanted to talk about various topics from my novels.

Kay and I were about to wrap things up when Olivia personally brought over a small man, probably in his early sixties, with a nervous smile and carrying one of my books.

"Vanessa, Kay, I'd like you to meet James Prescott, who is a professor at the University of Maine, teaching creative writing, I believe. He recorded your talk today to show to his students."

"Oh, yes, I remember now, hello professor, so nice to meet you," I offered, holding out my hand. "Thank you for coming this afternoon. Would you like me to sign that?" I asked, nodding towards his book.

"Very much so," he replied, rather shyly, as though by doing so I would save his life. "I'm a big fan. This," he continued, handing me the book, "is a first edition of your first novel, *Cards*."

"Then we must treat it with all the reverence it deserves," I answered lightly, as we all laughed. After signing my name, I politely enquired about the writing program he taught. "I hope your students are enthusiastic about the endeavor. How big is the class?"

"Classes," he corrected, again diffidently. "We currently have over fifty students enrolled at various stages in our degree program."

"Must keep you very busy," Kay said, helping me out in the conversation.

"They do, fresh young minds and all that, so full of wonderful ideas. Hard to keep up sometimes," he joked. "I can't wait to show them your talk."

"How long has your program been in existence?" I asked.

"Going on fifteen years now. We started with just five students and now look at us."

"Very impressive," I offered, trying hard to wind down the encounter.

"I wonder," he said, yet again tentatively, "whether I might leave my card with you. Perhaps at some point…whenever it's convenient, of course…you might consent to come and speak to the students. I know most of them are huge fans and it would be such a thrill to have you actually standing before them. We have quite a few aspiring novelists and I know they would appreciate and benefit from any advice you could pass on."

I quickly glanced at Kay, as I raised my eyebrows as if to say… *see, they're lining up already*…before turning my attention back to Professor Prescott.

As I took his card I replied, "Oh, certainly, professor, it is something I'll definitely bear in mind. Unfortunately, my agent here," I continued, feigning a deep frown at Kay, "has seen fit to encumber me with a rather extensive book tour once the new novel is published, so any talk would be months from now, I'm afraid."

"I quite understand, but a few months would take us into the new school year. A talk by you would be the perfect start to the semester. I live in hope," he offered, with an almost pleading smile.

"I'll see what can be arranged," I answered. "Right now that's the best I can do."

"As long as you keep us in mind I shall not pester you again. And, thank you so much for signing my book. Something I shall always treasure."

We cordially shook hands and he disappeared seemingly as quickly as he could. We, too, gathered up our things but before we bade farewell to Olivia I told her of a gesture I'd like to make.

"Olivia, you have such a wonderful library here that is a credit to you and the community. Your welcome to me and Kay far exceeded anything I had imagined. Thank you. It is an experience I shall not soon forget."

"No, no," she responded, "it's me who should be thanking you both for sparing so much of your valuable time. That you would do this for us is just amazing. Thank you. Thank you."

"Well, all that being said, I would like to make a donation to the library to be used in any way you think fit."

"Oh, my, I can hardly believe this."

"Yes, I'd like to give you ten thousand dollars."

"What? What did you say…ten…thousand…dollars!"

"That's right, and I'm sure Kay would like to give a little something, too, right Kay?"

Kay was temporarily stunned, too, by my offer but immediately redeemed herself by saying she would also give that amount to the library.

"It'll be money well spent and so richly deserved, Olivia," Kay offered, genuinely.

"We'll have our accountants get in touch within the next few days but, as Kay said, it will be money well spent."

Olivia immediately came over and hugged us both, tears of joy streaming down her face.

"This will make such an impact I promise, and you can be sure I'll keep you informed of how it is being spent. None of it will be wasted… not a penny."

And that it how we left her; amazed by the good fortune that had just fallen into her lap.

Before dinner we relaxed in the bar. Embarrassing for me, a few people came over and expressed their admiration for my talk, but on the whole we were left alone to enjoy our drinks. The same thing happened in the dining room, although two of the people who congratulated me were Jack and Clare Kenwright.

"We really learned a lot this afternoon," Clare began, pleasantly. "Not such an easy business after all, writing novels."

"Yes," I agreed, smiling, "not all fun and games for sure."

"Hope you didn't mind my question?" Jack asked. "Good to know you can sort out all of those different thoughts in your mind while you're hashing out a plot."

"Certainly not easy," I offered, as we tried to move on to our table, "but, as I said at the library, having a good, reliable memory helps."

My answer was pointed and it was meant to be. We exchanged some more small talk, but finally were able to disengage and sit down to dinner.

"Well, that was fun to watch," Kay enthused. "Game, set and match to you, I'd say."

On the way back to the hotel after my session at the library, I'd told Kay the back story to my and Jack's repartee and how he seemed to be trying to cast doubt on the veracity of the events I remembered from all those years ago.

"Oh, I don't think he, or she for that matter, are as confused or as dim-minded as they make out. For some reason they're trying to minimize his time at *The Announcer* and I appear to be their royal pain-in-the-ass."

Over dinner, Kay expanded on her thoughts for my book tour to celebrate the publication of the last book of the *Intimate Strangers* trilogy.

"Assuming you can let us have the final chapter very soon, I'd say the book will be released about two months later. That brings us to July. I would like to start the tour almost immediately to take advantage of what promises to be a blockbuster sales period. And it would end around early October. So…three months and you're done…for now," she said, with a wicked smile.

The talk of a three month tour boggled my mind, but I also knew Kay would take care of all the details and treat me with kid gloves the whole time, making sure my welfare was always uppermost in her mind. Nevertheless, it still seemed a daunting prospect to me.

"Of course, Kay, I'll do whatever to promote the book. That is *so* important to me. I've worked long and hard to complete the trilogy and I really think I've done a credible job…"

"*Credible?* Oh, no, that doesn't even come close to what you've accomplished here. It's a masterpiece, Vanessa, nothing less, believe me."

"Well, thank you. What I meant was I would like to give the old girl – in this case *Intimate Strangers* – a great send off. It would be a fitting end…"

"Vanessa, do not even go there! This is not the end, I hope, just a temporary lull."

Again, I didn't have the heart to smash her dreams of other novels from me, so I smiled and nodded that I understood.

"Anyway, the point is I will do what is necessary…with a smile on my face…to make the tour a success."

"That's all I ask," Kay responded. "That's all I ask."

We spent the rest of the evening on my balcony accompanied by an extremely lush bottle of our favorite red. The night was warm with a gentle breeze off the ocean, and for a long time we sat in silence just enjoying the moment.

Finally Kay said, "It's affected you, hasn't it?"

"What?" I asked, puzzled.

"All of your remembering. I sense a change in you; more pensive; more concerned with what was or may have been."

"In some ways, I suppose, but in other ways it's been fun and revealing. I love going back and reliving all over again how this writing seed germinated and grew in me."

"D'you think it cost you a lot in some ways?"

I knew what she was hinting at and for a few moments I considered her question.

"You mean Ralph?"

"Of course."

"We never should've married. It was a mistake on my part. I was selfish to think I could have it both ways."

"What happened? I never really knew, just that one day it was over and he left."

I quickly looked back over forty years and saw us as we were then, two souls adrift on a sea of trouble. I smiled ruefully and shrugged.

"It was me, mostly, my writing got in the way."

"Ralph couldn't handle your success?"

"Something like that. I guess my job was more important than the relationship."

"Did he ask you to choose?"

"Not in so many words but the inference was there."

"But it had become your life, hadn't it, writing?"

"I loved it more than anything...obviously...and that was the problem."

"More than him?"

I nodded.

"It was the right choice, Vanessa, you do know that, don't you?"

"I've been blessed for sure and I realized a long time ago I would have been miserable without it."

"Is that where the trilogy came from?"

"The original idea, yes. I thought it would be cathartic."

"Was it?"

"Well, one book turned into three, so I guess it was less costly than therapy," I replied, with a laugh.

"Did you ever keep in touch?"

"Never. Oh, I heard he passed about ten years ago but by then he was just someone I used to know."

"Any regrets, Vanessa?"

I turned and listened to the waves rolling in, almost feeling them roll over me.

"None. It wasn't meant to be and my writing was. I would have always resented him holding me back, so sooner or later everything would've crumbled. I've had the life I've had and I'm so grateful."

"And what about Rainbow Falls?"

"Right now, it's just fun trying to go back. Nostalgic, of course, but also kind of mysterious."

"Mysterious? How?"

"Well, I keep thinking there's something...an event of some importance...that I haven't yet discovered. I feel it definitely has some connection to the Kenwrights, particularly Jack, but I have to work up to it to eventually find out what it is."

"Vanessa, this is quite clearly your next book," Kay answered, not totally joking. "And you must keep me informed since now I'm intrigued."

"You will be the first to know," I promised, facetiously.

As the rest of the lazy evening wound down we reminisced as the contents of the bottle of wine diminished with every minute. Finally, we said our goodnights and I thanked her again for being my agent and my dearest friend down our years of growing and closeness.

As I settled in my room I suddenly had the urge to finish the last page of the book. I'm not sure whether it was the preceding conversation I'd had with Kay, or something entirely different, but I immediately knew how the book would end. Excitedly, I revved up my laptop and, within less than an hour, had finally written the conclusion to *Intimate Strangers*. I sent it to Kay's email, went to bed and again slept the sleep of the dead.

Chapter Fifteen

───◆───◆───

"Sensational!" Kay greeted me with, as we met in the lobby for breakfast. "Oh, Vanessa, I really don't know what to say except that this ending is beyond anything I imagined."

Her high praise was all the validation I needed that the trilogy had ended on the right note.

Bowing my head, I replied, "From you, Kay, that means everything to me. I'm so glad you liked it."

"*Liked it?* I loved it, Vanessa. I must've read it ten times this morning. Oh, what a way to wake up!"

"That being said," I answered, seriously, "there must be no editorial changes to it at all, none. This is how I want it to appear in the book. Understood?"

"Of course, I will personally see to that."

Smiling, I thanked her and we went into breakfast talking a mile a minute.

Kay left shortly after we'd eaten. I thanked her profusely again for taking the time to come all the way to Maine to see me, as well as for all her professional and personal support. She told me we'd get together again as soon as I returned home for the book launch and to finalize the details of the tour. I waved her off with feelings of regret and relief; regret, because I always valued her friendship and would miss her, but relief because I could once again return my thoughts to the past and Rainbow Falls.

I planned on staying in Maine for only another week, but with the book finally finished I intended on making the rest of my time as much a vacation as possible. I'd just walk, watch the ocean, shop, enjoy my wine and, of course, try to remember exactly what it was that continued to nag and bother me about the Kenwrights.

To that end, I made my way to my favorite spot on the beach, laid out my towel, closed my eyes and began recalling the past.

The incident with my Vietnam articles blew over and for a while at the paper things stayed relatively calm. Jack Kenwright seemed to be keeping a low profile, ostensibly learning as much as he could about the newspaper business and treating everyone with the respect they deserved as seasoned reporters.

In fact, he and Charles Barrington appeared to have settled some of their differences, although I didn't totally buy into Kenwright's apparent sudden conformity. He still asked a lot of slanted questions and always made sure that everybody knew his father owned *The Announcer*. He also began taking time off, often missing for days at a stretch with no discernable explanation which, as the boss's son, he obviously felt he could. And when he returned he was usually upbeat, as though he'd just won a huge jackpot in Las Vegas.

I continued to work hard at my craft as Mr. Barrington thrust more and more important stories in my lap. These were exciting times for me as I began to accumulate a great deal of knowledge and facts that would later be so beneficial with my novel writing.

The Barrington family also became more and more important to me and I now found myself firmly entrenched within their circle. As well as going often with April to their house in the woods, I always seemed to be invited to participate in any of their numerous and various fun activities. It was at one of these that I noticed Jack and Samantha still appeared to enjoy each other's company.

Rainbow Falls boasted, in those days, a first class theater named *The Bright Lights Company*. Although a small, regional venue, besides local productions it also managed to attract touring plays and musicals. Charles Barrington and his wife were huge benefactors, and he was particularly pleased with that night's production of *Hair*.

One of my new assignments for the paper was to write reviews of the local entertainment scene, so when I attended that night's performance with the rest of the Barrington family I had already seen it. My review was due to be published at the weekend but, of course, Mr. Barrington had already read it.

"Vanessa, your *Hair* piece, excellent and mouth-watering. I can't wait to see it. Should please a lot of folk in town but not, I think, our friend, Jack Kenwright." He uttered his last comment with a huge laugh.

I thanked him for his kind words and agreed Mr. Kenwright probably would not approve of the show's contents.

"Is he going?" I asked.

"Oh, yes, he and his wife. I invited him on purpose," he added, again with a chuckle.

"Should be an interesting night," I offered.

In fact, the whole family, as well as the Kenwrights, Samantha, April, my aunt and uncle and me attended. Being big donors to the theater, the Barringtons secured prime seats for all of us.

Remembering, as I lay on the sand, the musical, full of hippies, drug use, draft-dodgers, irreverence to the flag, near nudity and memorable songs such as *The Age of Aquarius* and *Good Morning Starshine* flashed before me. I also recalled a young, innocent nineteen year old being shocked and awed by what she saw. Within my shallow world I had little idea any of these things existed.

Apart from recollecting, quite clearly, the show, I also recalled one other important incident from that evening. During the intermission, while everyone gathered around the bar discussing the musical, I excused myself to use the restroom. The facility seemed quite a walk from the main lobby and being unfamiliar with its location I wandered around trying to find it. As I rounded one corner I was shocked to see in the distance Samantha and Jack Kenwright kissing. I quickly retreated, found the correct toilet and returned to my seat, stunned and confused. Shortly afterwards, Samantha came back followed a few minutes later by Jack. They took their seats, Jack beside his wife, Clare, as if nothing had happened.

Obviously, I couldn't concentrate very well on the rest of the show and, afterwards, when the rest of the family went on to dinner, I feigned not feeling well and drove myself home. I didn't mention the incident to anyone fearing a monumental backlash and upheaval of giant proportions. I wasn't sure anyone would believe me, anyway. But for me, what that moment confirmed was something I'd long suspected; that Samantha and Jack Kenwright were, indeed, having an affair of some kind. To recover somewhat from that experience, I took a couple of sick days off from the paper, stayed mostly in my room and concentrated on my debut novel.

Upon my return to *The Announcer* Betsy told me that Mr. Barrington was taking two weeks off for a minor surgical procedure. While he was absent he appointed his deputy editor, Ron Chabot, to take over the reins. Ron, like Charles Barrington, always had the pulse of the community in his heart and I imagined things at the paper would remain the same until Mr. Barrington returned.

Unfortunately, that's not what happened. Through the grapevine, I heard my review of *Hair* had suddenly been pulled from Sunday's edition, which puzzled me since Mr. Barrington told me personally how good and accurate it was. I immediately went to see Ron Chabot for an explanation and what he told me both bothered and annoyed me as never before.

"Sorry, Vanessa," he began, somewhat sheepishly for a senior editor, "but I got orders to ditch it from higher up."

Confused, I replied, "But Mr. Barrington himself approved and liked it. What happened?"

"It was Mr. Kenwright. He said his father would never allow a review of…and I quote *'pornographic, unpatriotic garbage'*…to defile the pages of any of his newspapers. And he ordered me to remove the review from Sunday's edition. I told him Mr. Barrington had approved the article but he said in his absence he was in charge of making executive editorial decisions. Sorry, Vanessa, but I had no choice."

Mr. Chabot's explanation almost brought me to tears. Even at my young age I recognized censorship when I saw it. But, just like Ron, I had no choice but to accept his ruling and no credible way to protest.

Over the two weeks Charles Barrington was laid up the paper either made no significant comments on the war, or published pieces written specifically by Kenwright himself. I imagined upon reading them Mr. Barrington would have had multiple heart attacks.

But the paper struggled through, albeit with a staff who mostly spent their days looking morose and defeated. Not so Jack Kenwright, who sauntered around the office, whenever he deigned to bless us with his company, without an apparent care in the world.

At one point I was in two minds whether to spill the beans to Edward about the kissing incident I witnessed between Samantha and Kenwright. As quickly as I thought I would I changed direction, fearing the damage it might do to the family would be devastating. I felt I just couldn't do it to them after all their kindnesses to me.

So, I buckled down and continued my regular reporting while counting the days until Mr. Barrington finally returned.

It was during this time, I remembered clearly, that Hugh, the Barrington's middle son, asked me to meet him for breakfast. Over the past months I had come to know him much better than either Edward or Simon, and it didn't hurt that he was extremely cute, although I never regarded him as anything but an older brother figure to me.

We met at a little place just outside of town and he warmly hugged me when I arrived.

"Thanks so much for coming, Vanessa, hope it hasn't disturbed your morning?"

I assured him it hadn't and that I was wondering what he wanted with me.

"Let's order and then I'd like to run something by you."

Since I had hunger pains and he was treating, I asked the waitress for a huge pile of French toast, bacon and coffee. Hugh simply had coffee and a bagel.

"So," I asked, "what's this all about, Hugh?"

"It's about my Dad."

"Didn't his operation go well?"

"Oh, yes, it's got nothing to do with that. He's fighting fit again. No, we're concerned he's under a lot of stress and it seems to be affecting him in a negative way."

"At the paper?"

"Yes. He's increasingly worried about this Jack Kenwright individual." I cocked my head, wanting to know more. "He feels Kenwright is trying to push him out over dad's opposition to the war."

"Well, Kenwright and his family have made no secret of their views, and I certainly have personal experience of what they're prepared to do to see the paper doesn't cross too many lines."

Agreeing, he said, "Now, my Dad doesn't know I'm talking to you…I don't think he'd approve…but he's getting more and more depressed by the moment, so I was wondering if you'd be prepared to keep your ear to the ground at the paper and let me know if you hear Kenwright doing or proposing to others anything that would undermine my Dad's job as editor."

I considered his proposal and, since I had a huge respect for his father and not that much for Kenwright, I agreed.

"I'd be happy to, Hugh, but in all honesty I'm not at that level where most people confide in me. But I will pay attention and certainly let you know if any tidbits drop into my lap."

"That's all I ask, Vanessa, but I don't want you putting your job in jeopardy in any way, so be careful, okay?"

"I'm now a seasoned reporter, Hugh," I replied, lightly and with a wide smile, "and a shrewd one at that. You needn't worry."

He thanked me again and we enjoyed our breakfast while chit-chatting over nothing in particular. Near the end I asked about Edward, who I'd only seen briefly at the *Hair* musical, and Simon, who was still away at college.

"How's his epilepsy?"

"Mostly under control," Hugh answered, "but Simon's the worrier in the family, so that doesn't help. Right now he's also concerned about Edward."

"Edward," I queried, "why?"

"Well, you know he and Samantha are a couple, but lately they seem to be going their separate ways more and more. At least, Samantha seems to be."

For a second I panicked as the kissing incident flashed before my eyes. Recovering, I replied, "And what does Simon think is happening?"

"He's fairly sure it's her music that's the important thing right now.

She's gone a lot and seems to be drifting farther and farther away from the family."

"Does he think she's interested in someone else?" I ventured, casually.

"Don't know, except he did say she seems quite smitten with that Kenwright guy, why," he continued, seriously, "have you noticed anything going on?"

I shook my head and told him I'd barely seen Samantha in weeks, which was true.

"And what about Edward, has he mentioned anything to you, Hugh?"

He laughed, before saying, "Oh, no, not our Edward. He wouldn't notice if the sky was about to fall in. He's very laid back, as I'm sure you've witnessed?"

I nodded and tried hard to think of something else to say to change the subject. When that didn't fly, I made work an excuse, told Hugh I had to go, gave him a hug and left. A half-mile down the road I pulled over and shook at what I was imagining.

Chapter Sixteen

◆——————◆

The tide started coming in and before the waves could tickle my
feet I moved my towel higher up on the beach, took a drink
and a bite from my granola bar, and settled down again to restart
my recollections.

I sighed as I thought about those difficult days at the paper. Up until
then my journey into journalism, apart from a couple of jolts of reality,
had moved along remarkably smoothly. Even with Jack Kenwright's
meddling I enjoyed the work, the writing and the people.

I cast my mind back to when Charles Barrington eventually returned
from his surgery and confronted Kenwright over his interference while
he was away.

"As soon as Mr. Kenwright shows up," he said, tersely, to all and
sundry, "please ask him to come and see me immediately." He then
firmly shut the door to his office and we all looked at each other as
though we feared the world was coming to an end.

Kenwright finally showed up around eleven and Ron Chabot quickly
intercepted him, joyfully, it seemed, and told him Mr. Barrington was
waiting to see him.

For the next hour we played at working as we listened to raised
voices coming from Mr. Barrington's office. We learned later from his
secretary, who overheard some of the back and forth, that Kenwright
threatened to have his father fire Barrington, and that Mr. Barrington
replied if he did that then it would effectively mean the death of the

paper in the community, since so many people supported the main opinions expressed in *The Announcer*.

Certainly, when Kenwright emerged from the meeting, he smiled at us all as he made for the door, and he wasn't seen around the office for the next three days. As requested by Hugh, I duly reported to him what I'd seen and heard, if only second- handedly, and Hugh later told me his father had assured the family he thought Kenwright's threat was an empty one because he felt sure Kenwright's father knew how much of a money maker the paper was for his company. The advertising revenue it generated was enormous.

To his credit, Mr. Barrington never involved any of us in the internal politics swarming around the office and, indeed, for the next few months everything settled down once more and the paper resumed its normal functions.

On my beat, which not only included covering the arts and local council matters, I also was entrusted to report on the openings of any new businesses in the area, which usually meant restaurants. That suited me fine because to write a valid article I always found it necessary to sample some of the delights on the new menus, all at the paper's expense, of course. But the downside was that it required me to work a lot more nights as well as adding several new inches to my waist.

But Mr. Barrington was very fair to me and gave me days off in lieu of my obvious dedication to the culinary scene. On those day I concentrated on my novel *Cards*, which surprisingly seemed to speed along at an impressive clip, if you count a new chapter every two weeks or so impressive!

However, my evening work obviated me to travel across the county in search of stories, and it was in some of these out-of-the-way places that I ran into Samantha performing with her band, as well as Jack Kenwright sitting in the audience. Sometimes they saw me, but more often than not I ate my dinner at a secluded table and was able to retreat before my presence was known. Of course, Kenwright's wife, Clare, was nowhere to be seen, which only fueled my reasoning that an affair was, indeed, happening.

To make matters worse, Simon, the Barrington's youngest son, who was home from college for the summer, sometimes accompanied me on my jaunts, and it was all I could do on occasions to stop him from confronting Samantha. But he confirmed what Hugh had told me earlier that he worried Edward was being blindsided by both Samantha and Kenwright.

"I've got to let him know somehow, Vanessa, what's going on. He seems oblivious to it all, but this isn't fair on him what's happening behind his back."

"Simon, I'm not sure that's a good idea or any of your business," I answered, trying to calm him down. "Edward's not a fool and sooner or later he'll see what might be going on. Please don't put yourself in the middle of this. You certainly don't need the stress."

He shrugged and after that he stopped coming with me on my assignments.

The next get-together of the Barrington clan and its friends occurred in late June when they threw a party to celebrate Simon's twenty-first birthday. We all gathered at their large town house, enjoyed impressive catering and drinks, and were looking forward to Samantha singing a special song she'd written for the occasion.

The party had been in full swing for over an hour, with cards and presents being thrust into Simon's arms from every angle. Not one for throngs of people, he, at times, seemed overwhelmed with the affection and love aimed in his direction. April and I tried our best to soothe his angst, and he seemed to appreciate our efforts as we joked about how it was all downhill for him now as he'd reached such an advanced age.

While we were joshing with Simon we heard Charles Barrington's booming voice welcoming some new guests who'd suddenly appeared through the lounge door.

"Come in, come in!" he exclaimed to the Kenwrights, who were accompanied by Samantha. Glancing over, I noticed Clare's face looked like stone as she faked a smile in Barrington's direction.

"And there's my girl!" Barrington yelled over the din, as he embraced Samantha in a warm bear hug.

Edward immediately went over to her and the pair kissed, although, as far as I could tell, not particularly enthusiastically on Samantha's part. But Edward did lead her to the buffet table and the two seemed to be getting on reasonably well. The Kenwrights on the other hand, while together, looked uncomfortable, and it was Clare who eventually left her husband's side to engage me, Simon and April in some light conversation.

As the evening wound down, Mr. Barrington called for everyone's attention. He gave a witty speech in praise of his son, proposed a toast, to which we all joyously raised our glasses, and then introduced Samantha and her guitar.

"For this extra special occasion our dear Samantha has written a song especially to celebrate Simon's twenty-first birthday. And knowing Sam's musical talent I'm sure this will be the highlight of the evening. Sam…"

Samantha stood and made her way to the center of the room before turning in Simon's direction and addressing him personally.

"Simon, on this your special day I hope this song will let you know how dear you are to me…to us…and to tell you how much we all love you." She took a second to adjust her guitar before saying, "It's simply called 'You'."

And for the next four or five minutes Samantha sang a sweet ballad that had all of us smiling and nodding our heads. Several times during her rendition, when she came to the repeated chorus line '…*But mostly I'm just grateful for you…*' I noticed she turned her head and eyes very slightly in Jack Kenwright's direction and smiled. This must have happened four or five times and apparently I wasn't the only person to notice this subtle acknowledgment. Just before she finished the song, Simon stood abruptly and fled the room, leaving everyone except me in a state of shock. I immediately knew why he'd had this sudden meltdown, but obviously I couldn't say anything to anyone as conjecture swirled around the room. Mrs. Barrington hurried after him, but that was the last we saw of Simon for the rest of the party.

On the beach the lunch hour beckoned, so I packed up my things and took a leisurely stroll back to the hotel. All the way I thought about young Simon, the darkness that seemed to surround him and the eventual tragedy that befell him. I wondered what, if anything, I could have done to have helped him or, indeed, the whole Barrington family, but then I realized I was only nineteen at the time and not experienced in the ways of the human heart or its emotions. All the way back to the hotel I was bugged by the 'what if?' questions. What if I had told Edward about seeing Samantha and Jack Kenwright so often together? What if I hadn't stopped Simon from informing his brother about his suspicions? And, what if I had never known the Barringtons at all? I shook my head and blew out my cheeks as I considered those possibilities. In the end I decided life is what it is sometimes, and all the regrets weren't worth a grain of sand.

To my surprise, when I entered the lobby Joyce Andrews intercepted me and told me Clare Kenwright asked if I'd join her for lunch. Taken aback by such an offer, since I was sure the Kenwrights were no longer keen on speaking with me, I nodded and made my way to the dining room where she was waiting for me.

"Mrs. Kenwright, this is so gracious of you to invite me to join you," I opened with, hoping that approach would set the standard for our conversation and demeanor.

She smiled sweetly, her eyes still as bright and piercing as I remembered from all those years ago, before saying, "Well, having lunch with such a world famous author I'll be the envy of the room." She raised her eyebrows and chuckled and continued, "But we're leaving tomorrow and, as Jack's upstairs packing his things, I thought we might talk a little about some of those days in Rainbow Falls which you seem to be so consumed with."

I couldn't tell from her inference whether her tone was accusatory or just factual, so I chose the later.

"It's been mostly fun," I replied, cheerfully, "remembering my youth, and I have to thank you and Mr. Kenwright for that. If you hadn't been staying here I doubt I would've ever gone back over those years like I have." I left that compliment on the table and waited for her to respond. Before she could do so our server showed up and we ordered lunch and a glass of wine each.

"You do realize things were different in those days, don't you?" she finally offered, a tad defensively I thought.

"You mean compared to today?"

"Of course, we were just coming out of the Swinging Sixties and nobody much cared about rules and consequences."

I agreed that people were pushing boundaries in the name of freedom.

"Yes, and we were all guilty to some extent or another, wouldn't you say?"

I shrugged and replied, "Well, not me. I lived a pretty down-the-line life, actually."

"So consumed with your new reporting job and your other writing, I dare say."

"That's exactly right. Those were my excitements," I continued, with a laugh.

"So, how far have you got," she asked, "with your walk down memory lane?"

"Quite far, actually," I responded, to what I felt was a disparaging question on her part. "I've passed the part where your husband was trying to exert his influence on the paper, particularly with regard to the Vietnam War which, of course, was raging back then. He even tried to suppress a series of articles of mine and, indeed, managed to do so with a review I had written of the musical *Hair*." If Clare thought for one minute I would not respond with facts to her general assertions, then she had badly mistaken me for some welcome mat she could wipe her feet on.

She took a sip of wine as our server brought out our sandwiches and salads. We ate in silence for a few minutes before she said, "You know, I was against the war, too. That put a lot of pressure on our relationship, so I buried myself in my painting and let Jack get on with whatever it was he was doing. You probably remember I didn't seem to be around very much?"

"Yes, I did recall that but I recollected he always said you were away visiting family somewhere."

"That was Jack for you, always could come up with some plausible explanation," she answered, with a chuckle. "But, in truth, we were going through a difficult period back then. We'd married young and he kind of swept me off my feet. As you know, his family owned lots of newspapers, so money was no object to Jack. He showered me with the good life and, I have to admit, I liked it, being a young girl from a small town.

"But, as I think I mentioned to you before, Jack had a roving eye and sometimes…well, let's say, often…he couldn't resist a pretty face."

"He had affairs, you mean?"

"Yes," she replied, shaking her head. "He always came home, tail between his legs, apologies streaming out of his mouth like water, and promising never to do it again. And for quite a while he kept his word, as far as I could tell. By the time we came to your little town I would say we were back on track with our marriage."

"Until he met Samantha, am I correct?"

"You are. Oh, it was all perfectly innocent at first, just him giving her rides home, and even me picking her up sometimes. But then I recognized the old familiar signs and I knew he'd fallen for her. Can I ask, did anyone in the Barrington family or any of her friends suspect what was going on?"

"I certainly did. I'd seen Samantha and your husband together on a number of occasions. I mentioned it to her close friend, April, but she dismissed the possibility. So I let it go until Simon told me he was going to talk to his brother, Edward, who was Samantha's boyfriend at the time."

"Now Simon," Clare asked, "which one was he?"

"He was the Barringtons' youngest son. Away at college most of the time, but he had a sharp mind and could tell there was something amiss with Edward and Samantha."

"Wasn't he sickly or something?"

"He had epilepsy and was a touch fragile, mentally."

"And he died quite suddenly didn't he?"

"Yes," I nodded, sadly, "such a tragedy and a loss."

"I seem to remember that for some reason."

"Perhaps you also remember his twenty-first birthday party?"

She frowned, before asking, "Should I?"

"It was when Simon ran out of the room when Samantha was singing a song she'd written for him. Both he and I noticed how often she cast a look in your husband's direction when singing a particular line. And that's about where I'm up in my reminiscences."

By this time we'd finished our lunch and decided to take our coffees in the lounge.

Once settled, Clare surprised me by saying, "He really, really loved her, you know."

"Samantha?"

"Yes, he adored her. After we left Rainbow Falls he and I parted. It was mutual and he was very honest with me. He still travelled to his father's different newspapers but for a short while he and Samantha were a couple."

"So, what happened?" I wanted to learn, seeing as she and Jack were still together after more than fifty years.

"I think she got tired of him and, of course, her music always got in the way. She toured a lot more and seemed to have less and less time for him and his way of life. The woman had a very strong free spirit and I guessed she didn't want to be tied down once the magic wore off. Eventually, we reconnected and have been together, obviously, ever since and, no, he has never strayed again," she ended, with a laugh.

"And what about you, how did you manage to cope?"

"Oh, don't worry I had my moments, too. I became quite a good painter, eventually having successful shows all over the country. And along the way there were quite a few admirers, I might add," she finished, with a huge mischievous grin. "So, there you have it, Ms. Parker, your mystery couple's secret life, dirt and all."

We chuckled at her description and I thanked her for being so honest and forthcoming with me.

"Well, I doubt we'll ever meet again, so I wanted you to know the truth and the background when you're remembering all the other stuff from all those years ago. That's important to me...that you know the truth."

I thanked her again and we parted with a tender embrace. And she was correct, we never met again but her divulgences certainly did help me piece together the remaining parts of the story.

Chapter Seventeen

———◆———◆———◆———

The next morning I ordered breakfast in my room specifically to avoid seeing the Kenwrights again. My respect for Clare grew somewhat after our chat the previous day, but my feelings about her husband's behavior all those years ago left me with a very bad taste in my mouth, so I thought it best we didn't see each other again.

After I was sure they had left the hotel I decided to spend a lot of my last three days in this part of Maine just mainly relaxing, trying not to think about the past but just enjoying some of the sights and amenities I hadn't yet taken in.

I booked a seat at the local theater for the next night's production of *Menopause The Musical*, and then took myself off for a massage and pedicure in town. Lunch was at one of Maine's famous diners where I indulged in one of their fabulous lobster rolls, French fries and a glass of wine, of course. This town also boasted quaint trolleys, so I spent some of the afternoon riding around and stopping at various shops, museums and art galleries, of which there were plenty.

At a local bookstore, specializing in rare and hard-to-find editions, I managed to pick up a very good copy of Thoreau's *Walden*, his 1854 series of essays of his life spent in the woods.

Back at the hotel after a full day I asked Keith and Joyce Andrews to join me for dinner, to thank them for all their hospitality, kindnesses and considerations they'd shown me during my stay. Unfortunately,

Keith was dealing with some crisis or other with the hotel's catering company, so Joyce came on her own.

"This is so nice," she began, a huge smile creasing her angelic face, "I'm going to miss having you around, Vanessa."

"No, Joyce, I'm the one who should be thanking you and Keith for making my stay here so enjoyable and peaceful, and for always guarding and respecting my privacy. You're a gem!"

We drank to those sentiments before she brought up the status of my remembrances.

"So, how far have you got?"

I gave her a brief run-down, omitting those parts I felt I should keep to myself.

"And to think none of this would've happened if the Kenwrights hadn't been staying here, too."

"I know, amazing eh? And I have to thank your oldies' night for finally putting me on the right track."

Joyce frowned and asked, "How so?"

"Well, I happened to be passing the bar area on one of those nights and blaring out from the speakers was Janis Joplin's version of '*Me and Bobby McGee*'. And it was that song that connected me to them and all the memories that have followed."

"Oh, that's *so* cool," Joyce replied, "a chance in a million. Now, I recall you telling me sometime ago that this experience has been difficult in lots of ways. How d'you feel about it now?"

I nodded and answered, "It has been for sure, but in other ways I've loved recalling those days and moments buried deep in my brain. Like, for instance, sadly remembering my mother's passing but also how dear she was and is to me. And how grateful I was, and still am, to my aunt and uncle for being there at the worst time in my life, for taking me under their wings and basically putting my soul back together again. So, I have to say the pluses have out weighed the minuses."

"And the Kenwrights, may I ask?"

Again, without revealing too much, I said, "Some help and some resistance. Mrs. Kenwright filled in a few blanks for me when we had dinner last night, but he never seemed too comfortable discussing the past. And that's all right because my own recollections have done a pretty good job, I'd say. And, they've given me lots of reasons why he's apparently been so reluctant to engage with me too much."

"Because they're at the center of the story?"

"Seems that way. You see, soon after I got my first job at a local newspaper Mr. Kenwright, whose father owned that one and quite a few other ones, came to town to ostensibly learn the trade. Instead, he seemed to create havoc everywhere he went and with everything and everyone he touched. I haven't finished yet with my memories but I do feel the Barrington family, who kind of adopted me back then, suffered greatly from his interference and actions. I'm sure it's those kinds of things he didn't want to talk about or even remember."

"I guess we all have our ghosts and secrets," Joyce offered, "but at least it's allowed you to perhaps come to terms with some issues important to you."

"You're so right, it has. I loved recalling my young self and the beginnings of my writing career. It's been quite a life."

"And you've finished your latest book?"

"I have. It's now with the publisher. So excited, I am, since I think this will be my last novel."

"Really?"

"Yes, for a long time now I've thought I'd like to give something back, to maybe encourage young writers with their efforts. So, I'm seriously thinking of taking a writer-in-residence position somewhere."

"With the professor from the University of Maine? He seemed awfully keen to have you join him."

"Who knows, Joyce? But it's definitely a possibility."

By this time we'd finished our dinner and she said she had to go and check on her errant husband before he killed someone. We hugged, told each other we'd certainly keep in touch, and I thanked her once more for taking such good care of me.

The next day I spent taking a trip to the famous Nubble Lighthouse and also a whale-watching boat ride. Unfortunately, the cold, gray water produced no sightings but the excursion on the water, feeling the wind blow on my face and soaking up the smell of the Atlantic made the experience so worthwhile. In the evening I took off for the theater, where I greatly enjoyed and was amused by the play. A quick drink back at the hotel made the evening complete.

I planned on going straight to bed but found my mind still alert and not ready for sleep. I took the remainder of my wine onto the balcony, put my feet up on the railing and looked again at the twinkling lights dotting the shoreline as far as the eye could see. I thought back over my day and decided it was well spent and well deserved. Since sleep still eluded me I closed my eyes and returned again to Rainbow Falls. A faint, flickering remembrance took me back to a few days after Simon's sudden departure from his party.

I hadn't seen much of my friend, April, mostly because she was studying hard to become a vet and I was occupied with my job at the paper. But one evening she called and asked if I'd like to join her on Saturday when she visited a family friend, who also happened to be something of a clairvoyant.

"Oh, I don't know, April," I replied, cautiously, "I don't really believe in all that ESP nonsense and telling people vague things that might," and I emphasized the word 'might', "or might not come true at some point in their lives."

"Oh, c'mon, Vanessa," she pleaded, "if nothing else it'll be fun. And my friend, who's English by the way, is quite a woman who I think you'll really like."

I countered by saying, "Perhaps I'll write an expose for the paper on these fortune-telling charlatans."

We both laughed at that comment before she added, "I think you'll be very surprised by Beatrice Bapp, Vanessa, and who knows, could be she'll make you a convert."

After some more hesitation and protests I eventually agreed to April's request that I accompany her on Saturday to see the formidable, and possibly frightening, Beatrice Bapp.

I picked April up at ten and, after stopping for coffee, we made it to Beatrice Bapp's house by ten-thirty. It was located by the same river that ran near the Barringtons' property, but farther down and more isolated. The house was tiny with a neat front garden that seemed to be mostly covered with all sorts of fancy bird-feeders. April knocked before opening the door and marching inside.

Mrs. Bapp was in her small front room, standing before a huge bird cage which contained a multi-colored parrot, whom she was feeding nuts and pieces of fruit. Turning, she welcomed us with a nice smile, telling us to take our places at the table.

"Bea," April said, looking at me, "this is my friend, Vanessa. I hope you don't mind that I brought her with me today?"

"Oh, no dear, not at all, always a pleasure to meet one of your friends." She reached out and gently shook my hand.

For a few seconds I studied Mrs. Bapp, who had a full head of close-cut white hair, very broad, substantial shoulders, a round face and thin, wire-framed glasses. She spoke with an English accent which I immediately took to.

"Hi, Mrs. Bapp, I'm so pleased to meet you."

"Well, any friend of April's is a friend of mine," she responded, cheerfully.

"I love your parrot, Mrs. Bapp. Does it talk?

"Oh yes, sometimes I have to cover him up to shut him up," she answered, with a chuckle. "And sometimes," she continued, in a sort of conspiratorial whisper, "his language is quite rich, if you know what I mean?"

"Does he have a name?"

"Knick-Knack Paddywhack, although that's not what I call him sometimes," she offered, with a wicked grin.

At that moment the parrot spewed out some very choice words, which made us all laugh and certainly broke the ice. Mrs. Bapp yelled back some choice words of her own in rebuke before throwing a blanket over the cage.

"There, that should keep him quiet for a while. Now, in order for me to read your tea leaves we need to make a nice, fresh pot. April, dear, would you mind?"

April smiled and trotted off to the small kitchen while I chatted with Mrs. Bapp.

"You have to use loose tea," she informed me, "and I have a cousin who sends some over from England every now and then. Honestly, dear, you can't beat a nice cup of English tea."

I nodded agreeably but, being a coffee drinker, I couldn't really confirm her theory.

"Well, I'm looking forward to a cup, Mrs. Bapp. It's been a long time since I had one."

"Now," she told me, pleasantly, "I should like it if you called me Bea, like everyone else does."

"Oh, all right, I'd love that...Bea," as we both giggled. It seemed odd and difficult for me to call a seventy something stranger by anything other than Mrs. or Ms., but she insisted. "I love your accent," I told her. "How long have you been here?"

She thought for a moment before saying, "Close on forty years now. It seems like home."

"Do you miss it?"

"No, not really, I don't have many ties there anymore, just a few cousins."

At that moment a cat jumped onto her lap and then onto mine.

"Oh, that's a good sign," she stated, firmly. "Beauty doesn't usually take to most people."

The cat purred, but before she could settle down Mrs. Bapp shooed her away.

"If you give her half a chance she'll smother you to death and I can see you're not too keen."

"Allergies," I responded, "cats and dogs."

By this time, April returned from the kitchen with a tray full of cups, saucers and a large pot of tea."

"Here we are," she said, setting it down on the table. "It's already steeped, so who's going to play Mom?"

Mrs. Bapp took charge, poured each of us a cup and handed them around

"These are beautiful, Bea," I exclaimed, as I took a gleaming white, bone china cup and saucer from her.

"A wedding-present, brought them all the way from England. Now, drink up."

We sipped our tea and made small talk before Mrs. Bapp instructed me on the tea leaf reading rituals.

"Now," she began, looking over the top of her glasses at me, "leave a tiny amount in the bottom of your cup." I drank up and followed her instructions. "Take the cup in your left hand and swirl it gently around in an anticlockwise direction."

I did that and she then told me to invert the cup into the saucer and leave it for a minute. I waited before she said for me to turn the cup up from the right and hand it to her. She took the cup while April and I stared like zombies at her not knowing what to expect next.

Mrs. Bapp peered inside the cup, turned it around several times, frowned, smiled and raised her eyebrows.

"I'm looking at the shapes, the figures, the lines and the dots," she revealed, as if about to divulge State secrets. "They tell me everything," she continued, as she hummed and hawed while still rotating the cup. I edged closer in my seat fully engrossed now in the spectacle.

"April, just so you know, has told me very little about you except you're a writer at *The Announcer*, and I can see that from the strong lines and letters here." She then stopped and looked directly at me and asked, "Your mother, she's dead, isn't she?"

I pursed my lips and nodded.

"You write for her, don't you, a lot of the time?"

"Yes, I do, she's always with me."

Mrs. Bapp nodded in agreement before adding, "I see her clearly, how she was and she's waving."

"Waving?" I queried. "What does that mean?"

"She wants you to go on with your life and let it take you wherever."

"She was always supportive, that was Mom."

Inside the rim Mrs. Bapp noticed two triangles.

"Oh, lots of good luck here," she professed. "Success in what you'll do...great success, mostly with your writing although it will be very different from what you're doing now." She glanced along the side of the cup and proclaimed sudden changes were in store in the near future. "I see upheaval and though you won't think so at the time it will be good for you."

As she continued she suddenly sat back and put her hand to her mouth.

"What? What is it?" I asked, engrossed.

"A square, like a coffin. Someone will go but not you, someone you know, though."

I looked quickly at April and she shrugged as if to say *'she's only telling you what she sees'*.

Mrs. Bapp then took hold of my hand and whispered, "Oh, you will get married. I clearly see a ring on the bottom, so some time into the future. And his name will begin with the letter 'R'. There's also an elephant, which means you will enjoy good health, but I advise you to take care of your eyes."

We waited for more and Mrs. Bapp finally finished by telling me she saw a star surrounded by dots, which denoted wealth and distinction. Looking directly at me again, she said, "You will live a long and successful life. Some disappointments, of course, but really, dear, there are no bad omens for you personally."

Sitting back, I breathed a huge sigh of relief. On the whole I think I believed most of what she predicted, although I obviously felt great trepidation about the death of someone I knew. I hoped she was wrong about that and tried very hard to dismiss the possibility from my mind.

"Now you, April," I said, but Mrs. Bapp replied, with a chuckle, she'd read her so many times there was nothing left to learn. "So, do you read your own?" I asked her.

"From time to time."

"Any things come to pass?" I enquired, again.

"I learned I will live to be a hundred," she answered, with a bigger chuckle this time. "I guess we'll see."

We spent another hour with Mrs. Bapp before heading home. I thanked her for taking the time and trouble to read my fortune and assured her I'd keep in touch to let her know how accurate she was with her predictions

In the car, April asked me what I thought of the whole experience.

"Actually, I was pleasantly surprised. I'll certainly be paying attention to see what, if anything, she was right about. The only worrying part was the death of someone I know. I'm sure she may say that to a lot of people because somewhere along the way all of us always lose somebody close or who we knew."

"So, you're not too concerned then?"

I shrugged before replying, "No, not really, are you?"

"Not at all," April offered, with a laugh, "as long as it's not you!"

"Yeah, that would be a bummer...for both of us, but since she told me I'm to live a long and successful life, I doubt the victim's me."

"Well, then, I guess it's one of those predictions you have to forget about and just concentrate on the good stuff. Que sera sera and all that."

As I opened my eyes I smiled fondly at those recollections. I ran Mrs. Bapp's predictions through my head again and was amazed at how close she was with the truth. I have lived a long and modestly successful life, and she was correct that my writing would be different from the reporting at *The Announcer*. I did marry, and she was right when she said his name would begin with the letter 'R'. Also, in my thirties I developed a problem with my left eye, which, if left unattended would have resulted in poor or no vision. Luckily, I saw a specialist who preserved my sight, but ever since I've made sure I receive regular check-ups.

As I finished my wine, my mind drifted back to her warning about the death of someone I knew in the not too distant future. Clearly seeing that person's face again, I shook my head, sniffed back a tear and decided that memory would be saved for another day.

As good as my word, I did keep in touch with Mrs. Bapp right up until her death at age ninety-nine. She didn't reach one hundred as she predicted, but being in her hundredth year certainly counts in my book as being correct.

Chapter Eighteen

————◆————

I spent my last full day packing, before walking into town and ordering a huge arrangement from the local florist to be delivered to Joyce and Keith after I'd left. My time in Maine had been very productive and I silently thanked Kay again for pushing me into it. I ate lunch at my favorite bistro and topped it off with ice cream from the place I now called my second home.

Before dinner I took one more walk along the beach, dipping my toes in the still frigid water and watching the birds dive and scamper after the bits of crackers I scattered as I went. It was a true bittersweet moment having to leave a scene I had grown so accustomed to over the last month.

Keith joined me for dinner this time while Joyce took care of the front desk. I hadn't spent a lot of time talking to him as I had Joyce, so I wondered if he, too, would inquire about my recollections which seemed to be general knowledge by now. To my surprise he never mentioned them, concentrating rather on my books, particularly the one I'd just finished.

"You got me reading again, Vanessa," he admitted, cheerfully, "all of yours, of course."

"Of course," I answered, with a knowing frown, and we both cracked up.

"Can't wait for the last one in the trilogy. Have my own theories, of course, about how it all will end, but I'm looking forward to being surprised."

"Oh, you will be, Keith," I assured him, "you will be, and I will send you a copy when it's published just so you can see how wrong you were." We both laughed before he told me he and Joyce had a surprise of their own in store for me after dinner.

"Love surprises," I offered, "care to give me a hint?"

He shook his head but told me it had something to do with my past. We finished dinner and he seemed to drag out eating dessert until around eight o'clock. Finally, he wiped his mouth, put down his napkin, took me by the hand and led me into the bar.

Of course, I'd forgotten it was oldies' night, so the place was crowded and the music blaring. But once the deejay saw me coming through the door he immediately stopped the noisy Stones' track and called for quiet from everyone. I frowned, looked in puzzlement at Keith as he led me to the center of the floor.

On his signal, the deejay announced, "Ladies and gentlemen, this next number is in honor of one of the hotel's favorite guests...Ms. Vanessa Parker." He then put on a fresh song and turned up the volume. I was still bemused by all the attention until I suddenly heard the familiar, raspy voice of Janis Joplin belting out *'Me and Bobby McGee'*.

My face lit up as Keith took me by the hand and we sort of danced crazily through the whole song. Joyce eventually came over and joined us, telling me they wanted to take me back to when I was nineteen again.

Over the din, I gave them both a hug as my eyes watered in gratitude and my mind cast itself back fifty years. How could it have gone by so fast, I kept asking myself, how could it have gone by so fast?

I stayed quite late, enjoying the hits of the past and, of course, drinking more than I should. But the oldies' evening was a fitting end to my stay and something I would always remember.

The next morning, after an early breakfast, Keith helped me pack my car before he and Joyce hugged me and waved a fond goodbye. I drove along the coast road for a while just to take one last look at the ocean. And then I was gone.

I arrived home by early evening, stopped by Jean's house to retrieve my dog, Wolf, who was naturally overjoyed to see me, spent some time catching up with Jean, gave her the gift I'd bought her in Maine for taking such good care of him and the house, and finally made it home by nine-thirty. Being exhausted, I fed Wolf and myself, took him for a quick walk and had an early night.

Kay called the next morning to inform me that the majority of the editing was complete and the publisher estimated the release date of the book would be in less than a month. She also said she'd been working hard on the tour dates and destinations, but that it looked like they would begin in July in New York City and would include a stop in Paris where, apparently, my novels were very popular.

"Thirty stops in all," she told me, excitedly. "I've already started promoting the book in all the main outlets and word on the street is the anticipation is almost at fever- pitch. Your hand will probably drop off by the time we've finished the tour," she only half joked.

That news gave me ambivalent feelings; the prospect of having another, but last, successful novel thrilled me to pieces, while on the other hand a tour that long I felt would leave me exhausted.

"Kay, I hope you are going to space the dates apart somewhat. I'm seventy-two for goodness sake. I need my rest."

"Oh, don't worry *old* girl, I'll make sure there's a wheelchair handy," she responded, lightly. "Of course you'll have plenty of time to rest. I'm not going to run the hand that feeds me into the ground!"

At once, I knew Kay, as usual, would make sure I was looked after and catered to. She'd always had my back and I confidently expected this time would be no different.

"I'm actually looking forward to it, Kay. Bittersweet, of course, because it'll be my farewell tour..."

"No, it won't, Vanessa," she insisted. "This is *not* going to be your last novel."

I didn't have the heart to argue even though the decision had been made and wouldn't be changed. So I just told her we'd see and left it at that.

Being back in my own home thrilled me. The house was comfortable with enough private land to enable me to be secluded when I used the pool. But the real gem for me was my sun room, with its large windows on all sides which allowed me to enjoy the outside views while being protected from too much sun and too many bugs. And it was in here, after dinner that I settled into my favorite comfy chair, put my feet up and returned once more to Rainbow Falls.

For some reason my mind suddenly filled with visions of the Barringtons' daughter, Chloe. At the time, she was nearly eighteen, still in school but heavily interested in the ever-changing fashion business of which I knew very little, except that the clothes I wore every day were probably laughable to her.

At get-togethers she always sought me out, asked how I was doing at the paper and genuinely seemed to want a friendship with someone nearer her own age. In return, I tried my best to learn as much as I could about her obvious obsession with the latest designs and trends in the ever-changing fashion scene.

The moment I recall quite clearly now occurred during the early summer when Chloe had just finished her junior year in high school. She asked to meet me for some advice, which seemed odd considering I was only a year older than her. But I agreed because I liked her and wanted to know what possible advice I might impart.

We met at a quiet spot in the local park, hugged warmly and, after some small- talk, she told me why she needed to see me.

"Vanessa, I've had an amazing offer," she gushed, "a summer internship in Paris!"

"Oh, wow, Chloe, that's fantastic," I exclaimed, "tell me more?"

"Well," she continued, calming down a little, "as you know I live and breathe fashion and over the past year I've been sending some of my designs all over the place hoping someone would take notice."

"Okay, and?"

"And finally somebody did…well, not just somebody, but Michel Fontaine of The Fontaine Fashion House!"

Of course, the name meant nothing to me but I assumed he was a top name in the world in which he worked.

To hide my obvious ignorance, I asked, "So, what's the deal then?"

"The deal is," Chloe eagerly told me, "I get to go to Paris for the summer and after that…who knows?"

"Jeez, Chloe, I'm jealous already…Paris for the summer."

"I know, trouble is it hasn't been received well in the family. Oh, Mom and Dad are okay with it but Edward doesn't want me to go. He thinks all the riots over the war will put me in some kind of danger. He's trying to persuade Mom and Dad to stop me from going."

"Okay, while I don't agree with him I do have a few questions, Chloe. Where will you live and…?"

"All taken care of. I'll be with three other summer interns… all female, by the way…," she giggled, "and one of Michel's other designers …a woman, by the way…" she laughed again, "will host us at her house. So, we'll be safe and fed but Edward still thinks I'll be taken advantage of in some way. Now," she said firmly, "I really want to know what you think…I need your advice, Vanessa."

"I don't think you have a choice, Chloe," I began, as her face immediately turned dark with a harsh frown before she heard the rest of what I had to say, "you *have* to go. You really, really do."

"What, you think so?"

"Of course, this is an opportunity of a lifetime. If you don't do this now you will regret it for the rest of your life. It doesn't matter what Edward or anyone else thinks, this is something you have to do, trust me. Fashion is your true passion. Anyone who knows you can see that. And having this once-in-a-lifetime chance with, apparently, one of the foremost fashion houses in Paris and, probably, the world…well, it's a no-brainer. As I say, you don't have a choice."

"You would've done the same?"

"I did, Chloe, I did. Writing is *my* passion, as you well know, so when your father offered me a job with his paper I didn't have a choice but to accept. That's what I wanted to do in life…write…so it wasn't simply a choice, it was destiny. The same goes for you. Fashion is your destiny, plain and simple."

For a few seconds Chloe just sat and stared at me and then, as if a light bulb had just gone off in her head, she smiled and nodded.

"That's why I came to you," she said, still nodding, "because I knew you'd give me an honest opinion without the onus of family breathing down your neck. Oh, Vanessa, thank you, thank you, you're so right."

"What exactly are you expecting out of the internship?" I asked.

"To learn a lot, have my designs and ideas critically looked at and, hopefully," she continued, with a sly grin, "parlay all of that into a job."

"You're thinking of staying in Paris, aren't you, Chloe?" I responded, clearly understanding her intentions for the first time.

"Done the research, Vanessa. There's an American school there where I can finish my high school requirements and graduate. So, yes, if I'm offered any sort of position I'm going to take it, just don't tell anyone, okay?"

"You're going to be an adult soon, Chloe, I don't see how they can stop you, but my lips are sealed."

We chatted some more but, before we parted, I told her how proud I was of her for forging her own path and believing in herself.

"Got most of that from just watching you, Vanessa," she confessed. "You're my role model for the way to pursue your dreams."

I took the compliment in stride because I knew she was taking more chances with her young life than I ever would. In fact, over the years, the choice she made back then to try and realize her ambitions continued to inspire *me* with my own goals and objectives.

My advice to Chloe did not go down well with one member of the Barrington clan. A few days after our conversation, Edward asked to see me. We met at his apartment and, after a terse *hello* on his part, he began taking me to task for advising Chloe in the way that I did.

"Vanessa, you had no right to butt into my family's affairs, none."

"But Edward...," I started to protest, before he rudely interrupted.

"No, you had no right at all. This is our business."

I had no idea why, apart from perhaps thinking his sister would be in some kind of danger, he was being so adamant. His attitude, as young as I was, really irritated me as being unfair and totally irrational. Since I was now quite a seasoned reporter who over the past few months had interviewed and pursued all sorts of difficult people, I certainly wasn't going to stand there and let Edward walk all over me.

"Number one," I retorted, firmly, "Chloe came to me and asked for my opinion, which, yes, I gave to her. And secondly, it's none of your business that I did so."

I went to leave but he towered over me, pointing his finger in my face.

"If she doesn't come back it'll be your fault," he continued, shouting.

"If she doesn't come back it'll be her *choice*, Edward, nobody else's. She's old enough to make that decision for herself. You should stop interfering in her life and take a good look at your own!"

As soon as those words left my mouth I instantly regretted them.

"And what's that supposed to mean?" he asked, indignantly

"Nothing, I meant nothing by it, just that you should let her be."

But the damage had been done and he wouldn't let the comment die.

"Have you been talking with that little rat, Simon?" he yelled, viciously.

His question slapped me in the face since I'd never heard anyone in the Barrington family disrespect another member.

"I don't know what you mean, Edward, so please forget what I said, okay?"

I was trying hard to calm the situation down but he still wouldn't let it go.

"If you've been listening to his rumors then shame on you, Vanessa. Sam and I are doing just great, okay?"

"Okay, but I have no idea what you're talking about."

I did, of course, because my suspicions were obviously as strong as Simon's, but that was something I wasn't going to discuss with Edward. He sneered which made me irate, so I ended our little spat on my own terms.

"I think you're jealous of Chloe, that's what I think. She's off to Paris to pursue her dreams and you're stuck here in the boring insurance business."

I think those words stung him because he left me, sat down and shook his head.

"Just leave," he barked, "and don't interfere any more with us. Go!"

I left quickly and that was the last time I ever spoke to Edward face to face.

Chapter Nineteen

———◆———◆———

D espite Edward's objection to her going, Chloe left for France a week after our conversation in the park. The Barringtons held a small farewell party for her, which I attended along with my Aunt Sheila and Uncle Brian, while Edward, Samantha and the Kenwrights were nowhere to be seen. That suited me because I was certain had he been there Edward would have confronted me again in front of everyone and spoiled Chloe's warm send off. What I didn't realize at the time was that Chloe's leaving signaled the beginning of the breakup of the Barrington family.

My job at *The Announcer* took on a whole new dimension a couple of weeks later when Mr. Barrington told me he was moving me to the editorial department for a few weeks so that I could learn that side of journalism. I'm glad he did because the training and discipline I received from those expert editors helped me so much with my subsequent novel writing.

Being with the editors was like entering a whole new world, where craft, nuances and attention to detail mattered more than anything else. They could take a reporter's story and turn it from the ordinary into something more significant by simply improving the grammar, altering the syntax or merely substituting a word for another word. It was quite magical witnessing the process which in no way corrupted the essence of the story as the reporter had originally written or intended it.

But after a few days Jack Kenwright began making it his business to spend quite a considerable amount of time with the editors, advising and insisting they bend a story more to his and his father's liking. Of course, his interference was met with vociferous objections from the editorial team, which in turn brought its concerns straight to the notice of Charles Barrington. Naturally, Mr. Barrington immediately confronted Jack Kenwright, but this time he was told, in no uncertain terms, he could accept his 'advice' or find another job. This left Mr. Barrington in an almost untenable position; he could leave and watch the paper totally change beyond recognition, or he could stay and still exert his influence in those areas of local news that mattered most. In the end, he chose to remain at its head but, again, although I didn't realize it at the time, this was essentially the end of his reign as editor of *The Announcer*.

One of the consequences of Kenwright's interference led to my Uncle Brian leaving his job at the paper. My uncle always steadfastly believed in the integrity of his friend and boss, Charles Barrington, so when he began reading some of the negative and slanted opinion pieces, he, too, took his concerns directly to Mr. Barrington, who told him what he'd told the editorial team.

My uncle later reported their conversation to me and Aunt Sheila this way... "Brian, I understand what you're saying and I don't like it any more than you, but if I leave the paper we love and cherish it will soon go to the dogs. This way I can still preserve its vital role in the community." But my uncle, a stubborn and proud man, would have none of that and so, within a few months he left and took another similar job with a bigger paper in the next city.

These recollections, while being so meaningful for me, also made me tired from their sheer volume. I loved remembering those times from fifty odd years ago but I decided I needed a break to recharge my batteries. So, for the next two weeks I reconnected with friends, took Wolf for long walks and tried to focus on the next stage in my life after the tour had ended.

Of course, my plans were often interrupted by Kay, who continued giving me updates on the progress of the book's publication and also the status of the tour. She had set a firm starting date for the second week of July, beginning in New York City, and from there we would make our way up and down the east coast. In August, the plan was to cover ten more dates beginning in New Jersey and continuing through the mid-west, finally ending up in Denver at the end of the month. The last leg would begin early in September covering the west, and finishing up in Los Angeles by the last week. My final stop was planned for Paris a week later and then I was done. The whole itinerary sounded like a nightmare to me but I put on a brave front, telling Kay I was fit and ready.

"Advanced orders are through the roof already," she exclaimed one day, as I relaxed in my sun room. "Honestly, Vanessa, this book is going to exceed even *my* wildest dreams. Congratulations, old girl, it must be so satisfying for you."

"I'm just hoping people won't be disappointed with the ending, but it's how I wanted to finish the trilogy."

"Oh, don't worry, they'll love it." Then she told me some other fantastic news. "Now, I hope you're sitting down because I've just heard from one of the largest streaming companies and they want to buy the rights and turn the three books into a mini-series!"

Since several of my previous novels had been turned into movies I wasn't surprised, but the news did validate my overall vision for the trilogy.

"Oh my gosh, Kay, that certainly is great news and I know who I have to thank for it."

"You're welcome and, by the way, I'm eyeing a nice little beach front property up in Maine with my share," she only half joked. "Wanna know how much they're offering for the rights?"

"Of course, I've got my old age to think about, too," I joshed in return.

"Two million up front and a share."

"What?" I answered, as I shook my head and blew out my cheeks.

"You heard right...two...million."

"When do I sign?"

"Contract should be ready to go before the start of the tour. I'm expecting lunch and dinner on you every day after this," she joked again.

After we chatted some more we arranged that I would go down

to the publisher's office as soon as the first copy rolled off the line and hold a press conference to announce the official publication of the book. I hated those events, too, but completely understood why they were necessary for a successful launch. We then hung-up and I flopped back in my easy chair totally exhausted.

That evening I digested Kay's fabulous news about the rights being sold and considered what I would like to do with the money. I certainly didn't need it to live on since I had been prudent with my previous earnings and made sure throughout the years I had invested wisely to see me through my old age. So, the question was…how to best use the windfall? I had a few ideas but decided I was in no desperate hurry to make any firm commitments just yet.

I ended my hiatus from remembering about Rainbow Falls, *The Announcer* and the Barringtons about two weeks later because I was still so interested in uncovering some important details of those times that were nagging at me like persistent sores. My remembrances usually occurred in the quiet of the evening when, with a glass of my favorite red, I could clear my mind and just concentrate on pulling up the past.

This particular evening I picked up the story after I'd completed my stint in the editorial department. I resumed my reporting rounds, still covering the opening of new businesses, particularly restaurants, the local council scene and some minor crime situations which always led me to interview interesting people, both good and bad. But any war protests were off limits on strict orders from Jack Kenwright, but we did manage to slip in a few references to it when a local soldier was either killed or wounded. He couldn't stop us from printing that person's obituary or doing a piece on the wounded soldier's experiences, so I always made sure to tell the family it was perfectly all right to state their own views on the war. Nine times out of ten their opinions coincided with ours.

On my travels around the county and surrounding areas I still occasionally saw Samantha and Jack Kenwright, usually in out-of-the-way places where, I'm sure, they imagined they'd be safe from prying eyes. They never saw me but it was still clear the affair was on-going.

My suspicions were confirmed by April a few days later when we met for coffee.

"You were *so* right, Vanessa, I saw them."

"Them?"

"Sam and Kenwright, the other day."

"Tell me more," I ordered, with a sly smile, "I'm all ears."

"I wanted to see her about something, so I drove to her apartment last Thursday fairly early since I had a stint at the local vet's beginning at nine. She rents half a house in Barnstead and as I'm cruising up her street I see them in the distance in her driveway."

"What time was this?" I asked, getting more interested by the second.

"Probably around eight. Anyway, I pulled over, parked and decided to watch what was going on. They talked for a short while before hugging and kissing, which looked quite hot to me. Then he left as she waved goodbye."

"So, eight o'clock, d'you think he stayed overnight?"

"Well, yeah, it was eight for goodness sake, I'm sure he wasn't delivering doughnuts! I still can't believe Sam's doing this."

"Believe it, April. It's been going on for quite a while."

"I should've listened to you and Simon. I'm thinking of confronting her and telling Edward. She's being so unfair to him."

"No, don't," I urged. "Edward won't believe you. I let something slip the other day when he got mad at me over the Chloe trip. He thinks Simon's just trying to make trouble. And besides, April, this really is none of our business. Sam, Kenwright and Edward are adults. It's not your job to interfere or report what everyone's doing."

April thought about my advice for a few seconds before finally agreeing with me.

"But it's so deceitful, sneaking around behind Edward's back. I feel so bad for him."

"If I'm not mistaken, April, I don't think Edward's as gullible as we think. He can't be that blind to what's been going on. I think he's choosing to ignore the whole situation for some reason."

"So, we just do nothing?"

I shrugged and replied, "Don't think we should get in the middle of this. Sooner or later Edward will find out for himself and hopefully deal with it."

"How am I going to face her knowing all this is going on?"

I shrugged again before saying, "Talk about anything but this."

"Fortunately, she told me last week she's off on a three week tour soon, so maybe I'll just avoid her for a while."

"Sounds like a plan, April, and if I happen to run into her I'll do the same. Let's hope this mess resolves itself soon."

Of course, I didn't realize it at the time but those words of mine were prophetic to say the least.

As the evening began to fade outside the windows of my sun room I recalled another incident involving Edward and, this time, Hugh. The Vietnam War caused a lot of hard choices to be made by young men called up to fight. Edward had already served his time and returned safely, but Hugh could have been called up at any time.

His aversion to the war matched his father's, so it was no surprise when he talked seriously about fleeing to Canada to avoid going. Apparently, this didn't sit well with Edward, who felt strongly that Hugh, if called up, should serve his country. Hugh's parents and Simon obviously didn't want to lose him and, since the body bags from the war had started to pile up at an alarming rate, decided they would support any decision he eventually made.

It was also noticeable at this time to anyone who saw him that Edward was drinking more than he should. He often appeared at his parents' house looking quite disheveled and he became more and more argumentative with everyone. Looking back at it now it was obvious the situation with Samantha was preying on his mind.

I had popped into the Barringtons' house one Saturday morning to see Mr. Barrington about a story I was working on. We were having a pleasant chat when we heard shouting coming from another room. Mr. Barrington abruptly left to investigate and I followed at a discreet distance. What we found was quite disturbing. Hugh and Edward were standing toe to toe, with Edward yelling into Hugh's face while Hugh was trying his best to calm his brother down. As we reached the room, Edward shoved Hugh hard and his younger sibling fell back, thankfully onto a couch.

Mr. Barrington quickly intervened, managing to lead Edward from the room. All the while Edward was shouting, "He's a coward! He's a coward! He's a coward!" As he passed me, Edward sneered but said nothing. Eventually, Mr. Barrington hustled his son into his car and drove him to his apartment. I, meanwhile, went over to see if Hugh was all right, and he brushed the incident off as lightly as he could. But, for me, it left me shocked that a family I so respected could act that way.

Later I found out the dispute was over Hugh's decision to abscond to Canada if called up and, indeed, that's what happened several months later. He never returned from Canada, marrying a local girl and building a family and a whole new life.

After recalling these incidents the time had shifted past one o'clock. Those memories, while illuminating, were also tiring, so I finished my wine and got ready for bed. In the stillness of the night, under the soft, warm covers, I reflected for a while on how much had happened to me in the short few months I had been living in Rainbow Falls. At the time I'm sure I took it all in stride but now, as I looked back, I realized how much those moments were indelibly imprinted in my mind. And I was grateful for that since it made remembering that much easier, that much more relevant to my life as a whole.

Chapter Twenty

◆───────◆

The two weeks before the tour started flashed by in a flurry of activities for me and Kay. The first order of business was to present myself at my publisher Bremmer Haldaine's corporate offices to ceremoniously receive the first copy of the last book in the trilogy. CEO Gordon Wallace, a friend for over thirty years, treated me like a queen with flowers and a lavish lunch before an invited audience from both the publishing and entertainment worlds. It was a good job Kay accompanied me because I found the whole experience somewhat overwhelming.

Gordon made a lovely speech in which he said, "Today is a monumental day in the annals of publishing. We are all gathered to celebrate and honor Vanessa Parker's latest magnificent novel, the last book in her wonderful trilogy *Intimate Strangers*. I'm sure you are all aware of the scope and essence of the first two and, let me assure you, you will not be disappointed in the last.

"Vanessa has crafted a story encompassing the nuances of human emotions to a degree I don't think has seldom been reached before. This is not melodrama but raw truth told in an uncompromising but believable manner that will allow *Intimate Strangers* to take its place among the very great novels of not only this century but all the previous ones, too. Quite simply, it is a work of art."

Listening to Gordon's high praise left me dumbfounded to say the least. I knew the book was good but an author never really can tell how it will be received by the readers. One can only do the best job possible and leave the rest to others to decide its fate. Some will like and enjoy your effort while some will not. All an author can do is put it out there and hope for the best, rather like, I imagine, raising a child and finally letting him or her go out into the world to find their own way.

The distinguished audience applauded Gordon's speech and he finally wound it down by turning to me and saying, "Vanessa, you have been such a valuable contributor to my company's foundation and longevity, so as this book comes off the presses I would like to offer you, on behalf of my board of directors, a seat on that same board so that we can benefit from your skill and knowledge. Please say yes and make my life easier!" His last remark was received with laughter from around the room.

I, of course, was dumbstruck again but enthusiastically nodded my head in acceptance. Gordon then asked me to join him at the podium where he presented me with leather bound copies of all three books in the trilogy. He passed the microphone over and I made a short and, I'm sure, totally inane speech in response before the audience once again broke out into a thunderous applause.

A week later Gordon contacted me about the directorship and told me, as well as having a seat on the board, he hoped I would become the company's main go to person when they decided if a manuscript was worth investing in. And for this he was willing to pay me a director's fee of two hundred, fifty thousand dollars a year in keeping with the others' remuneration on the board. Dumbfounded, yet again, I eagerly accepted and told him I hoped he wasn't making a huge mistake.

Just before we left on the tour Kay picked me up and took me to the offices of ModTelion, the streaming service that wanted to buy the rights to the trilogy. There were only two people from the company in attendance; the young owner who looked like he'd just left high school, and his lawyer who had the contract in front of her, and who Kay insisted she go through line by line for me even though Kay had dictated most of the terms.

I listened carefully, making sure the company could not change the story in any way except to vary the dialogue where applicable but not in any major way.

"It's very important to me that the movie be a true representation of the trilogy, even though I understand you may have to make some minor adjustments along the way to accommodate the mini series format. Selling you the rights doesn't mean I now become a disinterested party. In fact, before the film is streamed I would like to see it to give my final approval. I won't sign anything unless that, too, is written into the contract."

"Ms. Parker," Brent Vischer, the young owner, responded with a wide smile, "I loved the trilogy just as you wrote it. To change anything would be a travesty and I can assure you that will not happen. My team of superb writers has specific instructions to follow your story right down the line. And yes, of course, you will have final approval before it sees the light of day. Marjorie" he said, addressing his lawyer, "could you go and add that condition to the contract now? It should only take a minute."

Marjorie hustled out and within ten minutes returned with the last page amended accordingly. Both Kay and I went over the three page document before we both agreed it was perfectly acceptable. The price Kay had negotiated was indeed two million dollars and after I signed on the dotted line Brent presented me with a cashier's check for that amount. We all shook hands and had a celebratory glass of wine to cement the deal. It was all very painless and I couldn't wait to see my trilogy, my baby for so long, transferred to the big screen.

The evening before the start of the tour found me in my sun room thinking back to a strange encounter with Samantha one wet Saturday in my room in Rainbow Falls. The news scene, quiet that day, enabled me to take a well-earned rest and, since my aunt and uncle were away for a few days, I wanted to buckle down and work on my novel, *Cards*.

Just before lunch someone rang the bell and when I opened the door I found Samantha bouncing from one foot to the other on the stoop. She smiled and asked to come in.

"Sorry to just show up like this," she began, nervously twisting her hair, "but I need someone to talk to."

It always puzzled me that when people needed to speak to someone they invariably chose me. Maybe it was my youthful perspective being nearer their own age but it certainly couldn't have been my experience or wisdom. I took these encounters as compliments but they still bemused me just the same.

"Oh, sure, Samantha," I offered, pleasantly. "Come on in and sit down."

As she did so the conversation I'd had with April a few days before flashed into my head. I briefly studied her face which seemed tense and tired, as though something monumental bothered her. I waited as she seemed to be struggling with how to begin.

Finally, she said, "It's Edward, I'm very worried about him."

"Edward?" I queried.

"Yes, he hasn't been himself lately. You must've noticed?"

"Oh," I replied, trying hard to distance myself from where I thought this conversation might be headed, "I really haven't seen that much of him since he reamed me out over the advice I gave Chloe."

"That's exactly what I mean, Vanessa. He seemed to go overboard about Chloe's decision to go to Paris. Normally he would have just wished her well and left it at that."

I shrugged and said Chloe told me he was worried about her safety with all the riots going on over there.

"And then there was that incident with Hugh," Sam continued. "I mean, they used to be so close but now not so much. It's very sad."

I had to agree with her that that moment was disturbing but brothers, being brothers, do fight occasionally.

"And he seems to be drinking more and more. I'm concerned he may harm himself." She looked down and shook her head and I couldn't help thinking that the root cause of Edward's supposed change in character was down to her apparent affair with Jack Kenwright.

"Are you and he still okay?" I asked, gingerly.

"Not really. It's like he's in his own little world now. We don't do much together anymore."

"Have you talked to his parents about this?"

"No, I'm apprehensive about going to the house in case he's there and, you know, he starts something. And now I'm off on tour for three weeks so who knows what will happen while I'm gone."

Cautiously I asked if she could think of anything she'd done to make him suddenly change in this way.

"Only my singing. Edward's never been very enthusiastic about it and it's caused problems in the past. But I love it, it's my life and I'm determined not to give it up."

"Nor should you," I agreed, "but from what you've told me it seems more than that."

She shrugged this time, saying, "Don't know, Vanessa, he knew I was a free spirit when we met."

"Perhaps he's jealous for some reason," I offered, carefully.

"Well, yes, he's always been somewhat possessive of me but I can't live like a saint all the time."

"So, what can I do to help?"

"Talk with Hugh and Simon. Ask them to keep a close eye on him to make sure he doesn't...you know...harm himself. But I think when I get back from the tour I'm going to have to break it off with him for both our sakes."

Sadly, it seemed to me that Samantha had decided to lay all the blame at Edward's feet while knowing full well she was the one most responsible. It was as though she was trying to absolve herself of any involvement should anything happen to Edward. Knowing what I knew, that thought made me sick to my stomach. At that point all I wanted was her out of the house and it took all my restraint not to tell her what April, Simon and I knew was going on with her and Jack Kenwright. In my mind she was a first class manipulator who was determined to bend the truth in her direction.

"I'll do what I can," was all I offered in reply, "but I really don't see much of them anymore since we're all so busy."

She gave me a hug and I wished her well on her tour. The whole episode left me feeling angry at Sam for trying to drag me into her sordid little affair. I'm not completely sure but I think that may have been the last time we spoke.

The time had now moved beyond eleven and since Kay was due to show up fairly early the next morning to begin the book tour with me

I decided a decent night's rest was in order. So, I put Rainbow Falls on the backburner, rinsed my glass and settled into bed for what I hoped would be a peaceful night before tomorrow's madness began.

Jean, my dear neighbor, had agreed once again to take Wolf and to also check on the house once in a while. I planned on returning home when the breaks in the tour allowed, which I hoped might be every four or five days until, of course, we hit the mid-west, the west and finally the last stop in Paris. I would miss Wolf so much since he'd been really my sole companion for some five years now after I'd got him as a puppy. It broke my heart to leave him knowing how hard it would be for a pal like him to understand where I'd disappeared to. But I promised him this would be the last, long separation and wherever I ended up next he would come with me.

Right on time the next morning Kay showed up in the chauffeured driven car she'd hired for the entire trip around the east coast states. The driver loaded my bags into the trunk and we were off before ten in what I considered to be the lap of luxury.

"How are you feeling?" Kay asked, once we were settled in the back seat.

"Good, really. How are the sales?"

Kay pulled out an up to date statement from my publisher, handed it to me, grinned and said, "Not too bad, I'd say."

"Is this correct?"

"Sure is, amazing eh? I told you people love your novels."

"Kay it's only been out less than two weeks and I've sold close to half a million copies?"

"Yes, and that doesn't include downloads. Want to know something else that's very cool?"

"No," I replied facetiously, "I hate good news...what?"

"Only number one on The New York Times Best Seller list for new fiction."

"Oh, wow, I'm stunned."

That *was* amazing news for me. I'd been on the list a few times before with some of my other novels but this was way different. In fact, for almost six months *Intimate Strangers* remained the number one best seller in the nation.

The book signing the next day took place in one of the city's premier bookstores and, because of the lines, took me nearly four hours to satisfy every buyer. But people were very complimentary of my writing, wanted to talk, take selfies and even touch my hand. It was all quite overwhelming but gave me a clear insight into what I was to expect for the rest of the tour.

That evening, back at our hotel, we relaxed over a superb dinner before taking our coffees and desserts in the spacious lounge. My hand ached from all the signings but apart from that I actually felt good about the event and the rest of the upcoming dates.

"People were so gracious," I told Kay, "and they really seemed to love the ending in the last book."

"And if the size of that crowd is anything to go by then your legion of fans is only growing by the minute. I'm so happy for you, Vanessa, since I know you had your doubts."

"It's just that one never knows if your writing will be received in the same way you intended. So yes, it is both satisfying and, I suppose, validating."

"How are the recollections coming along?"

"I'm completely surprised by how much I'm remembering considering my old age," I joked. "It's all very interesting, like watching a movie you haven't seen for quite some time. Some of it has disturbed me and I know there's more of that to come. But a lot of it has been recalling some very good, happy moments, so all in all I'd say it's been worth the trip."

"You know, I'm in there somewhere, too?" she remarked, raising her eyebrows.

I frowned before realizing what she referred to.

"Oh, you mean how we met?"

"Exactly, a long time ago now."

"Haven't reached that part yet but I'm certainly looking forward to reliving the day you darkened my door," I joked again. "Jack Kenwright," I continued, more seriously, "turned out to be quite a piece of work in more ways than one. And the Barrington family wasn't all it was made out to be, either. So yes, interesting, revealing and hard to think it all really happened."

At that point I told Kay we should really turn in since our schedule was full for the next few days. We hugged and I thanked her again for all she'd done for me, and she answered that the beach house she was eyeing was growing closer and closer every day. I slapped her gently on the arm and we giggled as we made it to our rooms.

Chapter Twenty-One

———————◆———————

As much as I wanted to get a good night's rest I lay in bed and thought about how gratifying it was that the last book in the trilogy had been received so well. As I reflected on my good fortune my mind drifted back through the years to my early writing days while I was working at *The Announcer*.

I had begun my first novel *Cards* when I was nineteen and working at the paper, managing to write a little most days when I could. The process seemed totally different from my reporting, since I had to make everything up. Progress was moderate but I felt I needed other people's input to gauge whether or not this was worth continuing. At that age I never really felt confident enough to share my efforts with anyone, although I thought the book was quite good.

Through someone at the paper I learned of a local writing group and decided to take the plunge and join it. It met every Thursday in a room kindly donated by the nearby library and was run by a New York City literary agent who lived in the next town. His mission was to nurture, develop and support, as much as he could, new and burgeoning talent among up and coming young authors. His name was Alfred Collins and in the years to come he and, eventually his daughter, would guide my career to where it is today.

There were usually only five or six of us in attendance, so Alfred was able to spend quality time with us all. He didn't tell us how or what to write but instead offered his experience from dealing with some of his high profile clients. We all had to bring in each time at least two new chapters from the book we were working on, read the work aloud and listen to hopefully his and the other members' valuable criticism. That was the part I found most difficult both from a writing point of view and being required to judge others' offerings. But as the weeks went by and I became more familiar with the members of the group, I learned to take their comments in stride as an important tool for improving my book.

Alfred's criticism always focused on the positive aspects of our writing, making sure we never felt the task was beyond us or unworthy. I must admit, some of the work in progress I had to listen to and comment on left me in a difficult position for finding something positive and encouraging to say, even though I felt this particular piece of work lacked any sort of interest or merit. Surprisingly and gratifyingly, the novel I was working on, *Cards*, usually seemed to elicit enthusiastic and heartfelt assessments. Indeed, Alfred took me aside one day to tell me once I'd finished it he would take a serious look at the book with a view to possibly representing me to a publisher. That was the first time I really began to imagine I might make it as a serious novelist.

Those thoughts from so long ago made me smile as I saw myself then as a young girl trying her best to accomplish the only thing she wanted to do in life. My journey wasn't always the easiest but on the whole my early dreams and hopes had largely come true. In that perfect frame of mind I turned over and slept the sleep of a baby.

Our next stop on the tour took us to Boston, Massachusetts, a city I was familiar with and loved. On the way I related to Kay my reminiscences of the night before.

"You would've been about twelve I'm guessing," I told her, "and quite sassy even then," I joked.

"Oh, that's right," she confirmed, "I was a little you know what in those days."

"What d'you mean…those days?" I joked again, as she playfully slapped my arm.

She thought for a few seconds before saying, "Daddy, I remember clearly now, often came home after one of those writing group sessions he conducted and mentioned a young lady who he thought showed a lot of promise…and then he talked about you…" she joshed right back at me. "But, yes, even in those early days, Vanessa, you were quite clearly going to be a writer of some note."

"Your dad was always so kind and encouraging to all of us, it's such a pity some of his goodness didn't rub off on you, Kay," I teased again, as we fell back in the seat both giggling our heads off.

"You were his shining star, Vanessa. I'm sorry he didn't live long enough to enjoy your success."

I nodded knowingly, telling her his advice served me so well down the years.

"But he left the agency in very good hands, Kay. If anyone was going to carry on his legacy it was you. He would have been so proud how you've managed to expand it to where it is today."

"A great teacher, indeed," she acknowledged, "and I miss him every single day."

"Me, too. Me, too."

Boston the next day was fantastic, the line around the block and more, so many books signed, selfies taken and words of mine to nearly all the buyers. By now I was getting used to the pace of these events and certainly began to enjoy them more and more when I witnessed the enthusiasm and, dare I say, love shown by so many of my loyal readers.

From Boston we travelled down to Hartford, Connecticut and after the signing there managed a day by the beach at Mystic. But Kay was a hard task mistress and before I knew it we had taken in Atlantic City and finally Philadelphia. By this time nearly two weeks had passed so before we left again for the southern shores I told Kay I needed time at home to see Wolf and just relax for a while. Secretly, I felt she, too, needed a break from our hectic schedule and wasn't at all surprised when she agreed. We made plans to resume the tour the following Tuesday when she'd take me to Washington and then onto Virginia.

Back at my house, I collected Wolf, took Jean out to dinner and prepared to enjoy several days of doing absolutely nothing. My wish nearly came true since my hands were certainly idle but my mind and reminiscences eventually worked overtime as I found my way once again to Rainbow Falls…

As the summer wound down I found myself more and more in Simon's company, mostly because he was nearer my age, soon to return to college and I wanted to try and stop him from confronting Edward, as he wished to do on a daily basis, about Sam. Of the three brothers Simon always struck me as the most sensitive, the one who most of all cared about his family. He hadn't decided definitively about his future but seemed to be leaning towards the arts and documentary film making. His mind always seemed to be engaged with some difficult subject or problem, which fascinated me whenever we got together because his mouth would spew words, theories and ideas at a mile-a-minute and I actually managed to learn a lot from him. In return, he loved hearing about the latest stories and gossip I was involved with at the paper and often made outrageous suggestions as to how best to write my piece.

He had stopped accompanying me on my rounds of newly opened restaurants, so we mostly got together after work at a local café or diner. Generous to a fault, Simon usually picked up the tab which, for a struggling reporter like myself, helped a great deal with my finances. He also knew I was trying to write my first novel, asked constantly about it and even suggested some scenarios I might like to follow which, of course, I never did.

But, on this particular evening when we met, Simon seemed more subdued and not at all like his normal jovial self.

I noticed immediately and asked, "What's up, Simon, you seem a bit down tonight?"

He shrugged, trying to pass it off, but I insisted he tell me what was bothering him. Over the past few weeks I thought we had developed quite a good relationship, so I felt comfortable pressing him on the matter.

"It's Edward, he seems to be going downhill fast."

"How d'you mean?" I queried, remembering the conversation I recently had with Samantha.

"Drinking too much and angry all the time with everyone. And it's all because of that girl."

"Sam, you mean?"

"Of course. It's clearly over but Edward won't admit it."

"Has he spoken to you about any of this?"

"Ha! Fat chance of that," he answered, with a sneer. "He still thinks they're going to ride off into the sunset together."

"What are you going to do, Simon, this is so tricky to get into the middle of?" I warned.

"Already done something," he boasted. "Got in touch with Sam before she left on tour and told her when she gets back she has to tell Edward it's all over between them."

"And?"

"Sam said she couldn't possibly do that because she feared what Edward's reaction would be. That's Sam for you," Simon continued, disparagingly, "only concerned about her own well being. So then I suggested while she's away she compose an appropriate letter to Edward and I would willingly deliver it. Naturally, she seemed okay with that idea, so right now that's the plan. At least this way Edward will finally get the truth from the horse's mouth so to speak," he said, finishing with a snide laugh.

"So, sometime next week then?" I asked.

"Yup, Mom and Dad are having their usual end of summer picnic and get- together at the country house, which you are cordially invited to, of course, so I thought at the right time I'd get Edward on his own and deliver Sam's letter. Not going to be pleasant for him, but this seems like the only way to get it through his head."

For a few seconds I considered Simon's proposal and on the whole thought it might be the best solution to a very difficult problem.

"He's obviously not going to take it well, Simon. Are you sure you're the one to do this?"

"Well, I guess I'm the *only* one, Vanessa, since Hugh's not in Edward's good books right now and Chloe's in Paris. Of course, I'd gladly step aside if you or April wanted to do it," he offered, with a laugh.

"I think it best if this comes from a member of his family, so I suppose it's you or no one."

And that's how we left the situation. As Wolf's wet nose roused me back to the present, I clearly recall that at the time little did I realize Simon's plan would be a recipe for disaster.

My short break ended much too quickly and before I knew it we were off to our next stop Washington. Kay asked about my time at home and I told her I'd done some remembering and felt my recollections were about to reach a critical moment.

"I'm at the point, Kay, where I feel the whole thing will soon be resolved one way or another. Edward's a mess, Chloe is in Paris, Jack Kenwright is still causing all sorts of problems both at the paper and within the family, Sam seems to have finally made up her mind and Simon is trying his best to be some sort of judge and juror. My next memory will concentrate on an end of summer get-together the Barringtons were having at their house in the woods. But I'm not in any hurry to think about that just yet because of what eventually happened to Simon."

Kay listened but obviously had no conception of why all this retrospective thinking on my part mattered. All she saw was another book.

"I'm telling you, Vanessa, you have a gem of a story here from the little you've told me. Think about it please, will you?"

I was firm in my mind that there would be no more novels but it was hard for me to douse Kay's enthusiasm.

"Let's get the tour over with first, Kay, and then I promise I'll give it some serious thought." *Yes*, I said to myself, *about two seconds' worth of serious thought!*

Then she surprised me by asking a question about one of the characters from my past.

"Now, who was this Chloe girl again?"

"She was the Barringtons' only daughter. She left school after her junior year for an internship at some famous fashion house in Paris. As far as I know she never permanently returned, making quite a name for herself over there I understand, why?"

"Oh, no reason," she answered. "Merely curious," and left it at that.

I passed off Kay's question as just her trying to show some sort of interest in her crazy friend's seeming obsession with the past. We then settled down for the ride to Washington and, hopefully, another successful book signing.

This next leg of the trip was indeed successful. The folks in

Washington greeted me so enthusiastically that we decided to hold another signing the following day. At both events the lines stretched around the block and more, which made me humble beyond measure. Most spoke of their love of the trilogy and how the ending, although surprising, was totally believable. I even had a senator show up to get his signed copy which, again, had me pinching myself to see if all this acclaim was really happening.

After a good night's rest we drove to Richmond, Virginia where, after the signing, we said a grateful goodbye to our wonderful chauffeur. The rest of this leg of the tour to Charleston, Atlanta, Tampa and finally Miami we made by plane, with an eventual final flight back to New York at the end of July. Although totally exhausting the book signings, wherever we went, seemed to be affirmations of how deeply my writing had affected so many people. And for that I'd be eternally grateful.

Chapter Twenty-Two

Now that I had some time before the mid-west tour was due to start, I took care of a couple of promises I'd made while staying at the hotel in Maine. I dug out from among my collection of odd pieces of paper the name and address of the lovely woman who had nervously stopped by my table one day to compliment me on the first two books in the trilogy. Her name was Carol Beaumont and she was the mother of the two children who, at breakfast one day soon after I arrived, came over and started asking me all sorts of questions. I promised Carol a signed copy at the time and certainly didn't wish to disappoint her. When packaging up the book I also included a letter to each of the children hoping that their own writing efforts were going well.

The other people I promised books to were, of course, Joyce and Keith Andrews, owners of the hotel in Maine. They also received a note thanking them once again for taking such good care of me. I told them that at some time in the future I intended to be back in Maine and at their hotel.

Having completed those tasks I felt free to indulge myself and Wolfie for a lot of the time we had together before having to once again part for a month. The next two legs of the tour would not allow me to come home, so I wanted to make this time with my precious pet special for both of us. For the next week then I took him everywhere with me and our evenings were spent in closeness, with me spoiling him every moment I could, unable to resist his fuzzy head and gentle, appealing eyes. I was grateful he was still relatively young and, hopefully, would be with me for many years to come.

Having Wolfie by my side over the next two evenings certainly helped me cope with the difficult remembrances I called up. At crucial times he was there when I needed something tangible to touch as I recalled the most traumatic moment, apart from my mother's death, in my young life.

"Hope to see you at the get-together on Saturday, Vanessa," Mr. Barrington told me, as we passed in the press room a few day before the event.

"I'll be there and thanks so much for inviting me."

"Almost part of the family now," he continued, with a huge smile, "so sorry your aunt and uncle can't make it, too."

Aunt Sheila and Uncle Brian were away for a few days visiting her mother, my grandmother, in upstate New York. The unfortunate part about that was my aunt asked if I would take Jimmy to the picnic since she would be gone and his folks, unfortunately, were working. Naturally I agreed but I certainly wasn't thrilled about it. Jimmy, as a typical nine-year-old, had an inquisitive mind, liked to be involved with all things around him and generally needed to be kept an eye on. Fortunately, April would be joining us for the trip to the picnic and she could always be relied on to stimulate Jimmy with her tales from the vet's office.

Of course, at some time during the get-together Simon was due to hand Samantha's letter to Edward, so I warned April that there may well be an almighty flare up once Edward read the contents. Samantha, obviously, wouldn't be in attendance, nor I suspected the Kenwrights. I was wrong about that though, since Clare showed up to do some painting of the local countryside while Jack was nowhere to be seen. Just as well, I thought, considering Edward's fiery disposition at that time.

Jimmy's dad dropped him off at the house quite early, together with his backpack and fishing pole. Not having much in common with a nine-year-old boy, I asked him some general questions about how he'd spent his summer to pass the time until we left to pick up April.

He surprised me by saying, "I finished my story, Vanessa."

I frowned until my mind clicked into gear and I recalled on an earlier trip he'd found an animal skull by the river and told April and me he was going to write a story about it.

"How'd it come out, Jimmy, are you pleased with it?"

He nodded before fishing around in his backpack and producing a couple of crumpled up sheets of paper.

"Here," he ordered, "I'd like you to read it."

Smiling but not too sure, I took the paper, sat down and began to scan his very neat handwriting.

"Great penmanship, Jimmy," I complimented him. "Where did you learn that?"

"Oh, Mom taught me. She said it's important for people to understand what you write."

"And you mom's correct, of course," I agreed.

For the next ten minutes I read his story, *The Secret of the Skull*, and for a nine-year-old's first effort I thought he'd done a wonderful job.

"This is really good, Jimmy. I love all the details and the way you explained how the skull got by the river."

"You're not just saying that to be nice, are you, Vanessa?"

Shaking my head, I replied, "Not at all. And you know what?"

"What?'

"You kept my interest right up until the last word, and kept me guessing, too, which is always a good sign of a great writer. No, Jimmy, I really liked it and you know what else?"

"What?"

"At the paper, on Sundays, we have a children's section and I'm going to ask if we can include your story there one week. How about that?"

His eyes opened wide and for a few precious seconds there was silence.

"Really, you mean it? Oh, that would be so good, Vanessa. Thank you. Thank you."

"Not promising anything but I will ask and do my best, okay?"

"Okay."

"Now, I'm going to put this in a safe place and then we'd better be off otherwise April will think we've forgotten her."

In fact, the editor of the Sunday children's section also loved Jimmy's story and, with a few minor adjustments, it was published about four weeks later. To celebrate the moment I went to his house and presented him with a copy fresh off the press. He could hardly believe it and for weeks went around telling anyone who'd listen. For him, that was a moment that mattered for sure.

April was ready and waiting when we arrived at her apartment, so she threw her bag in the trunk and we sped off to make the ten mile drive to Beecher's Woods. The weather, pleasantly warm, promised a day without rain, which meant Jimmy wouldn't be confined to the house with little to do. After parking, we began our five mile hike to the Barringtons' house, which was mostly a gently walk along well-groomed sun-dappled paths, and only through a small amount of the woods at the end. The leaves crunched under our feet and all around us the sound of nature seemed to welcome us like old friends. We sat often, took in some water, chatted and tried our best to keep Jimmy occupied. He loved being outside, seemed fascinated by most things around him, and asked all sorts of questions, which we answered with plausible, but not always accurate, explanations.

As we approached the house across a newly mown field I noticed several people, including Edward, in the distance. He seemed to eagerly look our way, but just as quickly turned and meandered off when, I assumed, he didn't see Samantha with us. Mr. and Mrs. Barrington greeted us warmly and before long we found ourselves amid a throng of about twenty people. Fortunately, there were a couple of other children there around Jimmy's age and they went off for a while to amuse themselves. Quite a few of my fellow reporters were also present so I wasn't totally lost without my aunt and uncle.

The food, as usual, made you want to eat and eat, but Mrs. Barrington warned us to make room for the ice cream sundaes she was preparing. In that regard, and to keep Jimmy and the other kids occupied, she corralled them into helping her serve them up. Edward mixed with some of the people he knew but he didn't approach me. I guessed he was still miffed over the Chloe affair.

Around five I watched him wander off in the direction of the woods and the Hollow River. After a few minutes Simon came over, told us Edward needed to be alone for a while but that he'd be following him soon to deliver Samantha's letter.

"You're a brave man," April offered, "he's not going to take it very well."

"Time he faced the truth, April. Sam's not coming back to him."

"How much has he had to drink?" I asked.

"He's not drunk but he's definitely had his fair share."

"Just be careful, Simon," I advised, with a shrug. "I saw him with Hugh that time and it wasn't pretty."

"Oh, he'll just stomp off and I'll be back in no time."

As I remembered that moment all these years later, I suddenly realized those words were the last I'd ever hear Simon speak. I shook my head, acknowledging how sad it all was.

As Simon, too, disappeared into the woods, Jimmy came up to us and asked if we could go to the river so he could fish. April looked at me and smiled hopefully, which I took as a hint that she, like me, had had enough of the party for one afternoon.

"Good idea, Jimmy, I think we could all do with a break. Let's go!"

He gathered up his backpack and fishing pole and we set off for the river, which was basically following in Simon and Edward's footsteps, although we never caught up or saw them. We found an ideal spot and, while we girls made ourselves comfortable, Jimmy cast his line into the shallow water. He seemed contented for a while but said he hadn't seen any fish and could he go farther along the river where the water was deeper. The problem with that was the river turned around a blind corner for us and eventually cascaded over a dangerous looking rocky waterfall into a very deep pool.

"You can," I agreed, "but you have to promise on your life that you won't go near the waterfall, okay?"

"Okay," he quickly accepted before gathering up his things and moving along the bank until he was out of sight.

"I'll go check on him in a while," April offered, "but he's a good kid, so I doubt he'll disobey you."

We left it at that and continued our chat about our hopes for our future careers. I called out to him several times and he shouted back, so we knew he was all right. He must've been gone about fifteen minutes when the quiet of a wonderful late summer afternoon was split in two by desperate yells for help coming from Jimmy's direction. More frantic calls followed in quick succession but it was a man's voice we heard not a child's. These shouts, fervent and almost hysterical, cut through the silence of the moment and across the lives of the Barrington family.

After the first initial yells April and I looked at each other, stunned momentarily by the screams for help. In the next instant we jumped up and dashed along the river bank and around the blind bend, where we met Jimmy running for all he was worth in our direction and away from the noise. I firmly told him to stay where he was and wait for us to come back, but as I spoke to him I noticed the terrified look on his face as he began to cry.

We continued running at full speed and in the distance, by the dangerous waterfall, noticed Edward kneeling on the ground desperately trying to minister assistance to someone. As we got closer it was clear to us that person was Simon Barrington.

"What happened, Edward?" I frantically asked, as we knelt down by an apparently lifeless body and began our attempts at resuscitation. April, with some animal medical training, took charge, working feverishly to find a pulse, a breath or any sign of life. I joined in at her direction pounding Simon's chest and yelling for him to come around. For fifteen minutes we sweated in the late day sun to try and revive him but in the end it became clear he was already dead.

Edward, who was nearly soaked from head to foot, dashed off to call the emergency squad and the police. April and I sat on the bank, sobbing our hearts out, exhausted, angry and devastated. Then I remembered Jimmy, so I took off my light jacket and placed it over Simon's face before we hot-footed it back to the kid. Bless his heart, he hadn't moved an inch, but his sobs, still wracking, nearly cut us in two.

"It's all right, Jimmy, it's all right," was all I could manage, as I held him close and felt his body shake from his crying. We eventually led him away from the river and back up to the house, passing the medics and cops on the way. The police told us to remain at the house until they came back.

The rest of that dreadful afternoon was a bit of a blur. Mr. and Mrs. Barrington, of course, were beside themselves, and wanted to know from Edward what happened. His explanation, sketchy and at times fragmented, was fairly straightforward. Simon, he said, caught up to him and handed him Sam's letter. After reading the contents, Edward told his parents, he stormed off to be alone. Simon, he said, had wanted to go swimming in the pool by the waterfall and the last Edward heard of him was him diving into the water. According to Edward's version, which no one had any reason to doubt, after a few minutes he heard lots of splashing, turned and saw Simon flailing in the water by the waterfall. He assumed his brother was having a seizure, dashed back over some steep and rocky terrain, waded in and struggled to pull him out. Edward, comforted by his mother, couldn't go on and so we left him alone until the police eventually stopped by to also take his statement.

Throughout all this time we had largely forgotten about Jimmy, so we gathered up a now more composed boy and headed on our hike back to my car. During the trip we tried our best to talk to Jimmy about anything but the incident and, fortunately, it worked. He still seemed bemused and I noticed several times it was if he wanted to talk but couldn't express his feelings.

The ten mile drive back to April's apartment was mostly taken in silence. We dropped her off and made our way to Jimmy's house where, after getting out of the car, he held onto my hand as though he, too, might suddenly drown. Then he looked up at me and said he'd forgotten his backpack and fishing pole, before breaking down again. I walked him to his door and explained to his mother, after he'd disappeared into the house, what had happened. She told me she'd take extra special care of him and I left to spend the rest of the evening alone and desolate.

Chapter Twenty-Three

⬥

I heard through April a few weeks later that after an autopsy the county coroner ruled that Simon's death was caused by drowning after probably suffering a seizure. He recorded a verdict of death by misadventure and essentially the case was closed. The coroner, who is a medicolegal investigator, determines the cause and manner, as far as possible, of traumatic, suspicious or unexpected deaths. In this particular case he considered the police interviews with Edward, April and me, as well as looking into Simon's medical history. He noted that drowning can begin within the first seven seconds of a person being in difficulties in the water, and further proposed that if Simon had had a seizure, which he strongly suspected occurred, then drowning and death would have happened within the next two minutes. He absolved any other person in connection with Simon's death, noting that Edward made heroic efforts to save his brother, as well as acknowledging April and my contributions with regard to trying to resuscitate Simon once he was on the bank. All in all, the coroner concluded that this was nothing more than a tragic accident.

Within the Barrington family Mr. Barrington took Simon's death the hardest. It almost broke him in two, sending him into a deep depression from which, I learned later, he never recovered. I, along with my Aunt Sheila and Uncle Brian, attended Simon's funeral two weeks later, a very sad affair which only further served to affect Mr.

Barrington's health to a point of incapacity. Chloe came back from France to be there and support her parents, while Edward drifted farther away from the family and Hugh, until he bolted to Canada, became the titular head of the group. Samantha came and paid her respects but, due to the obvious awkwardness of her situation with Edward, stayed mostly apart and left as soon as the service was over.

"I never, never ever expected anything like this to happen in our family," Chloe said tearfully, as I tried my best to comfort her. "He was always there for me. I don't know how I'll carry on now."

"By having a full life as you know Simon would have wanted for you," I answered, trying to make the best of a bad situation for her. "He was a big supporter of you going to Paris, Chloe, so you can't disappoint him," I teased. "By the way, how are you doing over there?"

"The internship is so eye-opening, Vanessa. I'm learning so much…" She hesitated before continuing. "Can you keep a secret?"

"Anything you tell me goes no further…so?"

"I'm staying out there. I'm not coming back."

"Oh, Chloe, that's great news, but you'll complete your last year of high school, right?"

"Yes, there's an American one there and I'm already enrolled. I'll tell my folks just before I go back."

After what Chloe had just told me I knew that moment was the beginning of the end for the golden Barrington family. Simon was dead; Edward was drifting aimlessly; Hugh was destined to vanish into Canada at any time; Mr. Barrington was a mere shadow of his former self and now Chloe would be residing permanently in Paris.

I gave her a huge hug and let her know how happy I was for her.

"Oh Chloe, this is definitely the right choice for you, but I'm going to miss you like you wouldn't believe."

We parted with quite a few tears and I told her we must try and stay in touch somehow.

During the turmoil at the Barrington house I had neglected to check on how Jimmy was holding up after that terrible afternoon by the river. The police recovered his backpack and fishing pole and returned them to the house when they went to conduct their interviews. I rescued the items I knew were near and dear to Jimmy, bringing them to my house but forgetting to give them back. I made a special trip to see him and he was most pleased to get the backpack since it contained some of his most favorite treasures. His mother left us to talk and I naturally asked how he was.

He shrugged before saying he was bored and couldn't wait for school to start again so he could show his teacher his story in the paper. Neither of us mentioned what had happened at the river and it wasn't until I was just about to leave that he tugged on my arm.

"What's up, Jimmy, can I help you with something?"

He shook his head before saying, "I didn't do anything wrong, did I?" with eyes that seemed a second away from filling with tears.

I immediately hugged him before standing him at arms' length.

"No, no, no, Jimmy, of course you didn't do anything wrong. Nothing that happened was your fault, d'you understand me?" He nodded as I continued, "I'm just so sorry you had to be around when it happened. It was an accident, pure and simple."

He nodded slightly but didn't seem convinced of anything. He tried to speak but whatever he wanted to say just wouldn't leave his lips. I tried again to reassure him.

"Listen to me, okay? Simon had a medical problem, there was nothing anyone could have done to save him. He should never have gone swimming on his own. Now, I want you to try and forget about that afternoon because nothing was your fault, all right?"

He let go of my hand, sniffed back a tear and turned and left. That was the last I saw of Jimmy, since his parents decided the best course of action to help him heal from the trauma was to move right away and give him a completely fresh start.

Of course, while all this upheaval was taking place I still had to attend to my reporting duties at the paper. Mr. Barrington was still too upset, depressed and unable to carry out his editorial responsibilities so Ron Chabot quickly stepped into his shoes on a, hopefully, temporary basis. The atmosphere around the office was, of course, sad and disjointed without our leader to lead us in the right direction, but we managed to soldier on as best we could. Jack Kenwright showed up much more frequently, taking a more vigorous hand in the overall running of the paper and making subtle changes that none of us reporters liked or appreciated.

Since Mr. Barrington had been missing in action for nearly two months I decided, very apprehensively, to go round to his house one Saturday morning to see how he was. Hugh let me in and led me into the lounge.

"Don't think Dad's in any fit state to see you right now, Vanessa, sorry. Mom's with him constantly so you'll have to put up with me."

Shaking my head, I asked, "How bad is he, Hugh?"

"Not good, both physically and mentally. I'm really not sure he's coming back from this. Doesn't get out of bed most days and cries a lot. It's very sad."

"What about the paper? I mean, that was so much a part of his life. Is he ever coming back?"

Hugh shook his head before admitting that prospect didn't look great either.

"He's a broken man, Vanessa. All he keeps saying to me is that I have to leave soon for Canada. He just couldn't take another child of his dying, and he's convinced that's what would happen if I go to Nam."

"So?"

"So, yes, in the next two weeks I'm off."

"Oh, wow, Hugh, but I think you're doing the right thing."

As those words spilled out of my mouth the lounge door opened and standing there were Jack and Clare Kenwright.

"Sorry for bursting in but we did ring," Kenwright offered, weakly. "Just popped in to see how Mr. Barrington's doing."

Hugh's face changed immediately he saw the Kenwrights. His eyes blazed in their direction while his jaw set in a state of sheer contempt. I backed away to the corner of the lounge but couldn't escape what I suspected was about to happen.

"Oh," he shouted at them, "you want to know how my father is? He's very sick thanks to you!" Hugh, roughly six feet tall, towered over the smaller Kenwrights and I really thought he was about to hit Jack.

Jack backed away slightly before putting up his hands and saying, "Just worried about him, that's all."

But it was as if Hugh hadn't heard a word Jack said.

Almost in his face he yelled, "He's sick because of you! My brother is dead because of you! My father's beloved paper is dying because of you! You came here and ruined everything you piece of..."

Before he finished Clare butted in with, "Oh, now, just a minute, you don't know what you're saying. C'mon Jack, let's get out of here."

But Hugh blocked the door, sneered menacingly and folded his arms.

"You're going nowhere until I've told you what I think of you." Both of them backed off as Hugh continued. "You swaggered into town throwing your weight around the paper just because your father owns it, telling my father, who built the thing up from nothing how to do his job. You pushed your own views despite this town being nearly one hundred per cent behind my father. You insisted he follow your rules or be fired, and you took advantage of his absence when he was sick a few months ago."

Jack Kenwright looked at the floor as he was being harangued, shook his head and kept muttering under his breath. But Hugh hadn't finished his tirade just yet.

"And then you began to destroy not only Edward's life but all our lives by starting an affair with Samantha just because you couldn't keep your hands off of her. You're disgusting, cheap and the cause of Simon's death as well as being responsible for my father's breakdown." He then stood aside, opened the door and ended with, "Now get the hell out of this house and don't you ever let me see you here again!"

Needing not to be told twice, the Kenwrights hustled out and I was left stunned and, needless to say, very pleased by Hugh's words. Sitting down next to him I reached out and touched his hand. Smiling, he leaned over and surprised me by giving me a huge hug. That was the first time I could remember him doing anything of a physical nature with me. Just as quickly he released his arms as if he was sorry he'd done that.

Passing the incident off, I offered, "Wow, Hugh, that was some speech. Everything you said was true and he needed to hear it. Your dad would have been so proud to hear you stick up for him and the whole family like that."

He grinned and raised his eyebrows, before saying, "Yeah, probably cost dad his job now for sure."

"Well, from what you've told me it doesn't seem to matter now. Even if he gets better I don't see how he could possibly return under these circumstances. I'd say you've done him a favor."

We made more small talk before I decided I should go and leave the Barringtons in peace. And that was the last time I was ever in their house.

I thought my return to the paper on Monday morning might be awkward if Jack Kenwright was anywhere to be seen. I was correct since he ignored my existence, making it very clear I was obviously part of the enemy. My skin had been toughened over the months of working all sorts of stories so his blatant bad behavior didn't bother me in the least. I got on with the job best I could knowing all of us were now essentially working for him and not Mr. Barrington.

Ron Chabot, who had stepped into the editor's shoes in Mr. Barrington's absence was summarily fired two weeks later, with Kenwright bringing in one of his friends from the big city. The changes then came swiftly and the overall morale at the paper declined just as quickly. Reporters were now told how to write certain stories and what and what not to include. It seemed that Kenwright himself approved each and every one, with the overall tone of the paper changing in the public's view. Indeed, the office began receiving mounds of mail daily decrying the way the paper had gone from being a local mainstay representing the opinions of most of its readers to becoming a mouthpiece for the Kenwright family's slanted political views.

Naturally, advertising revenue, the main source of income for the paper, declined at a rapid pace along with a substantial drop-off in reader subscriptions. Kenwright also began replacing the more seasoned reporters with his own hand-picked sycophants, who seemed to have no problem towing the line.

My own position became more and more untenable as I was assigned mostly fluff and mundane stories which I knew held no real interest to our loyal readers. I stood it for about three months before I plucked up the courage one day to go and see him to let him know exactly how I felt. As usual, he was patronizing towards me, but before I told him I was quitting I managed to give him a piece of my mind, too.

"This is not the job for which Mr. Barrington hired me," I began, quite pleasantly. "All I'm doing is pretending to be a reporter. That's not what I signed up for."

While I talked he continually shuffled papers around, making sure I knew he wasn't really too interested in what I had to say.

Finally, he answered, "Really, so I take it you're not happy here?"

"No, Mr. Kenwright, I'm not. I came here to learn the trade and under Mr. Barrington's guidance I think I've made great strides. He trusted me to report worthwhile stories, stories that had an impact on people's lives. Now…well now…it looks like you've decided all I'm good for is to write about dog shows, school board meetings and the latest ice-cream shop to open. I'm used to getting out into the field and investigating the story behind the story. I have to tell you, Mr. Kenwright, I am definitely *not* a happy camper right now."

"Done, are we, with your little tirade," he responded, quite tediously. I looked at him and frowned, hardly believing what I was hearing, before he added, "You know, the door is over there and any time you want to leave I can assure you no one will try and stop you. Now, if there's nothing else of importance I have a lot of work to do." He then shifted his attention to his desk top and completely ignored me.

I imagined my face glowed beetroot by then and, being too flabbergasted to reply, I turned on my heels and left. Sitting at my desk I fumed with an anger I had not previously thought possible. After twenty minutes of thinking over my options I took a piece of paper from my desk drawer and began writing. When I'd finished I marched into Kenwright's office and literally threw it at him.

"Here, my resignation," I shouted before storming out. Just before I reached the door I turned and said, as contemptuously as I could, "You know, Hugh was right the other day, you did come here and ruin everything!" And with that pointed gesture I left *The Announcer* for ever.

Chapter Twenty-Four

———◆———

O ver the next few days I looked back at my time at the paper and felt strongly the work I did laid the foundation for my future writing endeavors. Certainly the people I learned most from were the seasoned reporters who took the time to share their craft with me. Remembering the unfortunate way I left filled me, even all those years later, with a lot of sadness, mostly because it was the end of working for Mr. Barrington, who meant so much to me in my early journalistic life.

On the other hand, if all those unfortunate incidents had not happened then I wondered if my writing career would have developed in the way it eventually did. I often pondered that question during my remembrances and surmised that on the whole things worked out for the best. Certainly I wasn't going to complain about the life I'd led or the amount of success of my novels. I came to the conclusion that some things are meant to be and no amount of second guessing would alter that. Take my amazing luck in securing Kay as my agent. If I'd never left *The Announcer* I doubt very much she and I would have experienced such a wonderful working relationship.

On my down time, when I wasn't recalling the past, I gave some serious thought to how I might distribute some of the two million dollars I'd received for selling the series' rights to *Intimate Strangers*. In my head I had already spent about a million on a beach house in Maine and, once the tour had ended, would hopefully make that happen. The other million gave me many options, most of which seemed, in the cold light of day, not to be practical or worthy. Talking with Kay one day, it was she who made a suggestion that seemed to fit perfectly with my passion for writing and education. Why I never thought of it astounded me, but that was the reason she was an agent and me a mere novelist.

When we talked about her idea Kay said, "I'm surprised *you* didn't think of this, Vanessa, after all you spent…what was it…three months at Yaddo upstate?"

And her memory hit the mark, since I did indeed spend quite some time there finishing one of my novels. The place was magical, an artists' retreat buried in gorgeous countryside, with nothing much to do but work on whatever it was you were creating at the time. Open to musicians, writers, playwrights and poets among others, Yaddo provided those it accepted with full free board and lodging for the time they were in residence. It wasn't just up and coming artists who took advantage of Yaddo's generosity. Some of the nation's and world's renowned artisans, covering the artistic spectrum, created or completed some of their most famous works there. The fact that you were left alone to start or finish a project took away the burden of pressure, leaving you with all the time you needed to just be creative. Of course, no stay at Yaddo was infinite and those terms were made crystal clear when your application was approved.

"Yes," I replied to Kay's question, "three months of heaven. That's where I finished *An Event of Some Importance*, a very difficult book to write but Yaddo gave me the time and space to complete it as I wished."

"One of your greatest, Vanessa, no doubt. So, what d'you think, will you give it some serious thought?"

"No need, Kay, you've sold me on the idea already. And what do I need a beach house for anyway? I'd only be there for maybe three or four months of the year in the summer. If I want to go to Maine I'll stay at Joyce and Keith Andrews' hotel. No taxes; no maintenance; housekeeping taken care of…no…it's a no-brainer, Kay."

"If you're really, really serious about making this writers' retreat a reality I'd love to be your partner. We'll form a board of some of our distinguished writer friends and hire some competent people to run it on a day-to-day basis."

"Oh, I'm deadly serious, Kay, my two million or more couldn't be better spent."

"I'll match whatever you put in, how about that?" she offered, generously.

"Sounds like we've got ourselves some project on our hands. Oh, wow, this is going to be so exciting."

The rest of my time before the tour began in earnest again flashed by so that I found myself on my last evening at home packing, going out to dinner with my neighbor, Jean, the ever-faithful guardian of Wolfie while I was away, and spending the last precious hours in his company before having to say goodbye for almost two months. But I was ready for the tour, looking forward to meeting some of my loyal readers in parts of the country I hadn't been to before, and finally ending up in Paris for a signing and a few days' rest.

Our first stop took us to Detroit and on the plane Kay revealed the latest sales figures for the book. Again I was stunned, noting the total sales had reached well over seven hundred thousand. At this rate, I told her with a laugh, our dream of opening a writers' retreat would happen sooner than we ever imagined. From Detroit we then took in Chicago, Louisville and Nashville, a city I particularly loved and enjoyed for its wide array of attractions, restaurants and, of course, music. Four stops in ten days left us tired, but we were buoyed by the great numbers of people who came out to the signings. It was also humbling for me to know so many folk were my loyal readers and followed my writing so closely.

After taking a rest for two days in New Orleans we made our way to a charming bookstore in Des Moines, Iowa, before moving onto Lincoln, Nebraska. Unfortunately, we didn't get a chance to see very much of the cities, but the warm welcomes we received certainly made up for that.

The final three stops, in Oklahoma and two in Texas, brought the largest lines we'd seen anywhere. My hand really ached from all the signings and we were both grateful we had a full week before we set out on the last leg of the tour at the beginning of September.

It was while we relaxed that I once again one late evening thought about the past. There seemed to be some unfinished business in my mind with regard to my leaving *The Announcer*. My memory stirred into life after Kay mentioned something to me at dinner that night.

"Do you remember, Vanessa, the very first time we met?"

Thinking for a second, I answered, "Sure, at your dad's house and you must've been, what, twelve, thirteen?"

"Thirteen just, and I believe I pestered you even then," she replied, with a giggle.

"Yes, you wanted to know if I'd worked on any murder stories for the paper. Strange question, I thought, for a young lady."

"Well I had read some of the books my Dad had taken on as an agent and a lot of those were murder stories."

I thought about those exchanges we had at dinner and they set me on a path later that night of recalling what I did when I'd left *The Announcer*. Settling down in my room I saw myself as I was then, a young girl scared of what might happen to her now she'd lost the job at the paper.

The first few days petrified me since I now had no regular source of income and not much likelihood of soon improving that situation. My aunt and uncle, as usual, told me not to worry, that I'd always have a roof over my head and food to eat. Comforting as that may have been, I began looking down on myself as a sort of failure, wondering all the while if I'd made the right decision by resigning. My Uncle Brian said he'd have a word with his new employer to see if there might be a position for me, but it was all very tentative and something I knew I couldn't count on.

Fortunately, I still attended on a regular basis the weekly writers' group organized and still led by Alfred Collins. These sessions kept me not only sane but focused on my love of writing. Without them I don't know what I would have done.

After one of those evenings when the other five or six participants left Mr. Collins asked me to remain behind. Puzzled, I agreed, and he began asking questions about *The Announcer* and how I was coping with all the changes he heard about.

"Actually, Mr. Collins, I quit."

Surprised, he asked why, since he knew I loved the reporting work there.

"Things aren't the same anymore now Mr. Barrington's gone. Mr. Kenwright fired a lot of the senior writers and brought in some of his close friends. He also took away any serious assignments from me, so that all I was left with was fluff and nothing. Very dispiriting, and when I went in to see him to raise my objections he really couldn't have cared less. So, on the spur of the moment I wrote out a quick resignation letter, threw it on his desk and walked out."

For a few seconds Mr. Collins looked at me and I imagined he was going to say how completely mad he thought I was for doing that. But he didn't, he surprised me with his next comment.

"Good girl. You did the right thing, Vanessa. I would've done the same. You stood up for what you believed in and preserved your integrity. Good girl."

"Except, now I don't have a job," I replied, smiling ruefully.

He sat down across from me, folded his arms and proceeded to make me an offer.

"As I've observed you and your writing skills in these sessions and after reading quite a few of your newspaper articles, I've formed the opinion that you are exceedingly talented with words. The novel you're currently working on, in my opinion, has a huge potential in the market. That's not to say it's perfect by any means or cannot stand to be purposely edited because, after all, it is your first attempt.

"My literacy agency is relative small, personnel-wise, but we do represent some high profile authors. I am eager to expand our current list of writers by discovering new and exciting talent. Unfortunately, that's not possibly right now because finding the right qualified people to assess these up and comings is quite difficult. So, if you would be at all interested in coming on board with my agency I would be quite overjoyed in having you as part of our team."

Flabbergasted, I couldn't speak for several seconds.

"Are you serious, Mr. Collins, you want me at your agency?"

"Indeed, but you don't have to decide this minute."

Smiling broadly, I replied, "Oh, yes I do and the answer's a resounding yes! Thank you! Thank you so much!"

"I have an office in my home so I'd like you to work from there rather than making the arduous trek to the city every day. I'll give you some of the many manuscripts piling up on my desk and we'll take it from there."

He also told me the salary he was prepared to pay which was generous to a fault. Honestly, I thought I'd died and gone to heaven. And so, for the next ten years until my first novel *Cards* was published with his massive help, I spent my days sorting through up and coming writers' efforts, deciding which to recommend to Mr. Collins for his ultimate approval, and editing some of the works before offering them to a publisher.

Working from his house obviated me seeing quite a lot of his thirteen year old daughter, Kay, an inquisitive young girl who seemed to take to me immediately. She always hung around the office after school, picking up manuscripts and telling me which ones she liked or disapproved of. She also asked lots of questions and by the time she reached high school I felt confident enough to ask her opinion on a number of different types of books, particularly authors who were appealing to the youth market. Invariably her thoughts coincided with mine, but on a number of occasions I recall we had fairly heated arguments over our conflicting opinions. But Kay always seemed to make sense, a trait I imagined she received from her father.

By the time she'd graduated high school it became clear she was destined to join the agency in some capacity or other. Four years later, after completing college, her father did indeed make her a junior partner. And quite right, too, since Kay had an innate sense for recognizing great talent when she saw it.

About this time I finally completed my own novel *Cards*, which became Kay's first real beginning-to-end project for the agency. Her editing, eye for detail and promotional expertise were phenomenal, which meant before too long she'd sold it to the same publisher I've had throughout my career.

With the success of the book and Kay's increasing stamp on the agency I took the plunge and gave up my day job to write full time, with Kay always available for any assistance and support I might need. Forty years later she is still doing the same phenomenal job for me.

The next morning over breakfast, I mentioned my previous night's reminiscences to Kay and she chipped in some of her own. All in all, we told each other how fortunate we were to have met the way we did, what we meant to each other down the years and our hopes for the future writers' retreat project. We laughed a lot over the next few days until we had to depart on the final leg of the tour, which went as smoothly, thanks to her extensive planning, as the first two. Taking in the last ten western states, we finally finished our journey in Los Angeles to the longest lines we'd seen. Although strenuous and hand-aching for me, the whole tour left me in disbelief that my writing meant so much to so many people. To say I was humbled beyond words would have been a massive understatement.

Our final book signing Kay had scheduled for Paris the following week. As we relaxed before making that arduous trip she surprised me one evening over dinner with an intriguing tidbit of information.

"While we're in Paris I've arranged for someone special to come see you. I'll say no more," she added, with a sly grin.

"Oh, really, can't you give me a clue?"

"No, it'll be a surprise, I hope. My lips are sealed."

Despite my continued pestering over the following days, Kay would not budge or bend an inch, so I was left to wonder who on earth she had lined up to see me in Paris.

Chapter Twenty-Five

After relaxing for a few days, catching up with Jean on how Wolfie was behaving himself and accompanying Kay on her various shopping expeditions to some of the finer stores in Los Angeles where, of course, I purchased nothing...hmm...hmm...we set out on our long, tiring and almost twenty-four hour journey to Paris. First class helped alleviate the hours spent in the air, while our first full day in the City of Lights was mostly spent catching up on our sleep.

Paris was a new experience for me so Kay, who had been there often, arranged quite a few sightseeing trips before the actual book signings, of which there were to be three. Over the next two days we took in all the major tourist attractions, including a magical afternoon at Versailles and a wonderful relaxing boat ride on the Seine.

But all good things come to an end and before I knew it I was sitting signing books in one of the biggest bookstores in Paris. Again, I could not get over how many people lined up to meet me and I was grateful that I had managed to retain a little of the French I learned in high school. That session took over five hours with the next two, spaced two days apart, taking almost close to that. Certainly my energy levels were well tested but my tiredness seemed to dissipate with every new book I autographed. The people could not have been nicer or more enthusiastic, so I was grateful that Kay decided to add Paris to my schedule.

Of course, from the moment I set foot in France I kept wondering who this mysterious person was who Kay told me she had arranged to come and see me, and when the event might happen. I continued to pester her but she still didn't divulge this person's identity.

We had reached the penultimate afternoon in Paris when Kay called from her suite and asked me to come to her room to discuss something to do with the latest promotional details of the book. I was in the middle of packing but dropped everything and hurried up because I thought she might be about to tell me she'd arranged an extension of the tour to Outer Mongolia or some such place. So I was in a disgruntled state of mind when she let me in and led me to her small sitting room.

"You'd better not have booked another stop, Kay," I barked on the way. "This has just about done me in."

Turning, she smiled but said nothing as we reached the cozy nook. Inside, sitting on the floral couch was an elegantly dressed woman, perhaps in her late sixties, whose face I recognized at once. By this time Kay had retreated with the words, "I'll leave you two to it and I'll see you later."

In front of me, appearing like a ghost from nowhere, was Chloe Barrington, the Chloe Barrington I hadn't seen since Simon's funeral some fifty years before.

"Oh, my god" I exclaimed. "is it really you, Chloe?"

She got up, came over and gave me the warmest hug I think I'd ever received.

"In the flesh, Vanessa, in the flesh, how are you?"

Still stunned by this apparition, I just stared at her for the longest time before she led me to the couch.

"Chloe, this is such a wonderful surprise. Let me take a good look at you."

She still had that amazing sparkle in her eyes, as well as the Chloe smile that I remembered so well. Her gray hair was pulled back into a neat bun, while her make-up was exquisite but not overly done. She wore casual but *haute couture* clothes and her whole appearance exuded a dignified elegance. It was a far cry from the seventeen or eighteen year old young girl I encouraged to leave school and go off to seek her dream in this great city so many years ago.

She beat me to it by saying, with a laugh, "A lot different from who you remember, I'm sure."

"Oh, no, Chloe, you're amazing...same sweet smile...same twinkling eyes...just wonderful. But how on earth did Kay get a hold of you, that's what I want to know?"

She grinned again and said, "Because she's representing me."

Puzzled, I asked, "Representing you how?"

"Only my autobiography...she's my agent, too, you know," she offered, raising her eyebrows.

"Oh, wow, that is so cool. But I'll be having a serious conversation with that sly old fox you can be sure, keeping something like this a secret; whatever was she thinking?"

"She just wanted to surprise you, Vanessa, to make our meeting special. Apparently you told her you've been thinking about those Rainbow Falls days and when my name came up...well, she could hardly believe the coincidence. She contacted me, said you were going on tour to promote your latest book and would I be up for a reunion here in September. I was just as stunned as you are now but, of course, I agreed immediately. Just the thought of seeing you again after all those years filled me with...oh you can't believe it...so much joy and happiness. Now let me look at you, Vanessa..."

She reached out, touched my cheek and said, "Still as lovely, still have the same beautiful smile...the years have treated you so well, Vanessa."

I thanked her for the kind words, which I honestly didn't feel were totally accurate, before moving on to concentrate just on her for a while. Because this was such a joyous occasion I decided not to begin with the last time we saw each other, which took place at Simon's funeral, or to ask just yet about her parents who I assumed must have passed away by now.

"So, Chloe, Paris, you must tell me everything beginning with when you first left Rainbow Falls."

Sitting back, she took in a big sigh and answered, "Oh, Vanessa, where to begin, so much has happened but all right, I'll do my best. The internship with The Fontaine Fashion House went better than I could ever have hoped. The first year just flashed by very quickly but I managed to learn so much from all the fabulous designers there."

"And school?" I asked, hoping she'd completed high school. "Did you graduate?"

"I did. Loved the place over here, very friendly, great set of teachers, couldn't have asked for anything better. And then, to my surprise, Michel took me aside one day after my first year with him and told me he thought my innovative designs so brilliant he was taking me out of the program and making me one of his regular designers. Me, at twenty, can you imagine?"

"Well, quite honestly, Chloe, I'm not surprised. I always thought your ideas and styles years ahead of most people's. I'd say he made the right decision."

"And five years later he made me head of design for the House and gave me carte blanche on the designs for his spring collection that year. I felt like I was living in some sort of fairyland and a whirlwind at the same time. But my ideas were received with quite overwhelming enthusiasm, so much so that The Fontaine Fashion House soon became the number one house in the country. And then…"

"And then?"

"And then when I was about twenty-five Michel asked me to marry him."

"What?"

"Yes, amazing eh?"

"So, did you?"

"Of course. Not only did we have a close business relationship but over the years had developed a close personal one, too. I couldn't have been happier."

"Oh, Chloe, that's marvelous. Any children?"

"Two. Amie and Michel junior, and both have followed us into the House and are now effectively running the show. I couldn't be prouder of them."

"So have you and Michel stepped down or something?"

"Pretty much, although I do attend meetings and still have final say over the spring and fall collections. That's how I came to have time to write my book. Michel unfortunately passed away in 2014. He was fifteen years older than me but always seemed like a big kid. I loved him so much, Vanessa."

"That's so sad, but at least you had him for such a long time and it sounds as though you two had a great marriage and partnership."

"Yes, we did, so I have no complaints at all. Michel gave me a wonderful life."

"So how did you meet Kay?"

"Mutual friend suggested her and the rest is history. The book should be out in the next six months or so."

"Can't wait to read it, Chloe, knowing you as I do."

"Well, Vanessa, it'll never be in your league, c'mon, you're a legend."

"Only in my own mind," I joked. "I'm flattered that you even know about my writing."

"Are you kidding? I have every one of your novels and can't wait to read the last in the trilogy. Sorry I couldn't come to the signing but Kay didn't want to spoil the surprise. But I'm not leaving here without a signed copy, okay?"

"Well, of course, providing you've got the cash!" I joked again.

"Now," she said, leaning forward, "we need to talk about you for a while. Bring me up to speed, Vanessa."

"I will, but first I need to know about the family, Chloe. I was so close to all of you...well, perhaps not Edward at the end there...so?"

She looked away, pursed her lips and took in a deep breath.

Finally, she answered, "After Simon's death Dad just went downhill really fast. Well, you know that since you were still around then. He didn't last too long, depressed, no motivation after losing his job at the paper, it was all so sad. Eventually he suffered a massive heart attack so at least the end was quick. Only fifty-one, so sad.

"Hugh did leave for Canada and, in fact, is still there with a great family. I saw him probably two years ago and we actually talked about you once in a while, so you see you weren't totally forgotten. Edward never got over that Samantha episode or Simon's death. He continued drinking and by the time he was in his mid sixties had cirrhosis of the liver. But honestly, it seemed a blessing. He was a complete mess, living hand to mouth, again so sad.

"Mom, bless her heart, came to Paris to live near me after Dad died. We had over thirty lovely years together. She absolutely adored Paris and the fact that I was someone of note here thrilled here so much. Unfortunately, when she was in her late seventies she developed ALS and went downhill very quickly. She couldn't walk but always retained her sense of humor and grace.

"I heard from a doctor friend that the hospital attached to The Curie Institute here seemed to be making great strides in coming up with possible life-improving treatments although, of course, there was no cure in sight. They saw her a few times but nothing seemed to help and Mom was determined not to end up in a totally dependent state. She didn't want that, saying she wanted to go out on her own terms. We all knew what that meant and supported her decision.

"Fortunately, it didn't come to that. One evening, and she was living with me at the time, she said she couldn't feel her right arm and was constantly falling sideways in her chair. I propped her up with cushions and she eventually went to sleep. When I checked on her a few hours later she was gone, peacefully and just how she wished. It was a blessing, Vanessa, you have no idea."

"Oh Chloe, I'm so sorry, that must've been so hard for you."

She nodded before adding, "Great lady and she'd had a wonderful life, full of love and laughter, a few heartaches, of course, and then she left on her own terms. Nothing to be sorry about, really."

"She always had time for me," I offered, "always kind and making sure at those picnics at your country house that I was included as a member of the family. I'm glad she didn't have to suffer." After letting that news fade from our conversation somewhat I asked about April and Samantha.

"Oh, April did become a vet. Mom kept in touch with her for quite a while so we knew how her life turned out. And Samantha…well, she was always the wild one, as you know. No one kept in touch, not that she would have wanted that anyway, but we did hear through April, actually, that she died in her early thirties from a drug overdose, which wasn't a total shock to anyone. I guess she had some moderate success with her music but on the whole I would say it was a sad life for her.

"So that brings you up to date with everyone, Vanessa, now, what about you?"

For the next hour or so I took her through my journey from when we knew each other in Rainbow Falls to now. She sat transfixed as I described leaving *The Announcer* after her father's departure, being offered and taking the job with Kay's father's literary agency, and finally settling down to write my novels.

"Not an exciting life by any means but I've enjoyed it."

"Did you ever marry?" she asked.

"Yes, his name was Ralph and for a few years I'd say we were happy."

"But..."

Shaking my head, I replied ruefully, "Don't think he could handle my growing success as an author. And the more notoriety I received the more it seemed to alienate him. In the end carrying on with the marriage just wasn't worth it for either of us. So, I got myself a dog for company, kept writing and *voila* here I am today on a thirty, no thirty-one with Paris, book tour and selling the rights to a number of my books over the years, including the trilogy, to the movies. So, no, no complaints at all, Chloe, it's been a great ride."

"And I hear it's not over yet according to Kay."

"Been spilling the beans again has she? Just wait until I catch up with that little...but, yes, we have some wonderful plans in mind for a writers' retreat and I'm also seriously thinking about attaching myself to a university writing program to give something back to up and coming young authors."

"Well if you give them half as good advice as you gave me they won't go far wrong. Do you remember what you told me when I was thinking about taking the internship all those years ago and Edward, in particular, was adamant I not come here to Paris?"

"I do recall I certainly encouraged you and got it in the neck from Edward for doing so," I answered, with a huge grin.

"You told me I didn't have a choice but to accept the offer, that being in the fashion industry was my destiny just as you hoped to be a writer was yours. That advice I always thought about as I made my way up the ladder here, and I know without those words constantly ringing in my ears I wouldn't have had the amazing career I've had or, indeed, the fortunate life as a whole. So, it's taken me over fifty years to thank you, Vanessa, but I do, I want you to know I shall be eternally grateful to you." She left the couch, came over and gave me another long, tight hug.

I held her at arm's length before replying, "No, Chloe, you did all that on your own. With or without my advice fashion was always going to be your destiny and your passion. All I did was give you the little push you needed. But I'm so glad and pleased for you that everything worked out so well." We hugged again as the door opened and Kay sailed in beaming from ear to ear.

"Hope I'm not disturbing you," she breezed, "but I've made a dinner reservation at *Chez Pierre's* and we really ought to be going. Can you finish catching up there?"

"Oh, we've pretty much covered all the bases, Kay, you little minx," I countered, with a fake frown. "Why on earth didn't you tell me you knew Chloe?"

"And spoil the surprise...never! That was part of the fun. Are you going to fire me now?" she responded, laughing.

"No, but I am gong to tell you you've given me one of the most perfect afternoons of my life. Seeing Chloe again has been magical, heartwarming and so, so unbelievable. So, no, I'm not going to fire you, you sly old fox, I'm going to thank you from the bottom of my heart."

Chapter Twenty-Six

———◆———

The encounter with Chloe Barrington, however brief, filled me with such joy and happiness knowing that at least two members of her family, she and Hugh, who had made his home in Canada, survived from that wonderful close-knit group from all those years ago despite the eventual tragedies which befell it. We promised faithfully to keep in touch and I offered any help I could give her as she was writing her autobiography.

It was now early October and I settled down at home again after the exhausting book tour. Kay also needed a break so we decided to put off our serious plans for the writers' retreat for a month or so. But both of us were eager to get started so she arranged for a real estate friend of hers to begin the process of finding a suitable site. Ideally, we wanted to buy an already established large estate complete with a sizeable house and plenty of land. Our idea centered around having accommodations large enough to house no more than ten authors at a time, with a good sized kitchen, dining room, lounges and private work spaces where they could write and create at their leisure. I was prepared to put up another two million and Kay said she would match it, too. We left everything in the hands of the realtor so that for a few months we didn't have to worry.

When I was writing my routine usually fell into a predictable pattern, which meant I devoted most of my afternoons and early evenings to the process while leaving the mornings free to take care of errands, household chores, seeing a friend for lunch and, of course, walking Wolfie. But now after a couple of weeks of basically doing nothing I began to get restless. I'd always been the type of person who needed to be busy most of the time and previously my writing certainly took care of that. It was then that I started thinking about my wish to perhaps attach myself to a college as a writer-in-residence somewhere. Over the years I'd received quite a few offers to give talks or perhaps spend a few months teaching a writing class but had turned them all down since I was usually in the middle of trying to finish one of my novels. But now I had the time and strongly felt this was something I should pursue.

It was then I remembered the talk I gave at the village library in Maine where a professor from the university up there stopped by and politely asked if I would at sometime consider speaking to his writing class. I recalled he seemed to be a decent sort of man, very diffident towards me and not at all pushy. I liked those qualities about him and began thinking we might be an academic match.

He gave me his card but, of course, with my penchant for being quite untidy around the house, it took me a couple of hours to find it. But find it I did and as I held the card in my hand I actually felt my heart beat a little faster at the prospect of possibly going back to Maine and helping this professor's students in some meaningful way.

His name was James Prescott and it was with not a little apprehension that I pulled out my phone, put in his number and waited.

"Yes, hi, James Prescott here."

"Oh, Mr. Prescott, it's Vanessa Parker, so sorry to bother you."

"Ms. Parker," he answered, definitely surprised, "no, no, no bother at all. This is indeed an honor."

"We met at the library talk in Maine a few months ago…"

"Yes, I shall never forget what a thrill that was for me," he interrupted.

"Well, you mentioned at the time that you'd like me to come up and talk with some of your creative writing students."

"Yes, yes, exactly, is that at all a possibility?"

"Actually, it is. I've just come off a three month book signing tour all over the country and Paris, so I definitely have some time on my hands right now and I'd be delighted to come up and mingle with your up and coming authors."

"That is wonderful news. We have three classes with some thirty students enrolled in the course. How much time do you think you might be able to devote?"

"Certainly at least a week and, depending on how things go, possibly a little longer. Would that be enough for now?"

"Oh, yes," Prescott answered, almost beside himself with joy, "any time you can spare would be gold, believe me, and we would, of course, cover all your expenses."

"Certainly not necessary but I appreciate the gesture. Now, today is Thursday so how about I set out on Sunday, and when I arrive perhaps we can meet for dinner and you can bring me up to speed with exactly where your students are in the course? I'll text my hotel details to you when I have them, how does that sound, Professor Prescott?"

"Sounds marvelous and please call me James."

"Oh, of course, and in return it's Vanessa as you well know."

"This is going to make such a difference to our students you have no idea, Vanessa."

"Hopefully," I offered, with a giggle, "only time will tell."

"Before you go," Prescott added, "I must tell you how much I enjoyed the last book in the trilogy. Quite sensational how you ended it all and managed to pull every theme and plot maneuver together in one satisfying conclusion."

Taken aback by the praise, I replied, "One never knows for sure how any book ending will be received by the reader, James, so thanks for the feedback."

"And that's one of the most interesting aspects of writing I'd like you to discuss...how to effectively construct a trilogy such as yours. One novel, fine, but three all connected is truly amazing."

Again, I thanked him for his compliment and told him that was something I'd be delighted to cover.

"All right, then, Vanessa, thank you so much again for doing this and I look forward to seeing you on Sunday."

After speaking with James I felt both excited and apprehensive. I hadn't been a part of academia for such a long time and I wondered how the younger generation would take to an old fogey like me. Their tastes certainly wouldn't gel with mine but I hoped to be able to provide at least a little guidance with the basic principles of writing and creating a novel. On the whole I looked at the experience as a sort of trial run to see if I was up to perhaps spending a whole school year as a writer-in-residence somewhere.

That evening I began packing for the trip to Maine after securing a room in a hotel near the college that also was willing to allow me to bring Wolfie. I certainly didn't want to leave him behind again and this hotel actually had a type of day care for pets which, for a substantial fee, I signed Wolfie up. Now we were all set and I went to bed that night feeling good about the whole trip.

"Still number one on the New York Times Bestseller list, Vanessa," Kay happily announced when she called me the next morning. "And sales have now surpassed a million. Congratulations, old girl."

"Oh, my, Kay, I can hardly believe it."

"That's good news number one. Number two, the realtor just called and she's found two properties upstate that she says look extremely promising. Can you ride with me tomorrow to check them out?"

"Of course. Are they in our price range?"

"Indeed, both around two million. Obviously they'll need some work but both seem to have what we need."

"That's fantastic, Kay, and I have a couple of pieces of news myself."

"Oh, tell me more."

"First, I'm off to Maine on Sunday. Do you remember that professor who came to my talk at the library?"

"Yes, wanted you to go and give some kind of pep talk to his students, right?"

"Exactly. Well I called him and I'm going to spend a few days up there checking things out. If all goes well, and he doesn't know this yet, I'm going to offer myself as a writer-in-residence for the rest of the school year. I'm taking Wolfie with me, too."

"That's good, Vanessa, but are you sure you want to commit so much time to this?"

"I do, I think it'll be like a breath of fresh air mingling with these young things for a while."

"Oh, you're just looking for a toy-boy, Vanessa, that's all," she responded, with a giggle.

"You know me so well, Kay, can't pull the wool over your eyes."

"No, I'm happy for you but you can't stop writing, that's an order. What was the other thing you had to tell me?"

"I've been busy working the phone, calling some of my closest fellow authors to rope them in to help with the retreat. So far four have offered to come in with us, money and expertise. I'm so excited."

"Wow, amazing, this is progressing much better than I ever imagined. You can tell me more when I see you tomorrow. The realtor will meet us at the first property at eleven, so I'll pick you up at nine. Okay, Sweetie, see you then, bye."

The first property we looked at had most of the amenities we required but not enough land in my opinion. We wanted space outside for our writers to be able to walk among nature, feel completely like time did not matter and to feel all of weather's elements as a source of inspiration. This location just didn't have that necessary feel although the house was perfect.

Undeterred, we moved on to the second one, with which we immediately fell in love.

"What d'you think, Vanessa?"

"With some minor renovations and furnishings I think this is our winner," I answered, nodding enthusiastically. Turning to the realtor, I asked, "How much again?"

"A flat two million and the seller won't budge a cent unfortunately."

"Give us a minute," Kay told her, as she guided me to a quiet spot. "Not going to do much better than this, old girl, shall we take it?"

"Absolutely, there's so much potential here and loads of room for improvements and additions should the need arise. Let's do it."

And so, that was that. In a short space of time we'd become the *de facto* proud owners of an impressive estate.

Since I was going to be away for who knew how long Kay undertook to negotiate the property deal and all the necessary arrangements. We didn't expect the closing to take place for a least two or three months so my presence at this time wasn't crucial.

Packing up my things and Wolfie in the car for the trip to Maine I felt a sense of freedom that this undertaking at the college could put me on a brand new path in my life. For so long all I had basically known day to day was settling down to write, finishing one book and looking to begin another. I loved that part of my existence, being able to create and articulate my stories for others to read and enjoy. But with the completion of the trilogy I wasn't sure I had much left to say anymore, that my style of writing and its content may not be relevant now. So in my mind it was time to move on, with no regrets or second guessing.

I arrived at the hotel in Maine in good time for my dinner appointment with James Prescott, checked in at reception, freshened up, walked and fed Wolfie before making my way to the dining room. It wasn't any more than five minutes after I'd settled into my seat that James arrived with a small bouquet for me.

"Oh, that is so sweet of you, James," I offered, "you really shouldn't have."

"I'm using all the weapons in my arsenal, Vanessa, to get you to sign up with us," he joked.

We briefly hugged and made small talk before the waiter came and took our orders.

"My students are chomping at the bit to meet you tomorrow. They're a lively bunch."

"Bright minds are what I'm looking forward to meeting. I just hope I won't disappoint them."

"Vanessa," he responded quite seriously, "you are one of the most famous authors in the country. You could recite your shopping list and they would be enthralled."

"So what exactly are your plans for me for the next few days, James?"

"Starting tomorrow…sharp at nine, I'm afraid…I'll do the introduction and then ask you to give a broad outline of a writer's life, the trials and tribulations etcetera and then I'd like you to get more specific with the actual nuts and bolts of constructing a novel. And don't hold anything back because they need to know what's in front of them if they choose to pursue a writing career."

We talked a little more about my agreeing to an eventual longer term commitment before I asked him about his journey to academia.

"I was encouraged to write at an early age," he confessed, "although I have to admit I preferred other outlets. In college I wasn't really sure what I wanted to do until I joined the campus newspaper because, I'm ashamed to say, it was run by mostly young women and, being quite shy, I thought I might meet someone who would take pity on me. Didn't work, of course," he continued, with a laugh, "but working at the paper spiked my interest in writing. To cut a long story short I enrolled the next year in their writing program, loving and enjoying every minute because the professor was an awesome guy who really thought I had some potential.

"Turns out I didn't but he suggested I switch my attention to studying the great writers throughout the centuries, including all the periods of classical literature, with a view to making that my area of expertise. So I did and I enjoyed the experience so much I eventually received my doctorate in comparative literature. From there it was a short jump to becoming a professor here. But just to make you laugh, at some point in the next few days I will show you my very first effort at story writing, and laugh you will, I promise, but not too loudly I hope!"

"Oh, I should love to see that, James. I'm sure it's not as bad as you make out."

We finished our dinner, thanked each other for the talk and looked forward to meeting again at nine the following morning at the college.

Chapter Twenty-Seven

———◆———

The week with Professor Prescott's students flashed by exceedingly well I thought. They were engaged, receptive, curious and respectful towards me. James, in the weeks before I arrived, and in the hope I might eventually contact him, assigned them some of my novels which, from their searching questions, they seemed to have thoroughly studied. Some connected with a few of my earlier works and wanted to know how I thought my writing had changed or matured since then. Others, quite a few, actually, concentrated their efforts on trying to understand the twists, nuances and complicated storylines of the trilogy *Intimate Strangers*.

Again, several asked pointed, detailed questions about my vision and motivation for the series, but one young lady, Jennifer, in a quiet aside with me went much further.

"Ms. Parker," she began, quite diffidently, "I have to tell you that these books," and she held up her copies, "have changed my life."

Taken aback by such a personal admission I asked how and in what way.

"So much of the story I can relate to. Things that you describe have happened to me and I've always struggled with knowing the best way to deal with them. Your books have made so many positive suggestions that, believe it or not, I've followed. They have helped tremendously. So, thank you."

I returned the compliment before asking her to be more specific.

194

"They've changed the way I look at my relationships now. It's almost as if I can see them in a new light, and my attitude to certain aspects of my behavior has changed, too. Believe me, you have helped me a lot going forward."

"I'm so pleased to hear you say that, Jennifer, but never forget the answers are inside you all the time. You just need to find a way to unlock them and if my books helped you do that then so much the better."

Receiving praise like that is always proof positive that even if you manage to reach only one person with your message then your efforts have not been wasted.

In my last sessions with the three classes I emphasized how well I thought they were doing as I also complimented them on their attention, dedication and work ethic. I also informed them that I hoped to be back sooner rather than later.

In that respect, before I left, James spent an hour trying to persuade me to return for the next semester as a permanent writer-in-residence. I let him go on but in truth I'd already made up my mind.

"James, it's all right, you don't have to try any harder because I've come to a decision."

He looked at me with a mixture of hope and disappointment in his eyes.

"And?"

"Cover my living expenses and you've got a deal."

"Really? Oh my god, this is wonderful news. No, no, we can pay you as well."

"Not necessary, let it be my gift to the college and these great students."

And so that was set and I would return on a full-time basis in a month.

During the next few weeks at home I busied myself making all the necessary arrangements for my prolonged stay in Maine. One important situation I needed to resolve centered on my recent appointment to the board of my publisher, Bremmer Haldaine. Since committing to now working with James and his students for the rest of the academic year, I realized I wouldn't have the time to fulfill my promise to its CEO,

Gordan Wallace, to help review some new manuscripts. In that respect, I also felt it unfair of me to continue on his board, so I respectfully resigned immediately.

Kay called regularly to give me updates on the progress of the retreat which she was pushing forward quickly, competently and responsibly.

"It looks like the closing will be early December. I'll let you know when I know but be prepared to come back for a couple of days, okay?"

"Sure, oh Kay, I can't wait to get going on this."

"How are the commitments from those author friends of yours?"

"Great. They're each putting up two hundred thousand, so with that million I think we should start a foundation to ensure the long-term health of the retreat."

"Good idea. By the way, how's the new novel coming along," she asked, which elicited a more than annoyed response from me.

"Kay, stop! There isn't going to be a new novel, I keep telling you that."

"A girl can dream, can't she? Did you hear any more from Chloe Barrington, I think she wants you to take a look at her book before it comes to me?"

"No, not yet, but, of course, I'd be glad to."

"Your sales are still pumping along quite nicely, Vanessa, and you're now four months at the top of the bestseller list, amazing."

"It is, quite honestly, so I'm enjoying the experience while I can."

We chatted some more about my time in Maine and I hung up rather abruptly when she pestered me again about writing a new novel. After I did so I chuckled to myself because I knew something that Kay did not.'

I'd quite forgotten her question about Chloe Barrington contacting me when a couple of days later I received an electronic file from her. Almost simultaneously, my phone buzzed and it was Chloe herself.

"Vanessa, hi, it's Chloe, did you get the file yet?"

"Hi Chloe, yes, just came in. What's up?"

"It's my autobiography. Could you read it over and let me know what you think?"

"I'd be honored. It'll be just like my old job with Kay's father's literary agency," I joshed.

"I'd really appreciate the feedback and, please, be ultra critical since I want the book to be as good as possible."

"You got it, Chloe, oh I can't wait to read it."

"You're on page forty-four, by the way."

"Really?"

"Yes, really, after all you were the one who set me on the path I took in the fashion world. I owe you everything."

"A little over the top, Chloe, but thanks for the mention."

"Well we won't argue the point now but I know the truth and so soon will all my readers...all ten of them I expect," she joked.

"Don't kid yourself, kid, you are and have been a top name in the Paris...no world...fashion industry. Millions of women wear your designs, so this is going to be a blockbuster. You also have Kay in your corner which means it'll be bigger still. Just as long as you don't knock me off the number one spot on The New York Times Bestseller list, okay?" I joked back.

"Don't think there's any fear of that, Vanessa, I design clothes, I'm not a writer, which is why I want you to help me by running a severe critical eye over my pathetic effort."

"Give me a week to take a look but I hope you won't take anything I say too personally. All I'll try and do is make the book a better read but I won't attempt to alter your style, okay?"

"Perfect, and again, thanks so much for doing this."

True to my word I spent a lot of the next few days reading, rereading and making copious notes on Chloe's manuscript. There were a lot of rough edges, a lot of redundant phases that I smoothed or removed altogether, but on the whole I found the contents of the book a remarkable read. I was often surprised and stunned by some of the details she revealed and I obviously knew nothing about. I called Kay after I'd finished my review and told her what an extraordinary piece of work she had on her hands.

"I thought as much, Vanessa, after we sat down and talked when she first approached me. She's led an amazing life and I'm grateful to you for taking the time to help out here."

"So much I never knew, Kay, and you're right, she's led a remarkable life over there in Paris. She was even honored by the French President for her service to the fashion industry. And she built The Fontaine Fashion House into the top brand almost singlehandedly after Michel stepped down."

"Yes, it's a story that needs to be told and her millions of admirers and customers will lap it up. I'm very lucky she chose me to represent her."

"Well that works both ways, Kay, because I know she couldn't have picked any one better."

"Most appreciated, old girl, but I'm still getting my twenty per cent," she joked. "By the way, I have a firm date for the retreat closing... December 10th, so book it in."

"That'll work perfectly since the school is on Christmas break."

We chatted some more before I told her I needed to go and call Chloe about the revisions I'd made to her manuscript.

"Chloe, hi, it's Vanessa."

"Vanessa, oh it's good to hear your voice. What's up?"

"Can we talk about your book? I have some suggestions for you."

"Wonderful, but I hope you didn't spend too much time on it as I know how busy you are."

"Not at all, but first, oh Chloe, so much I didn't know about you."

"It's been a life for sure," she agreed.

"Beauty queen at ten, and even at that age you designed and made your own dress?"

"Yup, and it still hangs in my closet," she answered, with a chuckle."

"And Edward, I never would have guessed he was such a troubled teenager."

"He was. I was about seven years younger than him but I can clearly recall the fights he had with my parents, the drinking even then and the trouble he got into. The only thing that saved him, the only thing that turned his life around was when he was drafted and went into the army. He received the structure and discipline he so desperately needed and probably saved him from ending up in prison."

"I never would have guessed that from what I saw of him, although he did turn on me pretty badly when he found out I was encouraging you to take the internship and move to Paris."

"He certainly had a streak in him which he never really lost. No wonder Samantha gave up on him."

"I don't think that was the only reason she gave up on him. She was having an affair, you know?"

"So it was true? Simon kind of hinted at it a couple of times but I never took him seriously."

"Oh, it was true, Chloe, with that Kenwright chap at your father's newspaper."

"The one who caused all that trouble for Dad?"

"Yes, the very same. I found out not too long ago from his wife that Jack Kenwright was seriously in love with her. Sam apparently broke it off because it was getting in the way of her music."

"God, I never knew any of that," she replied, totally surprised.

"Simon was really upset with Sam and wanted to tell Edward what was going on but I persuaded him not to, to not get involved. He finally managed to get Sam to write Edward a letter, which he gave to Edward before he went swimming and drowned. It was quite a mess, Chloe."

"I still miss him, Simon, after all these years. He always had time for me, always looked out for me. Tragic how he died but he should never have gone swimming alone when he knew he had epilepsy."

"I enjoyed him, too, Chloe, and the way you describe him in your book has certainly honored his memory, which brings me to my comments on your book, which I'll send you later in a file. I've cut out a lot of the clichés you've used and replaced them with fresh descriptions. I've also tightened up the sentences and paragraphs to make the words flow a little easier. There were several grammatical errors which I've corrected but I want you to know I haven't changed the feel of the book or made any factual alterations. On the whole I think you did a great job."

"Well, from you, Vanessa, that's a ringing endorsement, thank you, thank you so much."

"Kay will do the rest to bring the whole thing to fruition but as far as I'm concerned you've got a winner on your hands."

We finished our chat with promises to keep in touch more often and I told her how glad I was that she'd re-entered my life.

"Right back at you, Vanessa, right back at you."

Two days later, with three huge suitcases packed in my car along with all of Wolfie's essential belongings we made our journey back to the college in Maine. James met us on the main campus and directed me to my new digs for the duration of my stay. The apartment was spacious, clean and had great views over the rolling hills nearby. He'd been kind enough to stock the fridge with the essentials, as well as inviting me to dinner that evening.

The next morning on campus saw me holding my first tutorial with five writing students, and as the day progressed I became more comfortable with the new environment. Part of my plan was to hold individual sessions with all members of James' classes and to that end I began in the afternoon with three, spending at least an hour with each. They were nervous, I think, being so close to an established writer but I tried my best not to preach. My first priority was to gauge each person's level and go from there. At the end of the day I told James I thought he had some prize writers on his hands if I didn't mess them up on the way.

"Well, some of them need a reality check because they already feel they're the next Hemingway or J.K. Rowling. But I like your approach, Vanessa, and I'm sure as you get used to each other they will be more accepting of any suggestions you might make.

"Now, next Saturday I plan on holding a small get-together in your honor so that some of the other professors, staff and higher-ups can have the pleasure of meeting you. Nothing fancy just twenty or so at my house. Is that okay?"

"Sure, I'd be delighted," I responded, before packing up my papers and heading off to see Wolfie.

Chapter Twenty-Eight

—◆—◆—

All of the creative writing students had begun their novels, which ranged from futuristic sci-fi to a simple, sweet love story and all subjects in between. Their diversity pleased me since it gave me so many opportunities to question, advise and also ask about their depth of research, character growth and evolution as well as plot development. One of the many facets young writers don't tend to consider is how to pace a story in such a way that it flows naturally and not too much is given away in the first few chapters. On the other hand the story always needs to move forward without redundancy to bore the reader to death. The other important pointer I continually emphasized was the matter of surprise. It has always been my feeling and I have lived by the tenet that if you surprise yourself in your writing then the reader will be, too. One, of course, must be careful not to create situations merely for the sake of it or your whole effort becomes fanciful, contrived and eventually not believable. Some genres can accommodate some extremes but on the whole I advised the students to try and keep a firm hand on their more outlandish ideas.

Writing dialogue was another extremely relevant area that I extensively covered.

"You have to convey what you want a character to say in the appropriate style of that person's usual way of speaking. Very difficult sometimes, that's why it's so important to listen to everyday speech from people you meet in the course of your daily life. Pay attention to which words they use in a particular situation. Do they use unusual patterns of speech; are they articulate in what they're trying to say; what words do they use in various situations, and how do they express themselves emotionally or when they are under pressure? All of these traits can help you round out a character's persona so that your reader understands your intentions and believes what they are reading.

"The other matters I need to emphasize are grammatical uses, syntax and clichés. Do not overdo any of these especially clichés. Try and find a different, fresh way of saying 'as white as snow' for instance, or 'not the sharpest pencil in the box'. And definitely watch your grammar but don't go overboard and apply every rule in the book to your writing. For example, you can end a sentence with a preposition when appropriate. Sometimes sticking to the rules makes your words seem stilted and priggish. Don't do it."

By the end of the week as I sat down with the students one-on-one I have to say how pleased I was that they seemed to have taken my advice to heart. A marked improvement over their first efforts and I told them so.

"Excellent revisions, I have to say. Great job everyone. All you have to do now is keep it up," I finished, with a laugh.

I relaxed for the first part of Saturday, spending time with Wolfie and catching up with Kay's latest news on the progress of the retreat. But before I knew it I had to get ready for James' little soiree in the evening. I did the best I could with my appearance which was nowhere near Hollywood standards at the best of times. Giving my hair one more primp I hurried out the door and hoped for the best.

There were a few groups of people standing around and enjoying a drink as James escorted me into the fray. Heads turned as we entered and I smiled back as James got me a glass of wine and led me to meet two women and a man.

"Vanessa, I'd like to introduce the president of the college, Dr. Ottoline Bell, the chairwoman of the board of governors, Elizabeth Morton and the dean of student affairs, Gerald Johnson."

After shaking hands I told them how pleased I was to meet them and to be participating in the college's creative writing program.

"No, we're the ones who are thanking you, Ms. Parker, for agreeing to give our students so much of your valuable time. It's an honor to have someone of your distinction here on campus," Dr. Bell offered, graciously.

"Indeed," agreed Mrs. Morton, "and not only for our students. I'm a huge fan of your novels and just having this opportunity to meet you face-to-face is like a dream come true for me. The last book in the trilogy was just sensational. I'm almost overwhelmed right now."

Genuinely taken aback by all this praise, I replied, "So pleased to hear you say that, Mrs. Morton, and thank you. We authors don't look for validation but when it comes we are so grateful."

"And I must second what our chairwoman has said, Ms. Parker," Gerald Johnson piped up. "Thrilled to actually meet you and to also tell you what a wonderful story *Intimate Strangers* is. I hope James will make it required reading for his students from now on."

"Already on it, Gerald," James answered, with a grin, "already on it."

We chatted some more and I told them from my initial impressions that I thought they had a first class institution on their hands, and I was extremely thankful to James for persuading me to sign up.

"I just hope I will be of some use to your students and that they all don't decide to flee the class in horror," I said, as we all laughed at my silly aside.

The rest of the evening, which lasted about two hours, was spent mixing with other professors, one of whom asked, not at all jokingly she assured me, if she could sit in on one of my sessions so she might learn how to write as well as me.

"I would hope some of your magic might rub off on me," she continued, "but failing that, could you please put my name on the cover of your next novel as co-author," she joshed again, "so I can know what it's like to live in your shoes."

"Well, for a small fee," I joked back, "I'm sure we can arrange something."

As the last guests drifted off James asked me to stay a little longer while he went off to fetch us each another glass of wine and to retrieve something he wanted to show me. I was glad to be alone because all through the evening, as I made my way around his spacious lounge, I had noticed a painting on the wall which seemed vaguely familiar. Not a great work of art by any means but it did have a certain innocent charm that I found pleasing to the eye. As I heard him come back I returned to my seat not wishing him to think I was prying into his private world.

"Here we are," he said, setting down the two glasses and sitting across from me. "Went very well, I thought," he began. 'You've charmed them all."

"They're a lovely group, James, I can understand why you're so happy here, and very gracious, too."

"Good friends now, all of them, supportive and always open to the professors' new ideas. It's great to be part of a progressive institution like this, I can tell you. Now," he continued, "I want you to take a look at this," as he handed me what appeared to be a newspaper inside a clear plastic bag.

Carefully pulling apart the bag I removed the paper and gingerly opened it. To my astonishment it seemed to be a 1970s edition of *The Announcer.*

"Oh my goodness," I exclaimed, "what is this?"

"I don't know if you remember but when you came out for that week with us a few weeks ago I said I'd show you my first effort at story writing. Well, here it is."

I stared at the paper and at once knew what it was. Buried somewhere in my memories of recalling the time with the Barringtons I could see a boy named Jimmy excitedly showing me the story he'd written. I looked up at James, smiled and nodded.

"It's about an animal skull, isn't it?"

Cocking his head in disbelief, he replied, "Yes, yes, how do you know that?"

"Because you found the skull one day when you came on a hike with a young lady called April and me. And you told me at the time you were going to write a story about it. Back then I was working for *The Announcer* and I thought your story so good that I promised to help you get it published in the Sunday section one day. And I did and you were so proud. Oh, Jimmy, this is unbelievable!"

"You're right. You are so right," he answered. "I'd completely forgotten that. You used to take me with you when my parents were working. Didn't you have an aunt and uncle who made you do it?" he asked, with a laugh.

Nodding and raising my eyebrows, I told him that was about right but that I really enjoyed his company and explaining things about nature to him. I got up and went over to the painting on the wall.

"I've been staring at this for the longest time because I thought I recognized it. Clare Kenwright helped you with it when we met her one day on our hike. She was an artist and we came across her as she was finishing a landscape or something. You were fascinated and she let you paint a small part of the sky. Then she helped you paint this, the picture of a dog. Not bad, too, for a first effort. I'm amazed you still have it."

He suddenly looked at me and I thought he was on the point of saying something, as his eyes seemed to be searching back through the years with a hint of sadness and fright. But he remained quiet and asked how I managed to recall so much.

"When I was staying in Maine for a month trying to finish the trilogy I came across a couple in the dining room who seemed vaguely familiar. Eventually I remembered them as Jack and Clare Kenwright. His father owned a lot of newspapers across the country and Jack breezed into town one day to apparently learn the trade at *The Announcer*. Of course, he was really there to take the paper away from Charles Barrington, the long-time editor, because he opposed the Vietnam War which Jack's father fervently believed in."

"The Barringtons, ah yes, I can see them all now," he admitted. "Quite a family, weren't they?"

"Indeed they were and it was such a shame how it all changed for them in the end. When I first knew them they seemed to have it all, sort of the blessed and golden family of Rainbow Falls."

"Ah, yes, that was the name of the town – Rainbow Falls. Charming place I always thought."

"Do you know I actually met Chloe Barrington, the daughter, a while back?"

"Can't say I have any memories of her, but then I think I only saw them a few times during the summer. The mother, I faintly recall, always had time for me. I remember once she had me help her make ice cream sundaes, not very well, I'm sure. It's funny the things that come back to you, isn't it?"

"Chloe did very well for herself. She went to Paris and interned at a prestigious fashion house, where she became its top designer. She eventually married the owner and had two children but took over the running of the company when her husband died. So many women to this day wear her designs."

At this point James became noticeably quiet. He fidgeted with his hands and it seemed he had trouble looking me in the face. I took it that my recollections were boring him but I was soon to find out that wasn't the case.

"And three brothers," he finally offered, "isn't that right?"

"Yes, Edward the eldest, then Hugh, and the younger one, Simon. Hugh's the only one still alive and, according to Chloe, lives in Canada."

"I didn't really know them, either, but I do recall playing a pick-up game of softball once. What happened to Edward?"

"According to Chloe again, he had kind of a troubled life after Simon's death. Drank heavily and let himself go. Cirrhosis of the liver finally took him in his early sixties. And, of course, Simon died in that tragic swimming accident. So young and so much potential."

Again, James went strangely quiet. I cocked my head in his direction and it was then he spoke, softly and hauntingly.

"Except, it wasn't an accident, Vanessa."

Frowning at him, I replied, "What on earth do you mean, James, not an accident? Simon had a seizure while swimming. The coroner ruled it a clear accident."

Shaking his head, he replied, "I was nine and nobody paid much attention to me after all the shouting and running towards the waterfall. Someone, and it must have been you, passed me as I was running away and told me to stay where I was. And afterwards, when the hubbub had died down and the police were at the house, no one bothered to ask me anything. Of course, I was terrified and you saw how upset I was so you and your friend walked me back to your car and drove me home."

"Oh my god, James, this is unreal! So, what really happened to Simon?"

"I was fishing and I asked you if I could move farther down the river.

You agreed and I disappeared around a bend but still within earshot of you so you could check on me from time to time. A little way off I saw Simon hand Edward what looked like a piece of paper. Edward snatched it from him and read it. But then I could hear Simon really going after Edward about someone called Samantha. He was ranting and raving, getting right into Edward's face. Being so scared at that moment, I hid behind a tree but I could still see and hear what was going on. I heard Edward start to yell back and he pushed Simon, who responded with a push of his own. But then Edward, who seemed much bigger to me than Simon, went crazy, pushing Simon to the ground and wrestling him into the water. They were struggling but Edward was much too strong for Simon. He pushed him under the water and just held him there. I saw Simon's legs thrashing, trying to get himself free but Edward just held his head under the water until Simon didn't move anymore. Finally, Edward stood up, waited for a minute or two and then began pulling Simon from the water. He dragged him up the bank and that's when he started yelling for help. But, Vanessa, Simon was clearly dead and it was Edward who killed him."

As James' words washed over me it was hard to accept and really comprehend what he had just revealed. When someone tells you something totally contrary to what you have believed for most of your life, it is nearly impossible to immediately grasp the significance and meaning. For some minutes I sat, head drooped, turning his words over and over in my mind. *Edward killed Simon? Edward killed Simon?* I kept silently repeating the question in my head until I could look at James again.

"Are you sure, James? I mean, you were only nine, could you have been mistaken? It just doesn't seem possible that Edward would do that to his brother."

He shrugged and shook his head, before saying, "I know what I saw, Vanessa, even all these years later. I understand you're finding this difficult to process but I'm telling you the truth."

My thoughts switched to another implication which, shame on me, I'd completely overlooked.

"Then this means you've carried this knowledge with you for over fifty years, James. Oh my god, that's just terrible for you. How on earth have you managed to live with it for so long?"

"Time, I guess," he admitted. "Eventually time and distance enable you to forget or at least not think about it too often. I accepted what happened, realizing at nine I couldn't have changed anything. It's all water under the bridge now, but I thought you ought to know the truth. I'm sorry if it's upset you."

"No, no," I assured him, "I'm glad you told me. I mean, Edward always seemed to have a …I don't know how to describe it…an aggressive streak in him. He turned on me once and on Hugh, too. If you put that together with Samantha telling him their relationship was over, well…I can imagine him losing it when Simon gave him Sam's letter and then went on to perhaps tell Edward what a fool he was for not seeing what was clearly right in front of him with Sam's affair with Jack Kenwright. But still, it's shocking to think one of the Barringtons could have done that to another.

"I hope by telling me it will relieve some of the ghosts for you, James. You certainly didn't deserve to carry this with you all this time, I mean, you were only nine for goodness sake."

"As I say, it's all water under the bridge now. Will you tell Chloe?"

"No, no, she doesn't need to know this about Edward. What good would it do anyway? I'm happy for her to think Simon's death was an accident, so I'll leave it like that."

By this time the hour had grown late and James courteously walked me back to my apartment. I thanked him again for the reception and for trusting me with the secret he'd held for so long.

"You've come a long way, Jimmy Prescott," I told him, "since you were a kid in Rainbow Falls fishing and finding skulls. You should be so proud of yourself because I certainly am." And with that we said goodnight and he left me with my thoughts and memories.

Chapter Twenty-Nine

———————◆———————

"He killed him, Kay!"

"What? Who?" a startled Kay responded to my immediate outburst, as she answered her phone. "What are you on about, Vanessa?"

"Edward, he killed Simon. It wasn't an accident."

"Oh, the Barrington brothers, right?"

"Yes, James just told me what really happened that afternoon."

After returning to my apartment my mind still whirled from James' earlier revelation. I desperately needed to talk to someone, so I called Kay.

"And?"

"And Edward drowned Simon. He didn't have a seizure as we all thought."

"Why would he do such a thing?"

So I related what James had said and filled in some of the background story.

"And this all happened over fifty years ago? Amazing," she offered, before telling me this could be the basis for my next novel.

"No, Kay, I keep telling you there isn't going to be another novel," I answered firmly but even-temperedly.

"So how did it make you feel knowing the truth after all those years?"

"Well I never thought for one minute Edward would do something like that...murder his brother, never. It's still difficult for me to imagine him actually doing the deed, something so heinous. I've got to think about this some more, Kay, when I've calmed down and can look at things rationally. It was all so long ago now and yet it seems like yesterday."

"Are you going to tell Chloe?"

"James asked the same question, and I'm not. She doesn't need to know her brother was killed by her brother. Please, please don't mention it, either, okay?"

"Of course not and I thank you for trusting me with this. My lips are sealed."

"Look, I'm sorry to have bothered you with this, Kay, but I needed to talk to someone. I have to go and spend some time just mulling it over, so let me call you back in a little while."

"Okay, Sweetie, and I'm so sorry you had to hear this. Bye."

Although it was now around eleven I made some tea, brought my mug to the couch and settled down with my thoughts. I recalled when first meeting the Barringtons how I almost resented them for the apparent closeness they exhibited as a family. I had recently lost my mother and I felt I would never have what those kids had – loving parents to see them on through their lives. And as I became closer to them I actually started to feel that they were now my family. I was included in their outings, picnics and celebrations. I confided in Mrs. Barrington, given my big opportunity by Mr. Barrington and became close to Simon and Chloe. Looking back now I know they helped me shape my life for the better, showing me I could actually do things and make something valuable out of my life. Quite simply, I owed them so much.

But as I curled on the couch a sudden sadness filled my brain when I thought of what was and what it all became. That blessed and golden family ended up in ruins, torn apart by matters they sometimes couldn't control. As I searched my memory for reasons I realized Jack Kenwright's arrival at *The Announcer* almost certainly began the slow but steady descent into eventual turmoil and destruction.

It was Jack who almost at once began to undermine, little by little, Mr. Barrington's editorship until he finally drove the poor man to his wit's end. And it was Jack who came swooping in and stole Samantha from Edward without a thought for the consequences. Of course, Samantha was not an innocent bystander, but she had the right to make her own decisions regarding her relationship with Edward. But Kenwright, despite what Clare told me about him really being in love with Sam, did have a choice. But he chose his own lustful spirit over other concerns for anyone else's feelings.

I thought back to when I met the Kenwrights at the hotel in Maine and I raged at him for doing what he did. If I had known then what I know now I most certainly would have told him what I thought of him and his despicable actions. I remembered how he seemed to have trouble recollecting those times, putting on a good show of a failing memory when, I suspect, he clearly understood all the time and didn't have the guts to admit it.

Time makes you forget but it also makes you remember. All this happened so long ago now but curled up on the couch, in the middle of the night, it seemed, as I told Kay, that it happened yesterday. I clearly saw their faces like ghosts in front of me, talking, laughing, arguing... just being the Barringtons as I recalled them.

But now it was time to let them go, to close my book of memories and let them and me live in peace. I could do that, I knew I could, for a little while anyway.

Although now past two o'clock, I pulled up Kay's number and called her back.

"Too late, is it?" I asked, pleadingly.

"Never for you, Vanessa, never. Talk to me."

"I'm blaming Jack Kenwright for everything." I then went on to tell her what I'd been thinking and how sad I felt, even now, for the Barringtons and the way things turned out for them.

"And if it hadn't been for a nine year old boy seeing what he saw..."

"I know, I know," I interrupted, "I would've been none the wiser. But I'm still glad James told me."

"Ah, the past," Kay offered, "can't live without it however hard we try."

"But now I'm over it all...the Barringtons, *The Announcer*, Jack

Kenwright, Samantha, Edward, Simon, the whole lot of them...except Chloe and James, of course."

"So, on the whole, how was your trip down memory lane?" Kay asked, kindly.

"On the whole...I think it was worth it. Put my young life into perspective, validated my early hopes and dreams of becoming a writer and let me remember, mostly with fondness, some of my favorite people. So, yes, on the whole it was worth it, Kay."

"And I think these last few months have changed you somewhat, Vanessa. You seem more focused yet more relaxed in figuring out how you came to be what you came to be. I'm sure now that your remembrances are over you'll be more than satisfied with how your life has unfolded. Good job, old girl. Now, I have some news to share, too."

"That would be like a breath of fresh air, Kay, what've you got for me?"

"The closing for the retreat is definitely set for December 10th."

"That's in two weeks and is perfect since the college is on Christmas break for six weeks. I'll be coming home for a long rest so we can talk more about the renovations then."

"And Chloe's book...her autobiography...is done and should be released next month. You did a fantastic job with it, Vanessa, thank you."

I played down my part which, to be truthful, consisted of only tidying things up a little.

"It's a great story and will do very well especially as she has you behind her, Kay."

"We want you at the launch in Paris, which will be in mid-December, too."

"Wouldn't miss it."

"All right, and look, I'm sorry again for the Simon revelation and I hope you'll be able to move on now. Talk to you soon, bye."

I didn't know what mood I might find James in when I returned to school on Monday but I was determined to be upbeat and not dwell on what he had told me. He met me before the students arrived and only referred to the Simon incident once.

"I hope what I told you on Saturday didn't upset you too much,

Vanessa, but I just thought you ought to know the truth since you were so much a part of the family back then."

"No, I'm glad you told me, James. Must be a weight off your mind."

"I've put it to rest now and I honestly hope you can do the same."

"I've decided I'm over the Barringtons so, yes, I can."

And from that moment on we never spoke of what happened again.

The semester wound down and before I knew it I was back home for six weeks. Wolfie seemed so pleased to be back in familiar surroundings and so was I. Jean, as usual, had looked after the house in true neighborly fashion and I rewarded her with a sumptuous dinner and, next day, a session at the local spa.

Kay picked me up on the morning of the 10th to complete the closing on the retreat, which went off without a hitch. We then made our way to the property to meet with the contractor Kay hired to do the renovations. She had already laid out our chief specifications and the plans he showed us were spot on. He estimated the job would be completed within four months, so we were looking at early summer to finally open the place up to perhaps a dozen young writers. We celebrated the momentous occasion with lunch, champagne and lots of talk.

"Well, we did it," she enthused, as we touched glasses, "congratulations."

"Right back at you, Kay, couldn't be happier."

"And the foundation is taking shape, too. The lawyer's putting the finishing touches to it as we speak so all we need to do is come up with the money."

"Wonderful, just let me know."

We discussed how to best attract the kind of authors we wanted to support, mostly young with probably a first novel under their belt, but I told her it was important for established writers to also be included.

"I know how much going to Yaddo helped me, giving me the time and space I needed to really develop what was, I think, my third novel. Not having to worry about anything but the book lets you think and write much more clearly. Virginia Woolf had a room of her own where she could sit for hours, compose and write, in longhand, I might add, producing some of the finest novels of the 20th century. So, giving established authors such an environment to continue to do what they do best is a must for me."

"And I agree one hundred per cent, Vanessa, and in fact I have several clients who I know would benefit from the retreat."

We chatted some more about various other aspects including length of stay, social behavior and what amenities we should include, particularly for those authors suffering from some sort of handicap or disability. We wanted the retreat to be all inclusive so that anybody with proven talent had the opportunity to attend.

"By the way," I offered, "I've heard from three of my fellow writers who are anxious to come on board and serve in whatever capacity they can. Promised money, too, so this is going much better than I ever envisage. Having such noted people join us certainly will add to the overall image and atmosphere we want to create."

"Wonderful and I have two of my established authors lined up as well. Oh, Vanessa, I can't wait until we open our doors for the first time."

"Me, too, Kay, and with the foundation in place it'll be there long after we're gone."

"That's the idea. Now all we have to do it come up with an appropriate name for the place."

"I've been thinking long and hard about that, so how d'you feel about *The Chapter and Verse Retreat*?"

"Oh, I like that, yes, let's go with that since it encompasses prose and poetry." She brought up a couple of other matters before ending with, "By the way, Chloe Barrington's book launch for her autobiography is in a week's time in Paris. Can you make it?"

"Oh, absolutely, wouldn't miss it for the world."

"Good, I'll send you all the details in a day or two. She'll be so excited that you'll be there. Now, I have to run, so I'll drop you back home and catch up with you later."

December in Paris was a cold affair but my heart was warm at the prospect of seeing Chloe again. Since she still remained a shining star within the global fashion arena her book launch naturally called for an elaborate ceremony, full of glitz, celebrities and suffocating media coverage.

Kay and I had front row seats when the chairman of her publishing company stepped forward, after two songs by Adele and a short reading from her book by Meryl Streep. He spoke eloquently about Chloe's life, particularly how her designs had changed the fashion landscape throughout the world. He briefly touched on her family, her charitable work and the positive influence she had on millions of women around the globe. After he finished, fashion icons and fellow designers Gustave Miron and Martine Arbura, along with two of Chloe's most famous models, also gave heartwarming speeches about Chloe's life in the French fashion industry.

Finally, Chloe herself came to the podium and, after what seemed like a ten minute standing ovation, spoke graciously of her time in Paris, thanking her friends, her colleagues and everyone who had supported her fashion visions and for giving her so many opportunities to pursue the life she loved. Before she wrapped up her speech she warmly thanked both Kay and me for all the help we gave her whilst writing the book. That caught me by surprise and the applause we received was a little embarrassing to say the least. The reception afterwards went on into the early hours and before we left Chloe made me promise to come round the next day so we could talk in peace.

Kay and I met Chloe the next afternoon at her large house on the outskirts of Paris. Over coffee and delicious French pastries we talked about the book launch and how well it went, her plans for the future, which included setting up a brand new perfume company and spending time with Hugh in Canada.

As our visit wound down she suddenly turned to me and said, "You know, Vanessa, I still think of Simon every day. I know he drowned but I still don't completely understand all the circumstances. He was an excellent swimmer and even if he had a seizure I think he could have survived that long enough to save himself. Of course, I wasn't there that day but you were. Can you walk me through what happened as far as you remember?"

I saw Kay take a side glance at me before turning away. I looked at Chloe and smiled before beginning.

"April and I heard Edward's shouts for help and since we were nearby we ran to see what the problem was. When we got there he was kneeling over Simon and trying his best to revive him. April took over and worked on Simon for quite a while but it soon became clear he was gone. We then ran back to the house to call for help."

"My mother told me at the funeral that there was a small boy called Jimmy, I think she said his name was, around at the time and when I asked April about him she told me you and she had brought him to the picnic and that he was fishing down by the river. Did he ever say anything to you about what happened?"

Calmly, I replied, "We passed him on our way to help and all I can tell you is he looked scared, probably from all the shouting. We told him to stay where he was and after we'd seen there was nothing much we could do for Simon, took him up to the house with us. We then drove him home and I really didn't see much of him again."

"Did he say anything to you, anything at all?"

Honestly, I answered, "No, he didn't and we didn't want to make him any more anxious that he already was from the shouting and general hubbub. As I say I didn't see much of him again in Rainbow Falls because soon afterwards I left the area and went to work for Kay's father's literary agency."

She thought for a moment, shrugged and said, "Oh, okay, thanks for telling me. It's just that I can't imagine Simon drowning. But I guess his seizure was more severe that his usual ones."

"I guess so, Chloe. All I know is that it was a tragedy for everyone."

As soon as we could, Kay and I left Chloe's house, glad to be out in the fresh air again.

"Phew, that was close," Kay offered, as we returned to our hotel. "You handled that so well, Vanessa."

"I didn't say anything that wasn't the truth. And now, hopefully, she'll let it rest."

And that's exactly what happened. Whenever I saw Chloe in the future she never mentioned the incident again.

Chapter Thirty

———◆———

O nce back at college my life settled into a predictable routine which included a project I started in early January and with which I hoped to surprise Kay later in the year if I worked hard enough. I certainly had the time and space to devote to it, but once completed, I wasn't sure anybody would be much interested. Again I was totally wrong and the response stunned me to my core.

The senior students under my watchful eye continued to progress and most were in shouting distance of finishing their writing projects in time for graduation. One or two I felt were on the cusp of producing first novels of outstanding quality and I talked to them about the retreat Kay and I were setting up. They seemed blown away by my confidence in them but I countered by strongly suggesting their work was the result of their own talent and belief in themselves. They reminded me a lot of myself at that age and individually I told them as much.

"You have produced," I told one of them, Jennifer, the young lady who, in my early days at the college, came to me with an armful of my novels and related how they had literally changed her life, "in my humble opinion, a quite amazing first novel." It was called *The Incident* and encompassed an unusual story of how one incident affected the lives of so many unrelated people.

"The twists and turns you wrote into the plot were always believable, had me guessing and took me right to the end not knowing or having the faintest idea of the outcome," I continued. "Your characters achieved high levels of emotional connections to the story, which were never overplayed or written in just for the sake of it. Your words flowed naturally and the descriptive passages gave me just enough information to form a solid opinion of place and time. Jennifer, this is as good a first novel as I've ever read. Congratulations."

Jennifer covered her face and shook her head, hardly believing what she was hearing.

"Are you serious, Ms. Parker?"

"One hundred per cent and I have another piece of good news for you. This is so good that if you would like I will show it to my agent to see if she'll take you under her wing and move the novel forward. How does that sound?"

"Sounds unbelievable," Jennifer replied, still shocked at the praise. "You mean it might get published?"

"If I have anything to do with it, yes, yes it will."

The hug she gave me lasted forever it seemed until I pulled away and told her I still needed to advise her on a few more salient points. But in all honesty the book was a *tour de force* without any further intervention from me. As good as my word, I did eventually persuade Kay to take Jennifer on as a client, and six months later she was, indeed, a published author.

In early April James called me into a meeting with the president of the college, Dr. Bell who, after congratulating me on my work with the students, asked for a favor.

"As you know our graduation will be held in early May and I was wondering if I could convince you to be our commencement speaker?"

Of course, Dr. Bell caught me momentarily off guard as her proposal swirled around my head. I actually frowned at her, hardly believing her question.

"You want me to give the commencement address, really?" I asked, almost dumbstruck.

"Really, yes, we'd like that very much indeed. Will you consider it?"

"Well, yes, and I have," I replied, nodding and smiling broadly, "I'd be highly honored to do it."

"No, Vanessa," James piped up, "we're the ones who would be honored. Your presence would mean so much to the students and the college as a whole."

I scratched my head and still frowning answered, "Are you absolutely sure you want *me* as your speaker, after all their graduation is something they'll hopefully remember all their lives and I wouldn't want to encroach on that in any way?"

"Ms. Parker...Vanessa, if I may?" Dr. Bell chimed in, "your standing in the world of literature is monumental, second to none and having someone of your distinction to send our graduates on their way would be the icing on the cake of their education here. The subjects you have covered in your novels, the way you have spoken to generations of readers, the lessons you have imparted with your meaningful words... well...I know you will send these fine young women and men on their way with inspiration, love and hope ringing in their ears and bursting from their hearts."

Dr. Bell's eloquent homage, however misguided, touched me in such a profound way. I had never before thought my work could produce those kinds of benefits to my readers. Of course, I knew my books were well liked, even loved in some circles, but to think they went beyond that into perhaps the realms of enlightenment and motivation took me completely by surprise.

Honestly and humbly I replied, with a wide grin, "Well, we may have a difference of opinion there, Dr. Bell, but I thank you for your confidence in me to deliver an appropriate speech on the day."

"And," she offered, turning to James, "we are not quite done yet. James, would you please tell Vanessa what else we have in store for her on graduation day?"

"In light of your remarkable body of work, stretching over forty years now, the college would be honored to bestow upon you an honorary Doctorate of Letters."

Again I was temporarily speechless until the moment actually sank in.

"My, my," I offered, still stunned, "that would be...just wonderful... and I accept. Thank you. Thank you so much."

"I'll have James co-ordinate with you about length and so forth for your speech but I'm just so thrilled you will do this for us," Dr. Bell concluded.

Still excited at the prospect of delivering the college's graduation address, I called Kay to tell her and she immediately said she'd be there to support me. She also told me the retreat had reached almost completion and the grand opening, with the first ten authors in residence, was set for early June.

With that information under my belt I felt free enough to spend my spare time at the college working on the special project with which I hoped to eventually surprise Kay. Honestly, it was a labor of love and I enjoyed every minute constructing it. A lot of the details were already in my mind, so it was more or less a case of pulling all my thoughts together into one creative, interesting and personal piece of work.

Several times I took long weekends off to travel back home and dig through the attic and cellar to find some of the pieces of the puzzle or to confirm what I thought was really the truth. All too often in the process I was filled with a variety of emotions – sadness, joy, melancholy and downright amazement – but I always came away from my visits home with a true feeling of how, on the whole, my life had been blessed and fortunate.

Kay and I took the opportunity a couple of weeks before graduation to tour the now completed retreat to check out the renovations and make sure the staff we hired was in place and ready to go when the first residents arrived.

The contractor's work amazed and surprised us with its attention to detail, quality and small touches that added so much to the overall ambience of the place. We both agreed he deserved a bonus for going far beyond what he promised.

The director we hired to essentially run the place, Gabrella Turner, had nine years experience of running a high-class resort in her home country of Jamaica, before she immigrated to the States and became a citizen. Gabrella was recommended to Kay by one of her long-time clients who felt she would be a perfect fit for the job given her extensive and impressive resume. As well as being a top administrator she seemed to be well versed in any legal aspects, permit requirements and local laws that might affect the retreat. We now felt very confident the retreat would be in extremely capable hands.

My commencement speech took me over a week to write and was finished the day before I was due to deliver it. I asked James to run his eye over it to make sure the contents in no way offended the college.

"I don't need to do that, Vanessa," he emphatically told me over dinner. "Besides, we want your words to be your words, your advice to be your advice and your hopes for the students to be your hopes for them. Just be you and they will love and remember the moment all their lives. Of course, overstep the mark and your honorary doctorate will be toast," he joked.

"I will try and be on my best behavior, James, and limit the curse words to a minimum," I joshed back.

"Can't thank you enough for doing this for us, Vanessa," he added before asking about my plans for the summer.

"Probably spending quite a lot of time at the retreat, making sure things are running smoothly and to our satisfaction. And, then, I have a special project I'm hoping to surprise Kay with if I can finish it and, after that, just relaxing for a while."

"Both Ottoline and I were hoping you'd be back at the start of the new school year. Can I persuade you?"

"Try keeping me away, James, I love this place and the work I'm involved in. It's a long term commitment for me as long as the old brain holds out."

"Well, that is a relief. Now perhaps *I* can relax, too, for the summer knowing that. Thank you."

We parted early so that we both could get an early night before graduation the next day. I actually stayed up until the wee hours practicing my speech and trying hard not to get too nervous. In the end I gave up, went to bed and slept surprisingly well.

Kay, as promised, showed up early the next morning, took me to breakfast and then helped me into my gown and paraphernalia in time for assembling on a stage set up on the football field.

"You look a million dollars, old girl," Kay enthused, as James met us and guided Kay to her seat and me up onto the stage. By this time the horde of graduates began arriving and I felt calm and confident about delivering the address.

After the initial welcome by Dr. Bell we listened to two speeches by a couple of members of the graduating class, which were funny, sometimes self deprecating but always upbeat. Next came my turn and I was introduced by James.

"We are so privileged to have as our commencement speaker today Vanessa Parker, the esteemed novelist, whose career has spanned over forty years. Her novels have touched the hearts and minds of millions of readers throughout the world, and have been seen by millions more at the movies, on television and now on all the streaming services."

James went on like that for the next ten minutes but finally and thankfully, brought his laudatory remarks to a close.

"So please give a huge University of Maine welcome to our distinguished commencement speaker, Ms. Vanessa Parker."

I smiled broadly at James and took my place at the podium as the crowd of graduates, their families and friends applauded for what seemed like an age, Finally, I put up my hand and the touching reception slowly abated. I glanced at Kay who nodded as if to say, *You go, girl! You've got this!*

"Graduates, administrators, faculty members, distinguished guests, families and friends, I thank you from the bottom of my heart for that overwhelming welcome, and for allowing me the privilege of delivering this commencement address.

"During the past six months I have had the honor of working closely with some of you, as well as observing what a fine and close knit community the University of Maine is. It is a warm and encompassing seat of learning, which has certainly been enhanced beyond measure by the presence these past few years of this year's graduating class."

In my preparations for the address I had decided not to use too many of the usual sentiments expressed in such speeches, but rather to use my experience as an author and fashion my presentation in the form of a novel. I told the students as much and as I looked out over the crowd I saw puzzled stares on many faces.

"Our story...sorry...*your* story begins about four years ago when a cast of thousands descended on the University of Maine. There was hope and excitement bursting from the hearts of these characters as they began to plot how they could eventually earn a degree with as little effort as possible" The audience broke up at that description until I told them I had subsequently rewritten that chapter to be more kind.

"By chapter six, that is your sophomore year, these characters, or should I say heroes and heroines, developed friendships, some close, some strange and some...well...downright scary." Laughter again ensued. "And as the plot thickened so did some of their emotions. The villains of the piece, known to our main characters as professors, cooked up various schemes such as tests and audacious nonsense such as actual required reading and subsequent written papers, to try and thwart our super heroes at every turn.

"But by various twists and turns, known commonly as using their vast knowledge of the internet, the main principals in our story outwitted the evildoers at every juncture by finishing and handing in these dastardly assignments on time and with expert points of view."

I carried on in this vein until I'd reached the culmination of the story which was, of course, the end of their senior year.

"Finally, bewildered and grudgingly impressed, the wrongdoers... and you know who you are professors (more laughter)...came to realize that the important, enlightening and, hopefully, sustaining knowledge they had striven so hard to impart to their prodigies, previously referred to as...well...I have to keep this clean (more laughter)...so you know who you are...had actually been absorbed, so much so that the University of Maine...previously known to many as 'Sin City'...was proud to confer its appropriate accolade on each main character."

That ending was greeted with thunderous applause, laughter and whoops of delight and, after the din died down, I did give the graduates some traditional words of advice.

"So as you begin your life's journey away from here I would like you to often ask the question not 'why?' but 'why not?' when you are faced with difficult decisions or circumstances you think ought to be challenged or changed. Always try and be a pioneer or at least someone who makes a difference. Be well, congratulations and thank you so much"

More applause surrounded me as I sat down and I noticed Kay in the front row standing, smiling broadly, nodding and mouthing the words '*Good job! Good job!*' The next part of the ceremony consisted of conferring honorary doctorates on five people including myself. When my turn came, James stepped forward, took the sash and degree from Dr. Bell, made another short speech and presented me with the goodies. This was my third honorary doctorate but I felt the one that mattered most because of the connection to James and our past. Who could have known when I was nineteen and he only nine that we would be standing here today as colleagues and friends? Life certainly holds many surprises for us and I felt so blessed and fortunate.

The graduation wound down with the presentation of degrees to the eligible seniors and doctoral students. As those I had spent quite a considerable time with accepted their diplomas I warmly shook their hands and offered a few parting words of encouragement. Jennifer hugged me and whispered that she hoped to see me some time at the new retreat. In that moment I felt the pen had been passed and that the future of novel writing was in safe hands.

Chapter Thirty-One

The official opening of the retreat was scheduled for the second week of June. I made some calls among my author friends and managed to secure Stephen King's promise to come and speak and cut the ribbon for us. To have such an esteemed writer do this thrilled us beyond words but, as he told me over the phone, after hearing about my work at his *alma mater*, The University of Maine, he was only too pleased to support, in any way he could, our efforts in giving writers of all levels the opportunity to work in such a place.

I was glad of the break between commitments since it gave me the chance to try and complete the project with which I hoped to surprise Kay. So far it had gone exceedingly well and my confidence in being able to finish and hand it over before the start of the university's new school year, where I would once again be the writer-in-residence, remained sky high.

One of the other treasured moments of the summer occurred when Chloe Barrington, as good as her word about keeping in touch, called to ask if I could meet her in New York, where she was having a book signing, and spend a few hours catching up. Of course I agreed immediately and, since Kay also would be present at the event as Chloe's agent, we rode down together...

We arranged to meet that evening in the hotel dining room and when we arrived I was surprised to see Chloe was not alone. As I approached, this older gentleman slowly got up and greeted me with a huge smile. At that point I had no idea who he was.

"Vanessa Parker," he began. "Well, well, well, fancy seeing you again after all these years." We hugged but he could still see I was none the wiser. I looked at Chloe but all she offered were raised eyebrows and a nod. I quickly glanced at this man, who sported a full beard and heavy-rimmed glasses, before shaking my head and apologizing for my ignorance.

"Oh, that's quite all right," he acknowledged, "it's what fifty plus years will do to you."

As soon as he said that I knew at once who he was.

"Oh, my god, Hugh, is it really you?"

"In the flesh, so to speak," he replied, with an even bigger smile.

"This is so amazing to see you after so long!" I exclaimed. Turning, I introduced Kay before we all sat down. "What on earth are you doing here?" I asked. "I thought you lived in Canada."

"And I do but Chloe mentioned she was coming to New York and would I be up to a reunion with you. Well, how could refuse?"

We spent the rest of dinner catching up, talking about the old days in Rainbow Falls and all the good times we had there. As we chatted about his family we reminisced about his parents, with me reminding him how good and kind his father was to me, essentially launching my writing career by hiring me at *The Announcer.*

"Oh, Dad could always spot talent all right and it seems he made an excellent choice in you, Vanessa, considering where you are now in the literary world."

"I'm forever grateful to him, Hugh. His belief in me was quite astonishing when you realize I really had little experience. Such a pity how it all ended up for him."

Hugh ruefully shook his head before saying, "It was that damn Kenwright chap who started it all."

I briefly stole a glance in Kay's direction as I wondered where Hugh was going with this.

"Nothing was the same again," he continued, clearly still angry after all these years.

"I know, Hugh," I agreed, "Chloe and I have already talked about that."

"And then Simon's accident just about did us all in," he offered, shaking his head again.

To try and move the conversation away from Simon's death I asked about his life in Canada. He prattled on for a good ten minutes before he mentioned Edward for the first time.

"I came back to the States for his funeral in 2010. First time I'd been back since leaving. He was such a mess, you know, Edward. I really think he blamed himself for Simon's death." As he talked I noticed he stared off into the distance as though looking into the past. "I found his diary among his things after he died. Well, it wasn't a proper diary just a collection of his daily thoughts in a notebook. The day after Simon drowned he wrote, '*It's all my fault. He didn't deserve to die that way.*'"

I quickly looked at Kay again not knowing how this was going to end.

"Poor Edward," Hugh carried on, "he suffered so much over Simon's death. No wonder he spiraled out of control. I think he blamed himself for not being able to save him."

My eyes opened wide as I spread my hands in front of me and replied, "Honestly, Hugh, it was a tragedy for everyone. Edward, I'm sure, did his best but…" and I let my words trail off hoping that would be the end of conversation.

"Yeah, I guess you're right, Vanessa, he did the best he could, but it seemed to have cost him his life, too."

Fortunately our desserts arrived and the talk moved away from Simon's passing to questions about my career, and Kay and my efforts at starting a retreat. We parted a little while later and that was the last time I saw Hugh.

"Phew, that was dicey," Kay remarked, as we walked to our rooms. "But you handled it very well, old girl."

"Talk about your sins will find you out," I answered, with a smirk. "I just didn't know how much he knew."

"Well, no harm done and I don't think you need to worry about it anymore."

Later in the quiet of my room I questioned whether I had the right to withhold that information from Chloe and Hugh. Quite clearly they loved both their brothers and to learn one had murdered the other would have achieved…what? So I went to bed in the knowledge that I had done the right thing in letting them live with the memories they had always held and believed in.

The day before the retreat was to officially open Kay and I went over the place with a fine tooth comb to ensure the facility matched out strict guidelines. We needn't have worried since Gabrella Turner, our new director of operations, had the building and grounds in tip-top condition. The private rooms sparkled with such freshness it took your breath away and the manicured lawn, flowerbeds, pond and gazebos were as inviting as anything Eden had to offer.

"Oh, Gabrella," I gushed, "you've just done a fantastic job here. Thank you so much."

She bowed graciously before saying, "A labor of love. Now let's hope our authors think the same."

"If they don't," Kay interceded, joking with a fake frown, "they won't be invited back."

We spent the rest of the day going over some last minute changes we wanted made and Gabrella took those instructions in stride. Other than that, we told her she had a free hand to manage the place as she saw fit. Our confidence in her management style was solid and, indeed, over the many years she was with us she never once let us down but rather enhanced the retreat in so many ways.

Our fellow author/board members began arriving early the next morning, as well as our ten invited writers, Stephen King and various dignitaries from the local community. Gabrella took charge, taking them on a tour until it was time to attend the opening ceremony.

Kay welcomed everyone, particularly thanking Stephen for taking the time to celebrate the opening, and the ten authors who were essentially christening the place as a bona fide retreat. After Kay finished, I followed emphasizing how important we felt this retreat would be in years to come.

"I know from personal experience of having the opportunity to take advantage of the one in upstate New York, how instrumental it was in helping me have the time and space to just think and create." Looking directly at the bevy of young writers, I continued, "We hope this similar experience for all of you will offer the time and space you need." I then introduced our special guest, Stephen King, who gave a very funny speech, which he ended with this advice to our first residents.

"This place, as amazing as it is, could hold some pitfalls for you." We all frowned as he went on, tongue in cheek, to explain. "I grew up writing any place I could; dingy basements, cemeteries, public toilets and other equally squalid environments, but what those places gave me was a real sense of the macabre, and I'm sure I owe them a lot for helping train my mind into the horror place it eventually discovered and dwelled. So, don't get too comfortable or you'll never end up like me!"

Everyone broke up laughing at Stephen's advice, even if there was a hint of truth to it.

With the retreat in good hands I now had the time to complete the project I'd been assiduously working on to surprise Kay. Mostly a labor of love and discovery, it amazed me with the emotion, regret, longing and just plain happiness it brought me. I spent the next few days polishing and preparing it exactly how I wanted it to remain forever. There could be no changes once it was handed over since it came from the heart, complete with rough edges, truth and certainly most of my soul.

The next day, sure in my mind the time had come to let her see it, I called Kay and asked if I might stop by and see her.

"I have something for you. It's a surprise."

"Oh, I love surprises, come tomorrow," she offered. "And," she continued, "I have some news for you, too."

"Sweetie," Kay welcomed me, as we hugged and she led me to her patio. "Coffee's already made, so just give me a sec."

She returned a few minutes later carrying the coffees and a plate of cookies on a tray. She handed me a cup, offered the plate of goodies and then sat down expectantly.

With a huge smile I pulled a large manila envelope from my bag and handed it over.

"And what is this?" she asked, puzzled.

"I didn't want you to be out of work," I joked. "Open it."

"Oh, don't tell me…" she replied, her eyes lighting up anticipatingly.

From the envelope she took out a thick binder. Quickly opening it up, she immediately saw it was a manuscript.

"Oh my goodness, is this what I think it is? But I thought you told me no more books, Vanessa."

"No, I said no more novels...take a closer look."

She flipped through several pages, stopping now and then to read certain passages.

"No way...you're autobiography!" she gasped, totally flummoxed. "Oh, Vanessa, this is going to be gold."

"We can only hope."

"No, no, this is major, let me tell you. You're writing career is legendary and for people to know your history and some of the back stories to your books...well..."

"Kay, I've been as honest as I can with this. I've left nothing out except the true story surrounding Simon's death, of course. So, my rule here is nothing can or will be changed except for any stupid grammatical errors on my part. It has to be published precisely how I've written it or there will be no deal."

"It will be done. I will make sure of that. Oh, Vanessa, what a finale for you...and for me."

Her last remark caught my attention and I wasn't sure I'd heard it correctly.

"Did you say '*and for me*'?"

"Yes, this'll be my last book as an agent."

"Really, tell me more, *old girl*?"

"I'm handing the agency over to my daughter. As you know she's been with me for over twenty years and is more than capable of carrying on the good work. When you told me *Intimate Strangers* was going to be your last novel that made me take stock of my own life. I've been doing this for over forty years...as long as you've been writing...and you're right, it's time to move on to other things I want to do, including making sure the retreat is successful long after we're gone. So, yes, it's time."

"Well, I'm stunned but good for you. Over the years you've help launch the careers of so many authors, including yours truly here. That's a legacy you have to be proud of. Oh, Kay, I'm so happy for you."

"But it does mean I'll be bothering you a lot more because I'm not too good with my own company," she joshed.

"Well, I could certainly do with a dog walker for Wolfie," I joked back, "and drinking my wine on my own sucks sometimes, so you're company will be completely welcome anytime."

We chatted back and forth for the next couple of hours until it was time for me to go. As she walked me to my car she suddenly stopped and cocked her head.

"I forgot to ask, do you have a title in mind for the book?"

"Yes, yes I do. It's going to be called '*The Remembrance of Then*'"

Epilogue

---◆---

Sitting on my porch on this warm June evening, I suddenly begin to think where the last five years have gone. I'm due to start my sixth year as writer-in-residence at the University of Maine this coming September, which amazes me since it seems as if I began there only yesterday. James has become a really good friend and between the two of us I feel we have created something special for the writing students. Several have actually written first novels and Kay's daughter, who has run the agency since Kay retired, represents them as promising clients. Two of my former students have taken advantage of the retreat, which they tell me helped them so much to create and solely concentrate on their work.

And that thought brings me to the retreat. I shake my head in disbelief at how far it has progressed since its inception five years ago. According to Gabrella's last report the facility has been a temporary home to over four hundred authors. Not only that but at her suggestion, and with the help of a large donation from an artistic organization, we had another wing put on the house and opened it specifically for painters and visual artists.

Kay and I make several trips there every year and to know it has garnished a reputation for being perhaps now the leading facility of its kind in the nation thrills us beyond our wildest hopes and dreams.

As I pour myself another glass of my favorite red, Kay calls. It's always such a delight to hear from her and over the last five years she's become perhaps my closest friend.

"Vanessa," she says insistently, "what are you doing?"

"Having a glass and thinking," I reply.

"Did you watch it last night?"

"Of course."

"And?"

"A perfect end to the series, I thought."

"They kept true to your books, thank goodness otherwise it would have been a mess."

"Well, I was the script consultant, Kay, so I would hope so."

"I think *Intimate Strangers* is going to be a television classic for some time to come, old girl."

I hope she's right because the trilogy and now the three part series have been so much a part of my life. And I do feel they did a wonderful job of transferring the novel to the screen without losing any of the fundamental storylines along the way. On top of that they paid me handsomely, so icing on the cake all the way around.

"Let's meet for dinner tomorrow night," Kay offers, and I agree immediately since her company always cheers me up.

As she rings off I inadvertently hit a wrong app on my phone and a photo of Chloe Barrington appears. It was taken the last time I saw her earlier in the year before she became sick. Looking at her face I can't really believe she's gone. I quickly pull up a picture of Hugh, who passed away over three years ago now, and think how quickly nearly sixty years have passed by. He was two or three years older than me and Chloe was two years younger. Shaking my head, I can't believe I'm the only one left now apart from James, who didn't know them as closely as me, who remembers the Barringtons. I recall April telling me all those years ago not to make them into more than they were, that they were just a family like everyone else, with their own faults and foibles. How right she was! Oh, my goodness, how right she was!

At the time, in my youthful mind, they felt like a family who had it all, who were blessed with some kind of magic that I wanted to rub off on me. For a while that seemed to be the case when Mr. Barrington gave me the job at *The Announcer* and I was accepted into the family circle.

I sip my wine and gently shake my head at how easily their lives fell apart. Of course, I'm forever grateful for what they gave me, but I'm also happy to know I eventually had to make my own way in life and build the kind of future I did, in fact, fashion on my own.

As the sun slowly slips below the horizon, I smile and nod my head knowing the past will forever be with me but it's the present that always holds the most hope.

Printed in the United States
by Baker & Taylor Publisher Services